The Female Gothic

Also by Diana Wallace

THE WOMAN'S HISTORICAL NOVEL: British Women Writers, 1900–2000

SISTERS AND RIVALS IN BRITISH WOMEN'S FICTION, 1914–1939

Also by Andrew Smith

GOTHIC LITERATURE

VICTORIAN DEMONS: Medicine, Masculinity and the Gothic at the *fin de siècle*

GOTHIC RADICALISM: Literature, Philosophy and Psychoanalysis in the Nineteenth Century

QUEERING THE GOTHIC (*edited with William Hughes*)

TEACHING THE GOTHIC (*edited with Anna Powell*)

EMPIRE AND THE GOTHIC: The Politics of Genre (*edited with William Hughes*)

GOTHIC MODERNISMS (*edited with Jeff Wallace*)

BRAM STOKER: History, Psychoanalysis and the Gothic (*edited with William Hughes*)

FICTIONS OF UNEASE: The Gothic from Otranto to the X-Files (*edited with William Hughes and Diane Mason*)

DRACULA AND THE CRITICS

The Female Gothic

New Directions

Edited by

Diana Wallace

and

Andrew Smith

palgrave
macmillan

First published 2009 by
PALGRAVE MACMILLAN

Palgrave Macmillan in the UK is an imprint of Macmillan Publishers Limited, registered in England, company number 785998, of Houndmills, Basingstoke, Hampshire RG21 6XS.

Palgrave Macmillan in the US is a division of St Martin's Press LLC, 175 Fifth Avenue, New York, NY 10010.

Palgrave Macmillan is the global academic imprint of the above companies and has companies and representatives throughout the world.

Palgrave® and Macmillan® are registered trademarks in the United States, the United Kingdom, Europe and other countries.

ISBN: 978–0–230–22271–7 hardback

This book is printed on paper suitable for recycling and made from fully managed and sustained forest sources. Logging, pulping and manufacturing processes are expected to conform to the environmental regulations of the country of origin.

A catalogue record for this book is available from the British Library.

A catalog record for this book is available from the Library of Congress.

10 9 8 7 6 5 4 3 2 1
18 17 16 15 14 13 12 11 10 09

Printed and bound in Great Britain by
CPI Antony Rowe, Chippenham and Eastbourne

For Eugenia DeLamotte
In memoriam

Contents

Acknowledgements

We would like to thank the delegates of the Female Gothic conference which was held at the University of Glamorgan in 2004. In that year we edited a special double issue of the journal *Gothic Studies* on the Female Gothic which was a result of the many productive discussions at that conference and we would like to thank William Hughes, the journal's editor, for supporting the project, and the International Gothic Association for sponsoring it. Many of the discussions which began at that conference have continued and the present volume has been generated out of that shared enthusiasm. Alongside our general thanks to the delegates at that conference and for the stimulating dialogues which have been maintained, we also have our own friends and colleagues whom we would like to thank.

Diana Wallace would like to thank Gavin Edwards and Meredith Miller for several stimulating conversations about the Gothic, metaphor and history, and for useful comments on her essay in progress; her students on 'The Female Gothic' for their insights and humour over the years; and Jarlath and Seán for their forbearance during too many weekends spent working.

Andrew Smith would like to thank Carol Margaret Davison for inviting him to deliver a paper on Shirley Jackson, on which his chapter for this volume is based, on a panel on the Female Gothic that she organised for the 'Space, Haunting, Discourse' conference at Karlstad University, Sweden in 2006 and to thank the delegates for their helpful comments. He would also like to thank Benjamin F. Fisher for inviting him to speak on an 'American Gothic' panel at the American Literature Association conference in San Francisco in 2008 where he also discussed Shirley Jackson and received very helpful responses from delegates. He would also like to thank Joanne Benson for her love, tolerance and support during the editing of this book.

We would like to thank Paula Kennedy and Steven Hall at Palgrave for their forbearance and support. We would also like to thank Matthew Frost at Manchester University Press for permission to reproduce Lauren Fitzgerald's article from the Female Gothic special issue of *Gothic Studies* 6/1 May 2004. We would also like to thank Robert Miles for allowing us to reproduce the image used on the cover of this book.

At proposal stage this book included an abstract on Race, America and the Female Gothic from Eugenia DeLamotte who contributed a ground-breaking article on Pauline Hopkins and African-American identity for the Female Gothic special issue of *Gothic Studies*. Eugenia, who died in 2005, was the author of a landmark text in Gothic criticism, *Perils of the Night: A Feminist Study of Nineteenth-Century Gothic* (1990), although her scholarship transcended the Gothic field and included books on Paule Marshall (1998) and Voltairine De Cleyre (2004). She was a very fine and academically rigorous scholar whose work was always of the highest standard and it is to her memory that this book is respectfully dedicated.

Contributors

Kirsti Bohata is Lecturer in English and Assistant Director of the Centre for Research into the English Literature and Language of Wales (CREW) at Swansea University. She is the author of *Postcolonialism Revisited: Writing Wales in English* (2004). She has also published essays on race, nationality, gender and sexuality in Gothic writing and on *fin de siècle* fiction. Her most recent publication is an edited collection of short stories by the New Woman writer Bertha Thomas, *Stranger within the Gates* (2008).

Carol Margaret Davison is Associate Professor of English Literature at the University of Windsor. She is the author of *Anti-Semitism and British Gothic Literature* (2004) and *History of the Gothic: Gothic Literature 1764–1824* (forthcoming) and is researching on the Scottish Gothic tradition. She is also the editor of a special issue of *Gothic Studies* on the Gothic and Addiction (2009), has co-edited a special issue on Marie Corelli for *Women's Writing* (UK, 2006), and edited *Bram Stoker's Dracula: Sucking Through the Century, 1897–1997* (1997).

Lauren Fitzgerald is Associate Professor of English at Yeshiva University where she directs the Yeshiva College Writing Center. Her articles on the Gothic have appeared in *Gothic Studies, Romanticism on the Net, The Wordsworth Circle*, and edited collections. She also publishes in composition studies and is co-editor of *The Writing Center Journal*.

Anya Heise-von der Lippe is an external lecturer in English Literature and Cultural Studies at the Freie Universität in Berlin and an editor for language learning media with Cornelsen Publishers. She is currently completing her PhD dissertation on the aesthetics of contemporary Gothic literature. Her research focuses on a wide range of theories, forms and textual representations of aberrant, monstrous and posthuman corporeality. Recent publications include 'Post-apocalyptic Bodies' in *Narratives of Disaster* (2007) edited by Angela Stock and Cornelia Stott.

Avril Horner is an Emeritus Professor of English at Kingston University, London. She is currently writing on Iris Murdoch and the Gothic and, with Janet Beer, is completing a book on Edith Wharton's late fiction.

She has written three books with Sue Zlosnik, including *Gothic and the Comic Turn* (2005) as well as numerous articles and essays. They co-edited *Le Gothic* (2008) and have an edition of E. S. Barrett's *The Heroine* in press. They are Co-Presidents of the International Gothic Association.

Alison Milbank is an Associate Professor in the Department of Theology and Religious Studies at the University of Nottingham. Her research focuses on the relation of religion to culture in the post-Enlightenment period, with particular literary interest in non-realist literary and artistic expression, such as the Gothic, the fantastic, horror and fantasy. Her publications include *Chesterton and Tolkien as Theologians* (2009), *Dante and the Victorians* (1998) and *Daughters of the House: Modes of the Gothic in Victorian Fiction* (1992). She has co-edited, with Marie Mulvey-Roberts and Peter Otto, *Gothic Fiction, Rare Printed Works from the Sadleir-Black Collection* (2002–3), and edited the Oxford World's Classics edition of *A Sicilian Romance*.

Robert Miles is Professor and Chair of the Department of English at the University of Victoria. A past President of the International Gothic Association he has written widely on Gothic subjects. His books include *Gothic Writing 1750–1820: A Genealogy* (1993), *Ann Radcliffe: the Great Enchantress* (1995) and *Romantic Misfits* (2008).

Meredith Miller is Senior Lecturer in English at University College Falmouth in Cornwall. Her research interests are in cultural materialism, gender, sexuality and the history of the novel. She has published extensively on gender, sexuality and popular fiction and is currently working on a monograph entitled *The Meaning of a Woman: Modernity, Will and Desire*.

Marie Mulvey-Roberts is Reader in Literary Studies in the English Department of the University of the West of England, Bristol. She is the editor of *The Collected Letters of Rosina Bulwer Lytton*, 3 vols (2008), *Writing for their Lives: Death Row USA* (2007) and co-editor, with Alison Milbank and Peter Otto, of *Gothic Fiction, Rare Printed Works from the Sadleir-Black Collection* (2002–3). She is also the editor of the journal *Woman's Writing* and has published essays on blood, gender and the Gothic.

Andrew Smith is Professor of English Studies at the University of Glamorgan where he is Co-Director of the Research Centre for Literature, Arts and Science (RCLAS). His published books include

Gothic Literature (2007), *Victorian Demons* (2004) and *Gothic Radicalism* (2000). He is the co-series editor (with Benjamin F. Fisher) of *Gothic Literary Studies*, and *Gothic Authors: Critical Revisions*, published by the University of Wales Press. In 2004 he co-edited (with Diana Wallace) a special issue of *Gothic Studies* on 'The Female Gothic'.

Diana Wallace is Reader in English at the University of Glamorgan where her research and teaching focus on women's writing. She is the author of *The Woman's Historical Novel: British Women Writers, 1900–2000* (2005), *Sisters and Rivals in British Women's Fiction, 1914–39* (2000), and co-edited (with Andrew Smith) a special edition of *Gothic Studies* on 'The Female Gothic' (2004).

Angela Wright lectures in eighteenth-century Romantic and Gothic Literature at the University of Sheffield. She has published widely on Gothic literature between 1764 and 1820. Her particular research interests include Anglo-French literary exchanges, women's Gothic writing and the impact of translation during the Romantic period. She is the author of *Gothic Fiction* (2007), and has just completed a second book, entitled *The Import of Terror: Britain, France and the Gothic, 1780–1820*.

Sue Zlosnik is Professor of English at Manchester Metropolitan University. She has recently written on Hilary Mantel and is completing a monograph on Patrick McGrath. She and Avril Horner have written three books together, most recently *Gothic and the Comic Turn* (2005), as well as numerous articles and essays. They are co-editors of *Le Gothic* (2008) and have an edition of E. S. Barrett's *The Heroine* currently in press. They are Co-Presidents of the International Gothic Association.

Introduction: Defining the Female Gothic

Diana Wallace and Andrew Smith

The term 'Female Gothic' has become much contested. When Ellen Moers coined the term in 1976 she thought that it could be 'easily defined' as 'the work that women have done in the literary mode that, since the eighteenth century, we have called the Gothic'.[1] A definition of 'the Gothic' was, however, 'not so easily stated except that it has to do with fear' (90). Moers's pioneering work – two brief chapters in a book which was one of the earliest attempts to trace and value on its own terms a distinctive female tradition of writing – opened up what proved to be a very fertile field for critics. It can be seen as directly influential in the establishing of both women's writing and the Gothic as central areas in literary studies.

Since the early 1990s, however, there has been considerable debate over the usefulness of the 'Female Gothic' as a separate literary category or genre. A variety of other terms have been offered, some alternative, others more specific: 'women's Gothic', 'feminist Gothic', 'lesbian Gothic', 'Gothic feminism' and, most recently, 'postfeminist Gothic'. In a recent critique Chris Baldick and Robert Mighall have suggested that:

> the construction since the 1970s of the predominantly universal-
> ising category of the 'female Gothic', as an embodiment of some
> invariable female 'experience' or of the archetypal 'female principle',
> leads straight out of history into the timeless melodrama in which
> (wicked) 'male Gothic' texts always express terror of the eternal
> '(M)other' while (good) female Gothic texts are revealed to be – as
> Anne Williams claims – not just 'empowering' but 'revolutionary'.[2]

Their comments are part of a wider critique of what they see as a radically misguided tendency to privilege psychoanalytic interpretations

1

above historicist ones in the criticism of Gothic texts: 'the collapse of history into universal psychology' (218). While we would strongly support the necessity for historically aware criticism, their comments seem to simplify what is a far more complex and rigorous body of work than they allow here. Most importantly their account could be regarded as implicitly marginalising the (feminist) politics of this criticism.

In fact, in *Literary Women* Moers discusses two kinds of 'Female Gothic' – what she calls the 'travelling heroinism' of Ann Radcliffe's novels (chapter 7), and the 'birth myth' of *Frankenstein* (1831) (chapter 5). It is Radcliffe's novels with their heroines in flight from male tyrants across fantastical landscapes and in search of lost mothers entombed in womb-like dungeons beneath patriarchal castles which we now tend to characterise as the beginnings of 'Female Gothic'. Mary Shelley's *Frankenstein* (as Moers herself notes) is in many ways closer to the literature of the male overreacher and thus to what critics have more recently defined as 'Male Gothic'. Moers's chapters on the Gothic range from Radcliffe and Shelley through George Sand, Rossetti and Emily Brontë to Diane Arbus, Robin Morgan and Sylvia Plath. The connections she made between such diverse women writers offered new ways of reading and valuing them and that had a particular political importance in the context of 'the new wave of feminism called women's liberation' (xiii). It also proved inspiring to other critics who read the Female Gothic as a politically subversive genre articulating women's dissatisfactions with patriarchal structures and offering a coded expression of their fears of entrapment within the domestic and the female body.

Perhaps most widely influential has been *The Madwoman in the Attic* (1979) in which Sandra M. Gilbert and Susan Gubar utilised psychoanalytic theory to explore female anxieties about space and authorship, uncovering what they called the 'single secret message' of women's writing of the nineteenth century.[3] In reducing the diversity of women's writing to this single plot – the split psyche produced by the woman writer's 'quest for self-definition' (76) and best emblematised by the Gothic doubling of Jane Eyre and her monstrous 'Other', the imprisoned first wife Bertha Rochester – Gilbert and Gubar come closer to offering a universalising interpretation of women's writing than does Moers.

The essays in *The Female Gothic* (1983), edited by Juliann Fleenor, offer a more divergent series of voices, particularly in their contributions to the debate as to whether this is a conservative or a radical genre.[4] Fleenor quotes Margaret Anne Doody's earlier assertion regarding eighteenth-century novels that 'It is in the Gothic novel that women writers could first accuse the "real world" of falsehood and deep disorder.'[5] Rooted in 'the dreams of women', Doody suggested, the English Gothic novel became 'along one line of its evolution the novel of feminine radical protest'.[6] In contrast, several essays in Fleenor's collection see the Gothic, in particular the modern popular Gothic, as conservative, reinforcing the social roles of women. Following Claire Kahane's psychoanalytically informed work,[7] Fleenor herself locates at the centre of the Female Gothic an ambivalence over female identity, above all the conflict with the archaic all-powerful mother, often figured as a spectral presence and/or as the Gothic house itself. Fleenor's collection comes out of the beginnings of feminist literary criticism in the early 1980s and as such is underpinned by a politicised understanding of the 'historical reality' of women's position within patriarchal society, and the ways in which the Female Gothic is used by women as 'a metaphor for the female experience'.[8]

The 1990s saw the Female Gothic move from the margins into the mainstream of literary criticism, as well as a shift away from psychoanalytical interpretations to socio-cultural readings. Kate Ferguson Ellis's *The Contested Castle: Gothic Novels and the Subversion of Domestic Ideology* (1989) explored ideologies of gender and the domestic in relation to capitalism through a focus on the house or castle.[9] Locating the heart of the Gothic in anxieties about the boundaries of the self, Eugenia DeLamotte's *Perils of the Night: A Feminist Study of Nineteenth-Century Gothic* (1990), nevertheless insisted that these cannot be separated from social realities – of money, work and social rank – and the interrelated ways in which they limit women both socially and psychologically.[10]

Increasingly critics came to distinguish between Female Gothic and Male Gothic, initially identified with the gender of the writer. The Female Gothic plot, exemplified by Radcliffe, centralised the imprisoned and pursued heroine threatened by a tyrannical male figure, it explained the supernatural, and ended in the closure of marriage. In contrast, the Male Gothic plot, exemplified by Matthew Lewis's *The Monk* (1796), is one of masculine transgression of social taboos, characterised by violent rape and/or murder, which tends to resist closure, frequently leaving the supernatural unexplained. The common-sense correlation of plot or genre with authorial gender made by Moers, however, was broken down by Alison Milbank's *Daughters of the House: Modes of Gothic in Victorian Fiction* (1992) which discussed male writers' appropriation of Female Gothic to critique the ideologies of capitalism and their connection with those of gender.[11] In contrast, Anne Williams deployed psychoanalysis in *Art of Darkness: A Poetics of Gothic* (1995) to analyse the differences between 'Male' and 'Female' formulae in terms of narrative technique, plot, their assumptions about the supernatural and their use of horror/terror.[12] Revisiting the Freudian use of Greek mythology, she located the origins of the Female Gothic narrative (typified by female point of view, happy ending, explained ghosts and an adherence to terror), in the myth of Psyche and Eros rather than the Oedipal myth which underpins the male version.

In 1994, however, Robert Miles suggested in the introduction to a special number of *Women's Writing* on Female Gothic writing that the term had 'hardened into a literary category' and that, in particular, psychoanalytic readings which suggested the durability and universality of the Female Gothic plot had pushed critics into an 'impasse'.[13] His call for critics to reassess the critical validity of the Female Gothic, and particularly to investigate alternatives to psychoanalytic approaches, produced a collection of essays (by critics including Ellis, Milbank and Williams) which rose to the challenge of exploring and interrogating the term and arguably helped reinvigorate the field. Miles's own *Ann Radcliffe: The Great Enchantress* (1995) offered the most comprehensive account yet of the Radcliffean Female Gothic narrative of the persecuted heroine in flight from a villainous father-figure and in search of an absent mother.[14]

The debate over whether the Female Gothic could be seen as subversive or conservative was given a further twist by Diane Long Hoeveler's *Gothic Feminism: The Professionalisation of Gender from Charlotte Smith to the Brontës* (1998) which contentiously saw in it the origins of modern so-called 'victim feminism'. The heroines of Gothic novels, Hoeveler contended, masquerade as blameless victims of a corrupt and oppressive patriarchal society while utilising passive-aggressive and masochistic strategies to triumph over that system. This ideology of 'female power through pretended and staged weakness' is what Hoeveler calls 'Gothic feminism'.[15]

Although Moers and Fleenor had traced the Female Gothic through to modern and contemporary literature, much subsequent work focused on eighteenth- and nineteenth-century writing, with exceptions such as Tania Modleski and Joanna Russ's work on the modern or popular Gothic romance.[16] Post-1990, however, critics have increasingly turned their attention to the use of Gothic modes by twentieth-century women writers as diverse as Daphne du Maurier, May Sinclair, Barbara Comyns and Margaret Atwood. This work shows how the conventions and themes of the Female Gothic have repeatedly been both reused *and* reinvented by women writers. In *Daphne du Maurier: Writing, Identity and the Gothic Imagination* (1998), for instance, Avril Horner and Sue

Zlosnik argue that although du Maurier used the Gothic to explore the anxieties of modernity her texts do not fit what we have come to see as the typical Female Gothic plot.[17] Their work here and in the later *Gothic and the Comic Turn* (2005)[18] is an important reminder that any critical definitions need to be continually revisited and retested.

The continuing centrality of the Gothic, however transformed, in modern and contemporary writing by women is evidenced by two books published in 1999 which both in different ways draw on post-structuralist scepticism about essentialist categories, whether of gender, nationality, race or sexuality. Suzanne Becker's *Gothic Forms of Feminine Fiction* (1999) offers a study of English and Canadian women writers, most importantly Margaret Atwood's *Lady Oracle* (1976).[19] Becker chooses to use the term 'Feminine Gothic' to signal her focus on the gender of the speaking subject in the text rather than the gender of the author. Paulina Palmer's *Lesbian Gothic: Transgressive Fictions* (1999) explores how women writers have appropriated, reworked and parodied Gothic modes and motifs to articulate lesbian subjectivities. Palmer's concept of 'lesbian Gothic' draws on the understanding that 'Gothic and "queer" share a common emphasis on transgressive acts and subjectivities'.[20] Her study is concerned specifically with fiction which comes out of second-wave feminism but it has implications for a wider range of texts which have yet to be fully explored.

A recent turn to historicist readings has produced some valuable new readings of women's Gothic fictions. The title of E. J. Clery's *Women's Gothic: From Clara Reeve to Mary Shelley* (2000) signals a move away from the psychoanalytic readings of these texts as 'parables of patriarchy involving the heroine's danger from wicked father figures and her search for the absent mother'[21] which tend to confine women's texts to the private world of the family. Part of Clery's anxiety about the term 'Female Gothic', as in Horner and Zlosnik's work, is a concern that writers who do not fit what has come to be seen as the typical paradigms have been left out of critical accounts. In contrast to earlier emphases on the constraints and self-censorship suffered by women writers in the Romantic period, Clery's careful historical contextualisation reveals their often acknowledged status as professional writers, influenced and enabled by the powerful figure of Sarah Siddons as an ideal of female genius, and fully conscious of the profit motive.

The most recent engagement with Moers's term comes from the collection of essays, *Postfeminist Gothic: Critical Interventions in Contemporary Culture* (2007) edited by Benjamin A. Brabon and Stéphanie Genz. While they acknowledge the historical importance of Moers's term, Brabon and

Genz are convinced that 'Gothic and feminist categories now demand a self-criticism with respect to their own totalising gestures and assumptions'.[22] Noting recent assertions that we are no longer in the second wave of feminism, they suggest that 'by extension, we might also have crossed a barrier and reached a new critical space beyond the Female Gothic (and its ghosts of essentialism and universality)' (7). The new space they offer is 'postfeminist Gothic', although they admit that both terms are controversial and difficult to define. What is striking about this collection is that the majority of essays (9 out of 12) deal primarily with either film or television.

Despite, or rather, because of these debates, the Female Gothic remains a fertile field for investigation as well as an ever-popular subject for students. When in 2004 we edited a special number of *Gothic Studies* on the subject the response to our initial call for papers was such that the decision was made to make it a double issue of the journal.[23] The range of subjects covered – Mary Wollstonecraft, Eliza Fenwick, Pauline Hopkins, ghost stories, Bram Stoker, Sylvia Plath, lesbian Gothic – suggested the ongoing vitality and relevance of the area, and its capacity to tease out new meanings from canonical texts as well as offering a way to revalue neglected texts.

The current volume reprints one essay from that special number – Lauren Fitzgerald's valuable essay on Female Gothic and the institutionalisation of Gothic studies. The other essays here have been specially commissioned and develop a range of ideas on some of the areas which are currently of particular interest to scholars interested in the Female Gothic: national identity, sexuality, language, race and history. They are arranged in chronological order (although some overlap, of course) to retain that crucial sense of historical development and connection.

Lauren Fitzgerald in 'Female Gothic and the Institutionalisation of Gothic Studies' argues that Ellen Moers's account of the Female Gothic has its roots in a Lockean, European Enlightenment, philosophy of ownership. For Fitzgerald, this philosophy also influenced a 1970s feminist revision of the canon that involved identifying, and reclaiming, a 'herstory' of women's writing. Issues concerning the critical ownership of Ann Radcliffe, for example, illustrate how academic feminism has approached, and developed, the idea of what constitutes 'women's writing', while simultaneously indicating the extent to which Enlightenment ideas of ownership have shaped the Anglo-American feminist tradition.

Diana Wallace's ' "The haunting idea": Female Gothic metaphors and feminist theory' examines the traces of female Gothic metaphors – of women imprisoned, buried alive, and as 'ghosts' – which 'haunt' feminist theory and the relationship which exists between theory and female Gothic fiction. Mary Beard suggested that the 'haunting idea' has its roots in Mary Wollstonecraft's engagement with William Blackstone's legal doctrine that married women were 'civilly dead'. Wallace uses this insight to argue that feminist thinkers from Margaret Cavendish through Mary Wollstonecraft, Virginia Woolf, Hannah Gavron, Adrienne Rich, Luce Irigaray and Sarah Kofman to Diana Fuss and Judith Butler use female Gothic metaphors to theorise women's position or, rather, repression within history and society.

Robert Miles in '"Mother Radcliff": Ann Radcliffe and the Female Gothic' reassesses Moers's claims as regards Radcliffe and the Female Gothic. Miles argues that if Moers's version of the 'Female Gothic' is a tenable category, it must have an origin, in which case the origin is indubitably (as Keats implied) 'Mother Radcliff'. After reviewing the recent criticism, Miles argues that Norman Holland and Leona Sherman were fundamentally correct in asserting that Radcliffe's romances constituted a generative matrix for a distinct school of romance that has lasted to this day. Miles thus argues for a reconsideration of Radcliffe which locates her as a central figure in conceptualising the Female Gothic because her particular type of narrative grammar was informed by a wider gender-political unconscious that continues to shape the form.

Angela Wright's 'Disturbing the Female Gothic: An Excavation of the *Northanger* Novels' explores the significance of the Gothic novels mentioned in *Northanger Abbey* (1818). Titles mentioned by Isabella Thorpe include Eliza Parsons's *Castle of Wolfenbach* (1793); Regina Maria Roche's *Clermont* (1798); Peter Teuthold's translation of *The Necromancer: Or the Tale of the Black Forest* from the German of Lawrence Flammenberg (1794); Francis Lathom's *The Midnight Bell* anonymously published in 1798; Eleanor Sleath's *The Orphan of the Rhine* (1798); and Peter Will's adaptation of *Horrid Mysteries* from the German of the Marquis of Grosse in 1796. Very little has been done to examine these novels in detail, and yet Maria Regina Roche, Eliza Parsons and Eleanor Sleath in particular earned almost as much for their novelistic enterprises as Ann Radcliffe herself. Their immense popularity during the 1790s testifies to a strong female tradition which remains to be studied in detail. Wright argues that the development of a recognisably 'Female Gothic' form in the 1790s owed much to these pioneering novels. Wright's exploration of Parson's *Castle of Wolfenbach* and Lathom's *The Midnight Bell* argues that their particular blend of sentimental narrative and supernatural horror reworks, but moves them beyond, the Radcliffean Female Gothic. Wright also argues that the lack of discrimination in terms of authorial gender in Isabella's list indicates that the Female Gothic aesthetic is feminine, rather than female, as it was one that was widely used by both male and female authors (and was consumed by male and female readers). A 'Female Gothic' tradition, as it was conceived in the 'Northanger Novels', was thus very different from what Moers understood by the term 'Female Gothic'.

Alison Milbank in 'Bleeding Nuns: A Genealogy of the Female Gothic Grotesque' addresses the question of what happens to the Female Gothic in the nineteenth century, specifically in relation to the aesthetics of the sublime that underpins the plot of female emancipation from physical, psychical and temporal imprisonment in the earlier period. Milbank argues that the 'vertical' sublime by which female disempowerment is both dramatised and overcome in Ann Radcliffe is replaced by recourse to the 'horizontal' aesthetic of the grotesque, which puts physical embodiment itself to the question, and seeks scandalously to unite real and ideal, physical and spiritual in the monstrous body. Milbank explores the self-conscious use of the grotesque in writers including Horace Walpole, Matthew Lewis, Mary Shelley, Charlotte Brontë and Wilkie Collins. In particular she examines how the figure of the bleeding nun exemplifies issues relating to female subjectivity, authorship and metaphysical speculation.

Marie Mulvey-Roberts's 'From Bluebeard's Bloody Chamber to Demonic Stigmatic' explores how images of Bluebeard are reworked in Gothic narratives as potential narratives of resistance. By examining the transformations and appropriations of the Bluebeard tale from Perrault to Angela Carter, Mulvey-Roberts charts how connections between forbidden knowledge and dangerous reading practices inhere in the Female Gothic. Writers explored include Radcliffe, Charlotte Brontë, Daphne du Maurier, as well as male-authored versions of the Bluebeard story by the Brothers Grimm, and their implicit adaptations in Matthew Lewis and Bram Stoker.

Avril Horner and Sue Zlosnik in 'Keeping It in the Family: Incest and the Female Gothic Plot in du Maurier and Murdoch' explore images of father–daughter and sibling incest in the work of Daphne du Maurier and Iris Murdoch. They argue that these very different writers nevertheless develop incest as a trope through which to examine issues about the abuse of male power that are relevant to a reading of the Female Gothic. Horner and Zlosnik examine how du Maurier's representation of incest as an expression of invariably female horror and fear contrasts with how Murdoch elaborates incest in terms of issues about control and desire which invite moral evaluation.

Meredith Miller's ' "I Don't Want to be a [White] Girl": Gender, Race and Resistance in the Southern Gothic' focuses on how Gothic fiction articulates the relation between gendered and racialised categories of identity and positions of power. Miller traces a direct and specific relationship in the use of conventions between nineteenth-century British Gothic and twentieth-century Southern Gothic writers and argues that these conventions are useful to twentieth-century southern writers because they were originally developed in order to express a set of relationships between racial (national) and sexual positions of power. Race often remains under erasure as attempts are made to reclaim and canonise Southern Gothic writers as radically queer or feminist. Miller argues that this is a mistake which closes down the complexity of a very important period in queer American fiction. The interwar atmosphere of broadbased leftist politics made available to fiction writers a picture of racial and sexual identities as a set of complex interrelations. Using close readings of Carson McCullers' *The Member of the Wedding* (1946) and Truman Capote's *Other Voices, Other Rooms* (1948), Miller traces the use of established Gothic conventions to articulate a relationship between structures of masculinity and femininity and structures of race and culture.

Andrew Smith in 'Children of the Night: Shirley Jackson's Domestic Female Gothic' explores Jackson's tellingly entitled, if often jocular, accounts of domesticity, *Life Among the Savages* (1953) and its sequel *Raising Demons* (1957), where she repeatedly translates otherwise harmless childhood fantasies (concerning, for example imaginary friends) into adult terms which reconstitutes such fantasies as Gothic images of otherworldly 'Otherness'. Such texts suggest that motherhood requires a self-sacrifice that erodes identity, even while what is horrifying is the child's sense of developing and asserting identity. In Jackson's Female Gothic, as in *The Haunting of Hill House* (1959), the mother and child are frozen in a potentially self-destructive relationship. Jackson's writings should thus be seen as formulating a strategy of resistance in which the whole question of female identity and its construction within fraught familial bonds is foregrounded. Smith argues that how to find the way out of stifling domestic bonds is thus a key aspect of Jackson's Female Gothic and it constitutes a desire for a politics of liberation which represents a coming into being of what became a major political issue in America in the 1960s.

Anya Heise-von der Lippe's 'Others, Monsters, Ghosts: Representations of the Female Gothic Body in Toni Morrison's *Beloved* and *Love*' examines the metaphor of the monstrous body. She argues that as a thematically flexible concept it has the ability to both reinforce and challenge the established villain–victim structures of the Gothic tradition. The chapter explores how Toni Morrison's theory-conscious texts involve the reader in meta-fictional discussions of race, gender and genre. Morrison's representations of conjunctions between race, gender, history and the process of memory, or rememory, articulate a model of female African-American identity which is indebted to the structure of the Female Gothic.

Kirsti Bohata in '"Unhomely moments": Reading and Writing Nation in Welsh Female Gothic' follows David Punter and other postcolonial critics who have highlighted the importance of the Gothic for exploring the fractures, borders and hybridities created by colonial and post-colonial situations, in order to explore the Female Gothic as it appears in twentieth-century Anglophone Welsh writing in English. Her essay focuses in particular on the tensions produced by the figure of the house (here often ruined, deserted, cursed, haunted or burning) when it functions as both symbol of imprisoning patriarchal structures and as a trope of nationhood. Thus ideas of nation(hood) and gender intersect and complicate each other in the texts she discusses, notably Hilda Vaughan's *The Soldier and the Gentlewoman* (1932) and Mary Jones's *Resistance* (1985).

Carol Margaret Davison's 'Monstrous Regiments of Women and Brides of Frankenstein: Gendered Body Politics in Scottish Female Gothic Fiction' argues that early British Gothic novels set in Scotland often represent northern Britain as a divided, jingoistic nation unnaturally misguided by a monstrous regiment of passionate, treacherous, domineering women. While Scottish Gothic literature of the nineteenth century, written by Scottish writers, generally failed to take up the gendered aspect of a feminised, monstrous Scotland, it frequently exposed the dark underbelly of capitalism and British paternalism. However, it was only in the late twentieth century, against the backdrop of a growing Scottish independence movement, that Scottish Female Gothic narratives began to engage with the loaded and problematic conception of a feminised, 'castrated' Scotland. To that end Iain Banks's *The Wasp Factory* (1984) and Alasdair Gray's *Poor Things* (1992) – two works notably written by men – wield post-structural poetics to construct dark comic Gothic allegories about Scottish national identity and the Act of Union.

The Female Gothic, as the essays in this volume bear testimony, is shaped by many issues, including national identity, sexuality, language, race and history. It is also the case that the form challenges and complicates such issues and this is why it is of such major literary and cultural importance. As Juliann Fleenor argues, 'There is not just one Gothic, but Gothics' (4), with many different forms and levels. These change and shift as new writers transform and renew the form. But we need to retain a sense of history, of the line which runs from even further back than Radcliffe (from Sophia Lee's *The Recess* [1783] and Clara Reeve's *The Old English Baron* [1778]) down to Toni Morrison and to the new 'postfeminist Gothic' of Buffy and her peers. Retaining the term 'Female Gothic' as a broad and fluid category – while both interrogating it and acknowledging its many mutations (feminist Gothic, lesbian Gothic, comic Gothic, postfeminist Gothic) – is one way of doing this.

Notes

1. Ellen Moers, *Literary Women* (London: The Women's Press, [1976] 1978), 90. All subsequent references are to this edition and are given in the text.
2. Chris Baldick and Robert Mighall, 'Gothic Criticism' in David Punter, ed., *A Companion to the Gothic* (Oxford: Blackwell, 2000), 209–28, 227. All subsequent references are to this edition and are given in the text.
3. Sandra M. Gilbert and Susan Gubar, *The Madwoman in the Attic: The Woman Writer and the Nineteenth-century Literary Imagination* (New Haven and London: Yale University Press, [1979] 1984), 75. All subsequent references are to this edition and are given in the text.
4. Juliann Fleenor, ed., *The Female Gothic* (Montreal: Eden, 1983).
5. Margaret Ann Doody, 'Deserts, Ruins and Troubled Waters: Female Dreams in Fiction and the Development of the Gothic Novel', *Genre* 10 (Winter 1977), 529–72, 560; quoted in Fleenor, 13.
6. Doody, 562.
7. Claire Kahane, 'The Gothic Mirror' [1980] reprinted in Shirley Nelson Garner, Claire Kahane and Madelon Sprengnether, eds, *The (M)other Tongue: Essays in Feminist Psychoanalytic Interpretation* (Ithaca and London: Cornell University Press, 1985), 334–51.
8. Juliann Fleenor, ed., 'Introduction', *The Female Gothic* (Montreal: Eden, 1983), 27. All subsequent references are to this edition and are given in the text.
9. Kate Ferguson Ellis, *The Contested Castle: Gothic Novels and the Subversion of Domestic Ideology* (Urbana, IL: University of Illinois Press, 1989).
10. Eugenia DeLamotte, *Perils of the Night: A Feminist Study of Nineteenth-Century Gothic* (Oxford: Oxford University Press, 1990).
11. Alison Milbank, *Daughters of the House: Modes of Gothic in Victorian Fiction* (Basingstoke: Macmillan, 1992).
12. Anne Williams, *Art of Darkness: A Poetics of Gothic* (Chicago and London: Chicago University Press, 1995).
13. Robert Miles, ed., 'Introduction', *Women's Writing: The Elizabethan to the Victorian Period*, special number on Female Gothic 1/2 (1994), 131, 132.
14. Robert Miles, *Ann Radcliffe: The Great Enchantress* (Manchester: Manchester University Press, 1995).
15. Diane Long Hoeveler, *Gothic Feminism: The Professionalisation of Gender from Charlotte Smith to the Brontes* (Pennsylvania State University Press; Liverpool: Liverpool University Press, 1998), 7.

16. Tania Modleski, *Loving With a Vengeance: Mass-Produced Fantasies for Women* (New York and London: Routledge, [1982] 1990); Joanna Russ, 'Somebody's Trying to Kill Me and I Think it's My Husband: The Modern Gothic', *Journal of Popular Culture* 6 (Spring 1973), 666–91.
17. Avril Horner and Sue Zlosnik, *Daphne du Maurier: Writing, Identity and the Gothic Imagination* (Basingstoke: Macmillan, 1998).
18. Avril Horner and Sue Zlosnik, *Gothic and the Comic Turn* (Basingstoke: Palgrave, 2005).
19. Suzanne Becker, *Gothic Forms of Feminine Fiction* (Manchester: Manchester University Press, 1999).
20. Paulina Palmer, *Lesbian Gothic: Transgressive Fictions* (London: Cassell, 1999), 8.
21. E. J. Clery, *Women's Gothic: From Clara Reeve to Mary Shelley*, Writers and their Work series (Tavistock: Northcote, 2000), 2.
22. Benjamin A. Brabon and Stéphanie Genz, eds, 'Introduction', *Postfeminist Gothic: Critical Interventions in Contemporary Culture* (Basingstoke: Palgrave Macmillan, 2007), 7. All subsequent references are to this edition and are given in the text.
23. Andrew Smith and Diana Wallace, eds, *Gothic Studies* 6/1 (May 2004), special number on the Female Gothic.

1
Female Gothic and the Institutionalisation of Gothic Studies

Lauren Fitzgerald

Does Female Gothic have anything left to offer? Entrenched in Gothic studies for nearly thirty years and increasingly attacked during the past decade, this critical category seems to many to have outlived its usefulness. Nonetheless, there are still critical lessons to be learned from it, as much about the recent history of Gothic criticism as Gothic works themselves. Indeed, we would do well to contemplate what scholarly reputation not only feminist criticism of the Gothic but also Gothic criticism more generally would enjoy were it not for the intervention of Female Gothic.

Apparently first made public in a lecture delivered in the early 1970s at the University of Warwick (where 'Germaine Greer was a superbly scholarly heckler') and first published in articles for the *New York Review of Books* in 1974, Female Gothic is best known as the subject of a chapter in Ellen Moers's influential study of women's literature, *Literary Women* (1976).[1] Moers was not the first critic to be interested in the positive connections between women and the Gothic (as opposed to the eighteenth-century disparagement of the form's women readers), nor was she the only early feminist literary critic to express interest in the Gothic.[2] But through the telescoping effect of hindsight, her coinage has become a pivotal moment in the timeline often drawn of twentieth-century Gothic criticism, marking the point when, as Anne Williams puts it, 'feminist critics...recognized that gender is crucial in the Gothic.'[3]

Female Gothic is less noteworthy as an 'original' insight that emerged *sui generis* from Moers's critical sensibilities than as a product of a specific historical moment. Most important, the formulation of this category was the result of the rise of feminism and feminist literary criticism in the US during the late 1960s and 1970s. Moers herself makes the significance of this historical context clear in her preface to *Literary Women*. Recalling that though she had once believed it 'futile' to discuss women writers apart 'from the general course of literary history', feminism, and 'the dramatically unfolding, living literary history' of 'women's liberation' in particular, persuaded her otherwise (xi–xii). More specifically, as precisely the kind of singling out of women writers that Moers had initially rejected, Female Gothic was an expression of the 'second phase' of American feminist literary criticism, which focused on uncovering the lost tradition of women's literature, rather than revealing cultural traditions of misogyny as Kate Millett, for example, had done in her 'first phase' classic, *Sexual Politics* (1970).[4]

The advantages of hitching the Gothic's wagon to feminism's star by way of Female Gothic were many. As Robert Miles points out, doing so was essential to 'rescuing' the reputation of such women writers as Ann Radcliffe from critics who found her 'childish fantasies', 'gently spooky fiction' and 'concern for external circumstance' lacking the 'deeper implications' available in the work of such male writers as Matthew Lewis.[5] Maybe just as important, feminist literary criticism also rescued Gothic studies. David Richter, in an examination of the critical reception of the form, argues that feminism was 'perhaps the most obvious force at work' that transformed 'a field that was once neglected at best – and at worst a bastion of bibliophilic cranks' into 'a very important area of study'.[6] Similarly, David Punter and Victor Sage hold that feminist readings were on the cutting edge of late twentieth-century criticism of the Gothic, producing 'the most energetic' and 'interesting and important' of these discussions.[7] Feminism, in other words, was instrumental in institutionalising Gothic studies. Reflecting on the 'substantial gains' made since the late 1970s, Coral Ann Howells acknowledges that scholars no longer have 'to argue for the legitimacy of Gothic as a proper subject of literary study'.[8]

But there were also disadvantages to the feminist connection. Many of the problems with Female Gothic as a critical category which became evident in the 1990s – that it is 'unsatisfyingly simple' and 'common-sense', encouraging 'certain assumptions' about 'the intrinsic "femaleness" of Gothic fiction' by 'accepting gender as the bedrock of explanation' – were themselves difficulties that post-structuralist theory of the 1980s had discovered in American feminist literary criticism more generally.[9] (One could perhaps posit, then, that like Moers's coinage, the reaction against Female Gothic was a product of a specific historical moment, in this case, English studies after theory.) It might be too that just as feminism accrued costs through institutionalisation, as Ellen Messer-Davidow has recently charted, so did Gothic studies, though, admittedly, at a somewhat lower price. Whereas feminism failed to transform the academy that it was co-opted by, Gothic criticism, as Howells continues, merely fails to 'pay ... close attention to the slippages and oddities in these texts now that we have ready made theoretical perspectives through which to read them'.[10]

If feminist criticism, for better and worse, transformed how the Gothic is read and its status within the academy, the Gothic also changed feminist criticism. Feminist critics offered key insights into the centrality of property in Gothic fiction by women writers; Moers is almost as well known for 'pioneering' the view that 'property seems to loom larger than love in *Udolpho*' (136) as she is for her 'pioneer essay' on the Female Gothic.[11] Yet in pursuing these property interests, feminist critics of the Gothic often reproduce the plots and characters of their object of study. The critical tale of Radcliffe's place in the Gothic, and especially of her relationship with Lewis, is itself a kind of property plot – a tale of claims and counterclaims that finally inscribes both Ellen Moers and feminist criticism into this narrative. Female Gothic as defined by Moers may present difficulties as a critical category, but it still has the power to teach us an important lesson about the sway that the Gothic has had over readers, criticism and culture.

* * *

At least some of Moers's and other feminist critics' interest in property issues originates in Anglo-American feminist traditions. Mary Wollstonecraft's call for women's economic self-reliance in *A Vindication of the Rights of Woman* (1792), for example, reverberated in nineteenth-century 'feminist efforts ... directed to extending women's property rights and gaining recognized entry into employment'. These proprietary concerns continued in the twentieth century, from Virginia Woolf's demand for *A Room of One's Own* to Pro-Choice rhetoric of the abortion debates of the 1970s and 1980s, the latter forwarding a kind of feminist possessive individualism to argue that women have the right to choose because their bodies are their own.[12] Late twentieth-century American feminist literary criticism, with its claims for women's less literal ownership of a literary tradition, yields a similar concern.

Feminist criticism of the 1970s and 1980s is marked by a series of proprietary metaphors, including 'maps', 'territories', 'breaking ground', 'space', and 'landmarks' that, unremarkable individually, suggest a shared perspective when examined together. Elaine Showalter, for instance, punned on Woolf's demand in her title for *A Literature of Their Own* (1977), which with Moers's *Literary Women* and Sandra M. Gilbert and Susan Gubar's *The Madwoman in the Attic* (1979) formed the core of the second phase of feminist criticism in the US, what Showalter later described, in proprietary terms, as the moment 'when feminist criticism set out to map the territory of the female imagination'.[13] Mapping this territory did not come easily. In 1980, a year after the publication of *Madwoman*, Gilbert framed the difficulties she and Gubar faced in their initial 'attempt[s] to recover [...] the female literary tradition' as a tale of women denied property rights:

> The treasures of Western culture, it began to seem, were the patrimony of male writers, or to put it another way, Western culture itself was a grand ancestral property that educated men had inherited from their intellectual forefathers, while their female relatives, like characters in a Jane Austen novel, were relegated to modest dower houses on the edge of the estate.[14]

By 1985, the status of these 'female relatives' had improved enough for Showalter to write of their proprietary 'success'. Feminist criticism, she held, opened up a 'space' amidst those 'zealously guarded bastions of male intellectual endeavor' – literary criticism and theory – and recovered a lost inheritance, 'the whole body of texts that make up our literary heritage'.[15] The history of American feminist literary criticism, then, can be summed up by a story of property lost and regained.

In *Literary Women*, Moers similarly highlights the importance of women's 'possession of their own tradition' (42). And nowhere is this proprietary concern more significant than in her brief definition of Female Gothic and the manner in which it draws on a set of cultural connections between the body, ownership, and texts. 'What I mean by Female Gothic is easily defined,' she insists: 'the work that women writers have done in the literary mode that, since the eighteenth century, we have called the Gothic' (90). Moers's assertion of the 'ease' of this definition masks a number of crucial complications, not the least of which is the essentialist link between the biological sex of the writer and the 'gender' of the text. Similarly complex is her implicit claim for women's ownership of a substantial portion of the Gothic. This claim turns on Moers's use of the word 'work', and particularly the phrase 'the work that women writers have done', identifying simultaneously the literary productions of these women writers and the labour that produced them. Like much Pro-Choice rhetoric of the 1970s and 1980s, Moers draws on an argument for ownership based in the body. With literary property at stake, however, her allusion to Lockean posses-sive individualism also harkens back to reasoning used since the mid-eighteenth-century copyright debates to defend the author's rights to the property in his – or her – work. As Locke maintains in *Two Treatises of Government*, beginning with one's '*Property* in his own *Person*', own-ership extends outward to that which is produced by 'The *Labour* of his Body, and the *Work* of his Hands'. Eighteenth-century supporters of authorial rights in turn extended this premise to literary productions.[16] Moers's sex-based emphasis helps to clinch her case for Female Gothic, grounding ownership in the body of the *woman* writer. She outlines this point early on in *Literary Women*, detailing the way in which the 'great' women writers chose 'among the varying feminine facets of the human condition' and 'transformed this material...into literature'; 'Being women, women writers have women's bodies,' she asserts, 'which affect their senses and their imagery' (xi).

Feminism's (and post-enlightenment Western culture's) investment in property as the ground for rights and personhood help to account for some of the concern for ownership in Moers's definition of Female Gothic. But the particular shape of her and later feminist critics' narra-tives of women's claim to the Gothic more closely resembles Radcliffe's narratives and, in particular, the 'property interests' in *The Mysteries of Udolpho* (1794) that Moers was the first twentieth-century critic to remark upon. As Moers explains, 'property interests dominate the second half of the novel': 'the death of her aunt makes Emily an heiress; in most of the ensuing chapters, she is engaged gently, pensively, yet firmly in the consolidation of her property. Her struggle with the vil-lain Montoni is essentially legalistic, [and] concerns her property rights' (136). In its simplest terms, this plot charts Emily's initial claim to real estate (not only her aunt's but also her father's) that Montoni usurps from her but which she finally reclaims as her own. (The 'last page', notes Moers, 'is given over to legacies, estates, [and] marriage portions' [137].) Though especially pronounced in *Udolpho*, this property plot also forms the backbone of *The Romance of the Forest* (1791) and *The Italian* (1797), and is even suggested in Radcliffe's first romance, *The Castles of Athlin and Dunbayne* (1789).

Beginning with Moers's remarks on Radcliffe in her article-turned-chapter on Female Gothic, the feminist response to Radcliffe casts her as Emily in a critical tale that endures for several decades. Though

Moers is clearly more interested in the birth myth of Mary Shelley's *Frankenstein* (1818), at the onset of her discussion of Female Gothic she grants Radcliffe primacy in the Gothic domain (somewhat anachronistically, as we now know). According to Moers, Radcliffe 'firmly set the Gothic in one of the ways it would go ever after' and was consequently hailed 'as mistress of the pure Gothic form' (91). (Significantly, perhaps, Emily too is 'mistress', of herself and her father's and aunt's estates.[17]) Despite often explicitly positioning themselves against this early feminist project, many later feminist readers of the Gothic followed Moers's lead in their representations of Radcliffe's proprietary claims. Comments by Margaret Doody (in 1977), Cynthia Griffin Wolff (in 1983), and Eugenia DeLamotte (in 1990) plot a history of the Gothic in which Radcliffe takes precedence. Horace Walpole's *The Castle of Otranto* (1764) and its immediate successors, they argue, only offered 'the trappings of the Gothic story without its essence' and 'assembled the materials of Gothicism'.[18] As the 'great inaugurator of the genre', Radcliffe 'issued the "invitation to form" ' and 'introduced Gothic conventions into the mainstream of English fiction'.[19] If any single author could be said to 'own' the Gothic, they suggest, it is Radcliffe.

More tellingly Gothic is feminist criticism's representation of the literary transactions of Radcliffe, Matthew Lewis, and his scandalous novel *The Monk* (1796). Of course, feminist critics did not invent the story of Radcliffe's and Lewis's intertextual relationship; well before the 1970s it was common to read *The Monk* as a response to *Udolpho* and *The Italian* as a response to *The Monk*. By emphasising gender, however, Moers and subsequent feminist readers reformulated the relationship. As Kate Ferguson Ellis has recently observed, the Gothic's 'feminist defenders have argued that it was practically created by women writers ... From this perspective, the earliest male Gothicists undertook to wrest the form from the female hands in which they saw it too firmly grasped' – what Deborah Ross contends was 'an attempt to regain some lost ground' and 'masculinize, or remasculinize, Gothic fiction'.[20] From this rough outline it is but a short step to Gothic heroines and villains struggling over property rights, with Radcliffe playing Emily to Lewis's Montoni (a role he seems to have anticipated, likening himself to the 'Villain' of *Udolpho* in a letter that acknowledges his debt to Radcliffe).[21] Just as Emily is repeatedly 'shocked' by Montoni's acts of 'deliberate villainy' (*Udolpho* 270, 363, 436), Radcliffe was apparently 'shocked' by Lewis's attempt to 'wrest the form' from her, as well as to sully it with sexual content.[22]

In Moers's initiation of the feminist version of this literary relation-ship, Radcliffe, like Emily, does not retreat into feminine propriety in the face of such villainous transgressions. Though Radcliffe 'seems to have been dismayed by Matthew Lewis's avowed imitation of her work in his shocking novel called *The Monk*', writes Moers, 'in defense of her genre she then wrote *The Italian*, a work which is at once a bor-rowing from and a severe corrective to "Monk" Lewis's erotic fantasy' (137). And it is what Moers highlights as Emily's 'essentially legalistic' debates with Montoni over her aunt's property that structures much of the feminist reception of Radcliffe's response to *The Monk*.[23] According to Syndy Conger, *The Italian* is 'a sustained counterstatement' to and a 'near point-by-point refutation of' *The Monk*. And for many critics, Ross reports, 'Radcliffe had the last word in this "debate"'. Emily is finally able to reclaim her Gothic territory from Montoni; likewise, 'Radcliffe succeeded in claiming Gothic as "female"', Susan Wolstenholme argues, and in 'reclaiming a certain textual space' from male writers of the Gothic, particularly Lewis.[24]

The reproduction of this Gothic property plot is very likely due to a number of causes. As I've argued elsewhere, such critical Gothic tales are endemic to the history of Radcliffe's and Lewis's receptions, emer-ging almost from the moment their romances were first published.[25] Cultural and critical imperatives also help to explain the Gothic nature of feminist criticism. As we've seen, like post-enlightenment culture, both Female Gothic and Anglo-American feminism share a common fascination with property. Moreover, feminist literary criticism draws connections between its objects of study and its own project. Moers, for instance, attributes to Radcliffe influence not only on feminist criti-cism but feminism more broadly, declaring 'the Gothic fantasies of Mrs. Radcliffe...a locus of heroinism' – another of Moers's coinages – 'which, ever since, women have turned to feminist purposes' (126, 147). Similarly, Gilbert and Showalter find that feminist criticism repeats 'the revisionary imperative' and 'patterns of influence and rebellion that mark the female literary tradition'.[26] As a result, feminist critics see themselves and each other as part of the tradition they study. In a commemoration of the twentieth anniversary of *Literary Women*, for example, several scholars influenced by Moers figure her as the very type of 'literary woman' she described. Just as Moers saw her work as a 'celebration of the great women who have spoken for us all' (xv) and a 'tribute to the great women of the past who did in fact break ground for literary women' (63), so too do these later admirers 'celebrate the ongoing influence of Moers's work' through 'meditations on Moers's legacy'. Not surprisingly, they do so in proprietary terms. *Literary Women* is not only '*groundbreaking*'; it was part of a movement in feminist criticism 'that gave definition to the critical landscape', itself 'laying claim to great and unmarked territory' and enabling Moers to 'explore the significance of women's literary inheritance'.[27]

Although Moers might not have made such grand claims for herself, it seems clear that like much feminist criticism of the Gothic she was part of the Female Gothic tradition. As we have seen, the feminist response to Radcliffe, particularly in relation to Lewis, is often 'work that women writers have done' in the Gothic 'mode'. But it is not only the Gothic tale of Radcliffe and Lewis that incorporates these critics into the literary women's tradition of Female Gothic. Feminist criticism of the Gothic has also tended to vilify earlier (male) critics for attempting, like Lewis, to 'reclaim some lost ground' from women writers. When Leslie Fiedler, for example, finds that Radcliffe's 'gently spooky fiction' misses out on the 'deeper implications' of the Gothic, he is, insists DeLamotte, casting Radcliffe off of her own estate: 'Radcliffe...is defined out' and 'relegated to the periphery of the genre she herself did most to define'.[28] In countering this villainy, feminist criticism becomes more thoroughly embedded in the Female Gothic tradition, finally figuring critics themselves as heroines. By asserting Radcliffe's and other women writers' rights to the Gothic, feminist critics, like Emily and Radcliffe in their legalistic debates with Montoni and Lewis, offer their own 'point-by-point refutation of' and 'severe corrective to' the masculine counterclaim. Yet it is Moers who remains the most proprietary of these critical heroines. In naming Female Gothic, she initiated women's claim to the Gothic and reclaimed women's lost legacy from masculinising villains such as Fiedler.

* * *

By the early 1990s, it was increasingly difficult to maintain such claims for Female Gothic. In addition to the complications of making reference to, much less connections between, 'body', 'text', 'women' and 'literature', the influence of this category and the Gothic in general on Gothic criticism became both apparent and suspect.[29] For Diane Long Hoeveler, especially damaging was feminist criticism's reproduction of what she describes as 'victim feminism', 'an ideology of female power through pretended and staged weakness' that Female Gothic texts did not simply express but contributed to. 'Discussions of the female gothic,' she writes, 'have, unfortunately, uncritically participated in the very fantasies' that the Gothic helped to create.[30] By the late 1990s, then, Female Gothic was something to rid ourselves of. Indeed, not only has the familiar tale of Radcliffe's – and her feminist critics' – struggle with masculinist villains such as Lewis and Fiedler fallen by the wayside; it is now possible to publish on women's Gothic fiction with only cursory reference to Female Gothic and none at all to Moers.[31] The disappearance of this Gothic tale seems not to mean, however, that Gothic criticism has finally escaped the clutches of its object of study. Mark Edmundson, for instance, finds that aspects of the form have seeped into theory itself. 'Much, though surely not all, of what is called theory draws on Gothic idioms,' he argues. He cites Derrida and Žižek but concludes that 'the most intriguing exponent of Gothic theory is surely Michel Foucault' with his 'haunting agency' of 'Power'.[32] If Edmundson is correct, the very tools used to dismantle Female Gothic as a critical category are themselves Gothic.

Does the beginning of the twenty-first century mark the end of the story for Female Gothic and Ellen Moers's critical legacy? I realise that by attempting to recuperate Moers and make a claim for her rightful place in the history of Gothic criticism, I enter into the Gothic plot she laid out so well. Just as Moers positioned Radcliffe as her proprietary heroine, so too am I situating Moers as Radcliffe and asserting that she has an equally valid claim to the Gothic domain. The inevitability of this move is in fact part of my point. Moers has a place not only in the history of Gothic criticism but also in the Gothic tradition, as much, really, as Radcliffe. Neither is quite the 'originator' of Female Gothic, as tradition or critical category, as was once believed, but their importance as 'pioneers' in both is indisputable. My argument might be more persuasive if we consider the genre in which Moers wrote and what it implies for her work on Female Gothic. Though far from a Gothic romance, *Literary Women*, like her articles for *The New York Review of Books* and like Radcliffe's works as well, was intended for an educated, but essentially non-academic, reading public.[33] Moers remarks in her preface that one effect of the feminist movement was that it 'pulled [her] out of the stacks and made the writing of [her] book' something of 'an open-air activity' often born out of 'public lectures' (xii). Traces of this 'open-air' process of writing *Literary Women* can be seen in the ease with which she refers to such campy, contemporary, pseudo-feminist icons as Virginia Slims cigarettes and Patty Hearst (129) and 'present[s]...the critic herself', as Janet Todd notes, 'the writer situated in a specific time'.[34] If we do not acknowledge the ways in which *Literary Women* is deeply different from the kind of literary criticism we have come to expect in an age of super-specialisation, and instead continue to read and institutionalise it as *only* an academic project, we are doomed to relegate Moers to the periphery of a field she helped to define. In other words, Moers's discussion of Female Gothic is not only a lens through which to view the tradition of Gothic texts she mapped but also part of this tradition and therefore part of our object of study. Further, her work marks the point at which 1970s feminism began to participate in the Gothic tradition. Intriguingly, Anne Williams points out that 'The advent of feminist criticism in the early 1970s coincided with a decline of the '60s mass-market Gothic.'[35] It is perhaps feminist literary criticism of Female Gothic, with Moers as its chief contributor, that became the alternative.

Notes

1. Ellen Moers, 'Female Gothic: The Monster's Mother' and 'Female Gothic: Monsters, Goblins, Freaks,' *New York Review of Books* (21 March 1974), 24–8 and (4 April 1974), 35–9; Ellen Moers, *LiteraryWomen* (Garden City, NY: Doubleday, 1976; Rpt. New York: Oxford UP, 1985), xii. All subsequent references to *Literary Women* are to this edition and are given in the text.
2. David Richter attributes twentieth-century feminist critics' interest in the Gothic in part to the earlier, negative view of Gothic as 'female reading'. See *The Progress of Romance: Literary Historiography and the Gothic Novel* (Columbus, Ohio: Ohio State UP, 1996), 2; Bette B. Roberts, *The Gothic Romance: Its Appeal to Women Writers and Readers in Late Eighteenth-Century England* (New York: Arno Press [1975], 1980), 5–6 and Jacqueline Howard, *Reading Gothic Fiction: A Bakhtinian Approach* (Oxford: Clarendon Press, 1994), 60, point to several twentieth-century critics who addressed the connection between women and the Gothic before Moers. Feminist critics interested in the Gothic contemporary with Moers but apparently unaware of her work include Coral Ann Howells (as Howard notes, 59) and Roberts.
3. Anne Williams, *The Art of Darkness: A Poetics of the Gothic* (Chicago and London: University of Chicago Press, 1995), 100.
4. See Vincent B. Leitch, *American Literary Criticism from the Thirties to the Eighties* (New York: Columbia UP, 1988), chapter 11.
5. Robert Miles, *Gothic Writing 1750–1820: A Genealogy* (London and New York: Routledge, 1993), 124; Lowry Nelson, Jr, 'Night Thoughts on the Gothic Novel,' *Yale Review* 52 (1963), 236–57, 238; Leslie A. Fiedler, *Love and Death in the American Novel* (New York: Stein and Day [1960], 1966), 129; Robert D. Hume, 'Gothic Versus Romantic: A Revaluation of the Gothic Novel,' *PMLA* 84 (1969), 282–90, 285.
6. Richter, 2.
7. David Punter, *The Literature of Terror: A History of Gothic Fictions from 1765 to the Present Day. Vol. 1: The Gothic Tradition*, 2nd ed. (London and New York: Longman, 1996), 211; Victor Sage, 'Introduction,' *The Gothick Novel: A Casebook*, ed. Sage (London: MacMillan Education, 1990), 25.

8. Coral Ann Howells, *Love, Mystery and Misery: Feeling in Gothic Fiction* (London and Atlantic Highlands, NJ: Athlone [1978], 1995), vii.
9. Williams, 11; E. J. Clery, 'Ann Radcliffe and D. A. F. de Sade: Thoughts on Heroinism,' *Women's Writing*, special number: 'Female Gothic Writing,' ed. Robert Miles 1/2 (1994), 203–14, 203; Robert Miles, 'Introduction,' *Women's Writing* 1/2 (1994), 134. For discussions of the shortcomings of American feminist criticism, see Toril Moi, *Sexual/Textual Politics: Feminist Literary Theory* (London and New York: Methuen, 1985); Janet Todd, *Feminist Literary History* (New York: Routledge, 1998) 1, 76; and Ellen Messer-Davidow, *Disciplining Feminism: From Social Activism to Academic Discourse* (Durham and London: Duke UP, 2002), chapter 5.
10. Howells, vii.
11. E. J. Clery, *The Rise of Supernatural Fiction, 1762–1800* (Cambridge and New York: Cambridge UP, 1995), 194n.; Sage, 25. For subsequent feminist discussions of the importance of property in Radcliffe's works, see Mary Poovey, 'Ideology and *The Mysteries of Udolpho*,' *Criticism* 21 (1979), 307–30; Kate Ferguson Ellis, *The Contested Castle: Gothic Novels and the Subversion of Domestic Ideology* (Urbana, IL: University of Illinois Press, 1989), chapter 6; and Diane Long Hoeveler, *Gothic Feminism: The Professionalization of Gender from Charlotte Smith to the Brontës* (University Park, PA: The Pennsylvania State UP, 1998), chapters 2–3.
12. Mary Wollstonecraft, *A Vindication of the Rights of Woman* (1792), in *Mary Wollstonecraft: The Political Writings*, ed. Janet Todd (Toronto: University of Toronto Press, 1993), 67–296; Lenore Davidoff and Catherine Hall, *Family Fortunes: Men and Women of the English Middle Class, 1780–1850* (Chicago, IL: Chicago UP, 1987), 453; Virginia Woolf, *A Room of One's Own* (San Diego, CA and New York: Harcourt Brace Jovanovich [1929], 1957). See Lauren Fitzgerald '(In)alienable Rights: Property, Feminism, and the Female Body from Ann Radcliffe to the *Alien* Films,' *Romanticism on the Net* 21 (February 2001) [Accessed 17 April 2001], http://users.ox.ac.uk/~scat0385/21fitzgerald.html.
13. Elaine Showalter, *A Literature of Their Own: British Women Novelists from Brontë to Lessing* (Princeton, NJ: Princeton UP, 1977); Sandra M. Gilbert and Susan Gubar, *The Madwoman in the Attic: The Woman Writer and the Nineteenth-Century Literary Imagination* (New Haven, CT: Yale UP, 1979); Showalter, 'Introduction,' *The New Feminist Criticism: Essays on Women, Literature, and Theory*, ed. Showalter (New York: Pantheon, 1985), 3, 6.
14. Sandra M. Gilbert, 'What Do Feminist Critics Want? A Postcard from the Volcano,' *ADE Bulletin* 66 (1980), rpt. in *The New Feminist Criticism*, ed. Showalter, 29–45, 33.
15. Showalter, 'Introduction,' 3.
16. John Locke, *Two Treatises of Government: A Critical Edition with an Introduction and Apparatus Criticus*, ed. Peter Laslett, 2nd ed. (New York: Cambridge UP, 1967), 305–6, Locke's emphasis. Mark Rose holds that the copyright debates disseminated a 'blending of the Lockean discourse [of private property] and the aesthetic discourse of originality'. See 'The Author as Proprietor: *Donaldson v. Becket* and the Genealogy of Modern Authorship,' *Representations* (1988), 51–85, 56. William Enfield, for example, a contemporary man of letters involved in the debates (as well as a reviewer of Radcliffe's works for the *Monthly Review*) maintained that because 'Literary

compositions are the effect of labour[,] authors have therefore a natural right of property in their work'. *Observations on Literary Property* (1774), in *The Literary Property Debate: Eight Tracts, 1774–1775*, ed. Stephen Parks (New York and London: Garland, 1975), 1–52, 21.

17. Ann Radcliffe, *The Mysteries of Udolpho*, ed. Bonamy Dobrée, introd. Terry Castle (Oxford and New York: Oxford UP, 1998), 516. All subsequent references are to this edition and are given in the text.

18. Margaret Anne Doody, 'Deserts, Ruins, and Troubled Waters: Female Dreams in Fiction and the Development of the Gothic Novel,' *Genre* 10 (1977), 529–72, 552; Eugenia C. DeLamotte, *Perils of the Night: A Feminist Study of Nineteenth-Century Gothic* (New York and Oxford: Oxford UP, 1990), 10.

19. DeLamotte, 10, 12; Cynthia Griffin Wolff, 'The Radcliffean Gothic Model: A Form for Feminine Sexuality,' in *The Female Gothic*, ed. Juliann E. Fleenor (Montreal: Eden Press, 1983), 207–23, 223.

20. Kate Ferguson Ellis, 'Can You Forgive Her? The Gothic Heroine and Her Critics' in *A Companion to the Gothic*, ed. David Punter (Oxford and Malden, MA: Blackwell, 2000), 257–68, 257; Deborah Ross, *The Excellence of Falsehood: Romance, Realism, and Women's Contribution to the Novel* (Lexington, KY: University Press of Kentucky, 1991), 140.

21. Quoted in Louis F. Peck, *A Life of Matthew G. Lewis* (Cambridge, MA: Harvard UP, 1961), 209.

22. Patricia Meyer Spacks, *Desire and Truth: Functions of Plot in Eighteenth-Century English Novels* (Chicago, IL: University of Chicago Press, 1990), 150; Syndy Conger, 'Sensibility Restored: Radcliffe's Answer to Lewis's *The Monk*,' in *Gothic Fictions: Prohibition/Transgression*, ed. Kenneth W. Graham (New York: AMS Press, 1989), 113–49, 113.

23. At least a few feminist critics, however, have read Radcliffe and Lewis's literary relationship not through *Udolpho* but *The Monk*. See Lauren Fitzgerald, 'Crime, Punishment, Criticism: *The Monk* as Prolepsis,' *Gothic Studies* 5/1 (2003): 43–54.

24. Conger, 129, 144; Ross, 141; Susan Wolstoneholme, *Gothic (Re)Visions: Writing Women as Readers* (Albany, NY: State University of New York Press, 1993), 16.

25. Lauren Fitzgerald, 'Gothic Properties of Walpole's Legacy: Ann Radcliffe's Contemporary Reception,' in *Fictions of Unease: The Gothic from Otranto to The X-Files*, ed. Andrew Smith, Diane Mason and William Hughes (Bath: Sulis Press, 2002), 29–42.

26. Gilbert, 35; Showalter, 'Introduction,' 4.

27. Deborah Epstein Nord, 'Introduction,' 'Commemorating *Literary Women*: Ellen Moers and Feminist Criticism after Twenty Years,' *Signs* 24 (1999), 733–7, 733, 736; Sharon O'Brien, ' "I Can Dare to Generalize": Celebrating *Literary Women*,' *Signs* 24 (1999), 757–62, 757–8, her emphasis.

28. DeLamotte, 12.

29. See, for example, Eve Kosofsky Sedgwick, *The Coherence of Gothic Conventions* (New York: Methuen [1975], 1986), 140; Elizabeth Napier, *The Failure of Gothic: Problems of Disjunction in an Eighteenth-century Literary Form* (Oxford: Clarendon Press, 1987), 2; Chris Baldick and Robert Mighall, 'Gothic Criticism' in *A Companion to the Gothic*, ed. David Punter (Oxford and Malden, MA: Blackwell, 2000), 209–28, 210.

30. Hoeveler, 7, 3.
31. See E. J. Clery, *Women's Gothic: From Clara Reeve to Mary Shelley* (Tavistock: Northcote 2000).
32. Mark Edmundson, *Nightmare on Main Street: Angels, Sadomasochism, and the Culture of Gothic* (Cambridge, MA and London: Harvard UP, 1997), 40–1.
33. *Literary Women* was initially published by a commercial press, Doubleday, before being reprinted by Oxford in 1985. As such it seems to be on the cusp of a change Messer-Davidow finds in the publication of feminist works in the 1960s and 1970s. Initially commercial presses were 'careful to select only [works] that would attract a crossover audience' – which excerpted reviews from such popular US magazines as *Saturday Review*, *Newsweek* and *Ms. Magazine* reprinted on the back of the Oxford paperback edition suggest *Literary Women* did. Soon, however, these presses 'backed away from feminist trade books that hybridized the elements of movement and academic discourses' – which *Literary Women* did also. Messer-Davidow, 133.
34. Todd, 25.
35. Williams, 7.

2

'The Haunting Idea': Female Gothic Metaphors and Feminist Theory

Diana Wallace

In *Woman as Force in History* (1946) Mary R. Beard identifies 'one obtruding idea that haunts thousands of printed pages' dealing with women: 'It is the image of woman throughout long ages of the past as a being always and everywhere subject to *male* man or as a ghostly creature too shadowy to be even that real.'[1] This is what Beard calls 'the haunting idea' (77), a phrase which has two suggestive meanings. In the first place, she is arguing that this is an idea that 'haunts' writing about women, in the sense that it is a notion to which such writing repeatedly, indeed, uncannily, returns. In the second, she is pointing to the way in which woman has been depicted as 'ghostly', haunting in the sense that she is disembodied/disempowered through being subjected to '*male* man'. Beard wants to expose this notion as a fallacy, to argue that women have had power and 'force' in history. But what she does here is to draw attention to what has been one of the most powerful metaphors in feminist theory, the idea of woman as 'dead' or 'buried (alive)' within male power structures which render her 'ghostly'. This is, of course, the metaphor which is played out again and again at the heart of Female Gothic fiction, made literal in the supposedly dead mother incarcerated in a cave-dungeon in Ann Radcliffe's *A Sicilian Romance* (1790) whose ghostly groans haunt the castle of Mazzini.

In this essay I want to explore this metaphor by looking at some of the ways in which it has been deployed in feminist theory or, rather, in Beard's phrase, the way it has 'haunted' feminist theory. Beard argued that an engagement with what she called 'long history' (vi) is mandatory for any genuine understanding of human life. Bearing this in mind, I want to trace the use of what we can call female Gothic metaphors – of women imprisoned, buried alive, and as 'ghosts' – over a period which encompasses two major 'Gothic' moments, that of the 1790s and that of the late twentieth century.

'Gothic' is a notoriously slippery term, 'Female Gothic' perhaps even more contentiously so. Critics have argued over whether the Gothic is a literary form, genre or sub-genre, a mode of writing, a set of conventions or a historical period. In her essay in this volume Meredith Miller suggests that the Gothic is itself a kind of theory. The Gothic mode is powerful, she suggests, 'not because we can theorise it as a relation between self and historical trauma but because it is, *in itself,* the perfect method for the articulation of this relationship...In this sense, the Gothic mode is already theoretical.'[2] I want to approach this slightly differently by looking at the way in which the Gothic is a kind of metaphor or, rather, a series of inter-connected metaphors. Although Eve Kosofsky Sedgwick is primarily interested in the Gothic as a set of coherent 'conventions', as indeed the 'conventional genre par excellence', she acknowledges the 'set of connected metaphors' or 'the web of metaphors' that 'underlie Gothic conventions'.[3] Equally importantly for my purposes, she draws attention to the way in which words such as 'unspeakable' or 'buried' can be used almost 'casually' (62) in the Gothic text, not because another word would do but because our familiarity with the 'latent coherence of corresponding conventions' (63) ensures that we will recognise even half-submerged associations.

We often turn to metaphor as a figure of comparison when something is 'unspeakable' (itself a key Gothic trope) or cannot be articulated in any other way. Traditional literary criticism suggested that we say that something (the tenor) is 'like...' something else (the vehicle), based on a certain similarity (ground). Metaphor is usually understood in contrast to simile as being covert rather than overt since it drops the indicator 'like' or 'as if' which characterises the latter, and as being more complex. Thus it both hides and reveals meaning. Recent criticism, drawing on post-structural understandings of language, has suggested that we cannot simply separate out or unpack the constituent parts of a metaphor. David Punter, for instance, draws attention to the range of metaphors in early Gothic novels and the difficulty of assigning a specific meaning to them: what exactly, for example, is the ubiquitous castle a metaphor *for*?[4] Psychoanalysis, Punter suggests, can be useful in considering metaphor because 'metaphor is seen as being the very ground on which a text constantly goes beyond itself in an uncanny fashion, saying both more and less than it knows' (8). But he also reminds us of the historicity of metaphor, that metaphors are not always newly minted by writers: 'we construct metaphors for our times, but we also construct a concept of the metaphorical for our times' (139). Metaphor thus is 'something inherited, something unexamined, something belonging to the cultural unconscious' (140–1).

The ghost as metaphor is a case in point in that its meanings both exceed exact analysis and shift across time. We may no longer believe in ghosts, but Peter Buse and Andrew Stott have drawn attention to 'the persistence of the *trope* of spectrality in culture'.[5] In the twentieth century, they argue, the most sustained engagement with the figure of the ghost was in 'what has come to be called "theory"'(5). The ghost, they suggest, has been a theoretical tool, a useful metaphor for what is not to be believed in. '[M]odern theory,' they conclude, 'owes a debt to ghosts' (6). Their major interests are in the use of spectrality in psychoanalysis and deconstruction, with particular reference to Derrida's *Specters of Marx* (1993).[6] Derrida's deconstructive reading of the spectres in and of Marx argues that 'the figure of the ghost is not just one figure among others. It is perhaps the hidden figure of all figures' (120). Spectrality as metaphor has particular attractions for deconstructionists who are engaged in teasing out Derridean 'phantom texts', glossed by Nicholas Royle as 'textual phantoms which do not necessarily have the solidity or objectivity of a quotation, an intertext or explicit, acknowledged presence and which do not in fact come to rest anywhere'.[7] My own interest here is in the use of female Gothic metaphors, including that of the ghost, as a useful tool in feminist theory. As Beard's use of the word 'haunting' suggests, feminist theory often bears almost invisible traces of female Gothic metaphors, through key words which evoke the coherence of Gothic conventions.[8]

Beard traces the 'haunting idea' back to Mary Wollstonecraft, but in fact such metaphors go back well beyond what we normally think of as the first 'Gothic' period. In 'Female Orations' (1662), Margaret Cavendish, Duchess of Newcastle, wrote:

> ...men are so unconscionable and cruel against us, as they endeavour to bar us of all sorts and kinds of liberty, so as not to suffer us freely to associate amongst our own sex, but would fain *bury us in their houses or beds, as in a grave*; the truth is, we live like bats or owls, labour like beasts, and die like worms.[9]

The accumulation of figurative language here – the transitive verb 'bury' acts as a metaphor but is explained and re-emphasised by the simile 'as in a grave' – gives the imagery considerable force. Both men's houses and 'their' beds – the domestic and sexual spaces, equally under male ownership – are compared to 'graves' within which women are to be 'buried', potentially 'buried alive', a state which Freud called the 'most uncanny thing of all'.[10] This is tripled by three further connected similes, offering comparisons with bats and owls, nocturnal creatures associated with graveyards, and worms, underground creatures associated with corpses, all of which have become intimately connected with what we now think of as the Gothic.

Since this is the beginning of a series of rhetorical arguments about women's position, to be spoken by different orators, it is not necessarily Cavendish's own or final position. However, the emotional force of the metaphor of burial here makes it stand out and potentially undermines the even-handedness of Cavendish's rhetorical structures. Other orations also highlight the vulnerability of women within marriage because of their lack of legal status, notably the case of a woman afraid of her violent husband who is refused protection by a judge on the grounds that it is 'lawful for a husband to govern, rule and correct his wife' (179). In her autobiography, as Elaine Hobby has shown, Cavendish defends herself from the possibility of being thought vain for having written it by asserting that she has done so

> ...lest after-ages should mistake, in not knowing I was daughter to one Master Lucas of St Johns, near Colchester, in Essex, second wife to the Lord Marquis of Newcastle, for my Lord having two wives, I might easily have been mistaken, especially if I should die, and my Lord marry again.[11]

As Hobby comments, 'There is irony in the fact that when Cavendish comes to define explicitly who she is, the only criteria she has available are the names of her father and husband' (82). What Cavendish fears here is an erasure of her identity within history ('after-ages'). The legal definition of marriage at this point, as Hobby succinctly notes, meant that 'Husband and wife were one person, and that person was the husband' (4). Given that loss of identity, it is easy to see why Cavendish might argue that men 'would fain bury us in their houses or beds, as in a grave'. The 'house' here (like the Gothic castle of later texts) is not just the domestic space, but itself a metaphor for the legal institutions of marriage and patrilineal inheritance (enacted through the 'bed') which erase the female name. Moreover, Cavendish's dramatisation of the wife in fear of her husband's violence draws attention to women's vulnerability in a legal system where, as Cavendish pointed out, they were 'subjects', not to the Commonwealth, but to their husbands (xix).

It is the powerful passage quoted above which Virginia Woolf picks out by which to characterise Cavendish herself in *A Room of One's Own* (1929): 'both [Cavendish and Lady Winchilsea] are disfigured and deformed by the same causes. Open the Duchess and one finds the same outburst of rage. "Women live like Bats or Owls, labour like Beasts, and die like Worms"'.[12] For Woolf this kind of writing is 'disfigured' by anger, an emotion she also finds in one of the most famously 'Gothic' *and* feminist moments of *Jane Eyre* (1847), the laugh Jane hears when she is on the battlements of Thornfield musing on the position of women (66–7). Moreover, in a Gothic metonomy here the 'Duchess' stands in for her book, to be 'open[ed]' like a corpse to reveal the festering or cancer-like 'rage'.

The metaphor of 'burial', then, is a particularly powerful way of figuring the erasure of the female self within a construct of marriage which only allowed the legal existence of one person – the husband. In her suggestive study, *Marriage and Violence: The Early Modern Legacy* (2008), Frances E. Dolan explores the contradictions and conflicts between three common figures for marriage in the early modern period: the Christian model of the couple as 'one flesh' but (in seeming contradiction) with the husband as 'head'; the 'legal fiction' of common law coverture whereby the husband subsumed his wife; and the comic tradition of two separate but equal individuals battling for mastery.[13] The suggestion in all three is that marriage is an 'economy of scarcity in which there is only room for one full person', thus leaving violence as the only method of resolution (3). This has left its legacy in our own period, as Dolan suggests in Gothic terms which echo Beard's claim that, 'the early modern apprehension of scarcity *haunts* the present as a *conceptual structure or plot* that concentrates entitlements and capacities in one spouse, and achieves resolution only when that spouse absorbs, subordinates, or eliminates the other' (4, emphasis added). This legacy can be seen, Dolan argues, in modern films such as *Double Indemnity* (1944 and 1999) or *Sleeping with the Enemy* (1991) where abused wives kill their husbands and in the current fashion for historical novels, like those of Philippa Gregory, set in the Tudor period which take Anne Boleyn and Elizabeth I as exemplary figures to imply the deadly nature of marriage for women. Dolan does not look at Gothic texts but her own use of Gothic metaphors suggests the relevance of her thesis to the centuries she leapfrogs. The doctrine of male headship might offer an easy answer to the question of who's in charge in marriage, she suggests for instance, but 'the *specter* of the *erased*, *dead* or *zero* wife *haunts* that happy ending' (39, emphasis added).

The most explicit statement of the legal concepts of *coverture* and the *feme covert* is William Blackstone's influential *Commentaries on the Laws of England* (1765–9), the standard textbook for trainee lawyers. In the key and much-quoted passage he stated:

> By marriage, the husband and wife are one person in law; that is, the very being or legal existence of the woman is suspended during marriage, or at least is incorporated and consolidated into that of the husband; under whose wing, protection, and cover, she performs everything...[14]

It is to this passage and the notion that married women are thereby 'civilly dead' (80),[15] that Beard traces the origin of the 'haunting idea'. As Beard demonstrates at length, Blackstone misrepresented and over-simplified the legal position of married women, partly by focusing on common law and ignoring Equity and the provisions which could be made for them through trusts and so on.[16] But, she argues, the doctrine that married women were 'civilly dead' (95) was reinforced through reiteration by Mary Wollstonecraft, John Stuart Mill and American feminists.

'Civil *death*' is, of course, a kind of (Gothic) metaphor. From my point of view, it is Beard's assertion that when Blackstone declared that 'husband and wife are one' he was, as a rhetorician prone to 'elegant' language, 'using metaphors' (82) which is most interesting. A poet *manqué*, Blackstone had a fondness for figurative language, famously comparing the English constitution and laws to 'an old Gothic castle, erected in the days of chivalry, but fitted up for a modern inhabitant'.[17] His metaphorical statement of the legal position of the married woman became, Beard argues, 'the very basis, of a great fiction...that women were, historically, members of a subject sex – "civilly dead", their very being suspended during marriage...' (84). Dolan makes the same point, referring to the 'legal fiction of coverture' (77), but she goes on to explore its 'enduring and far-reaching *imaginary* resonance' (77, my emphasis). In the 1890s, she suggests, the notion of coverture was 'redrawn as a back-formation, an exaggerated view of the powers men used to have' (79). 'Because unity of person was always a fiction,' she suggests, 'perhaps it is not surprising that it endures as one' (95). Thus it continues to haunt our imaginations and shape our plots and narratives even in the twentieth-century texts Dolan explores.

In Beard's account Mary Wollstonecraft bears much of the responsibility for helping to 'vitalise the doctrine that married women were civilly dead' (95). At first glance the central metaphor for women's position in *A Vindication of the Rights of Woman* (1792) is that of slavery, but the two ideas are closely connected. Wollstonecraft explains the metaphor thus: 'When therefore I call women slaves, I mean in a political and civil sense' (286). In the dedication to Talleyrand, Wollstonecraft signals the issue of women's legal non-status through a Gothic metaphor of imprisonment: 'when you *force* all women, by denying them civil and political rights, to remain *immured in their families groping in the dark*'.[18] Wollstonecraft's summary of Blackstone's model of marriage, although it does not name him, draws attention to precisely the kinds of internal contradictions Dolan notes:

> The laws respecting woman, which I mean to discuss in a future part, make an absurd unit of a man and his wife; and then, by the easy transition of only considering him as responsible, she is reduced to a mere cipher. (257)

It is 'absurd' to make husband and wife one 'unit', especially if that unit actually consists of a hierarchy whereby the man is 'responsible' and the woman a 'mere cipher'. The phrase 'easy transition' suggests the specious nature of the argument, even its ('absurd') fictionality. The word 'cipher', originating from the Arabic word for 'zero', and meaning a symbol which denotes 'no amount' but is used to occupy vacant space (*OED*), anticipates Dolan's 'specter of the erased, dead or zero wife'. Wollstonecraft goes on to argue that 'in order to render their private virtue a public benefit, [women] must have a civil existence in the State, married or single' (262), indicating their current lack of 'existence' (or their 'civil death').

Wollstonecraft indicates in the passage above her intention of discussing women's legal position in 'a future part'. The subtitle of *Maria or The Wrongs of Woman* (1798) explicitly suggests its status as that 'future part', albeit in fictional form. In the *Vindication* Wollstonecraft's overriding concern is to represent women as potentially rational beings. As Woolf's response to Cavendish's writing indicates, Gothic metaphors are associated with anger and with the irrational. To say that women are 'like' slaves is a rational argument, to say that they are 'dead' or 'buried' might be considered irrational, even hysterical. It is perhaps not surprising that Wollstonecraft turned to fiction to explore the Gothic metaphors which haunt the *Vindication*, never quite articulated within it. Diane Long Hoeveler has argued that 'the *Vindication* exists as the buried content of [Wollstonecraft's earlier novella] *Mary*, or rather...the novella is buried as the subtext of the *Vindication*.[19] As its subtitle suggests, it is in *Maria* that Wollstonecraft excavated the 'buried' subtext or, in Derridean terms, the 'phantom text' of the *Vindication*.

The much-quoted opening of *Maria* consciously invokes the imagery of Gothic novels, only to undercut it:

> Abodes of horror have frequently been described, and castles, filled with spectres and chimeras, conjured up by the magic spell of genius to harrow the soul and absorb the wondering mind. But, formed of such stuff as dreams are made of, what were they to the mansion of despair, in one corner of which Maria sat ... .[20]

Here Wollstonecraft both draws attention to the importance of the Gothic as metaphor and claims to make the metaphor real in her own fiction. Markman Ellis argues that her depiction of Maria's prison (as both real madhouse and symbol of oppressive political structures) consciously reworks Blackstone's image of the English constitution as an 'old Gothic castle'.[21] It is thus through a fictional engagement with metaphor that Wollstonecraft is able to offer her most radical analysis of Blackstone's account of women's status as 'civilly dead' within marriage and the very real impact that has on women's material experience. 'Marriage had bastilled me for life,' declares Maria (115),[22] who loses her property, her home and her child and is 'buried alive' (135) in the madhouse. Moreover, like Cavendish, Wollstonecraft suggests that if women are subject primarily to their husbands then their status in relation to their country is ambiguous: 'the laws of her country – *if women have a country* – afford her no protection or redress from the oppressor' (118, emphasis added).

Wollstonecraft herself has attained a kind of oddly spectral presence within feminist theory. Barbara Caine has drawn attention to the omission of her name from the public writings of mid-Victorian feminists (although private letters seem to tell a different story), attributing this to rejection of her sexual radicalism as revealed in William Godwin's memoir of his wife.[23] Godwin's laudable intention of keeping Wollstonecraft's work alive led, ironically, to its erasure. The 'ghost of Mary Wollstonecraft' (93), Caine suggests, is a 'silent presence...haunting' (96) Victorian feminism.

The work of John Stuart Mill, the second theorist Beard singles out as responsible for promulgating the 'haunting idea' of women's subjection, is a case in point. *The Subjection of Women* (1869) opens with the Wollstonecraftesque assertion that 'the principle which regulates the

existing social relations between the two sexes – the legal subordin-
ation of one sex to the other – is wrong in itself...'.[24] It goes on to attack
Blackstoneian doctrine: 'The two [husband and wife] are called "one
person in law" for the purpose of inferring that whatever is hers is his,
but the parallel inference is never drawn that whatever is his is hers;...'
(166). Like Wollstonecraft, Mill develops the analogy between marriage
and slavery, asserting that: 'Marriage is the only actual bondage known
to our law. There remain no legal slaves, except the mistress of every
house' (220). Within marriage, then, woman is 'an upper servant, a nurse
or a mistress', or (echoing Wollstonecraft's 'cipher'), 'a nothing' (235).

Yet, Caine suggests, Mill himself showed no interest in 'women's own
contribution to their emancipation' or in allowing them their own
voice (106). That voice, epitomised by the already dead Wollstonecraft,
is what is repressed in his own text. Moreover, there is another ghost
haunting *The Subjection of Women*, that of Harriet Taylor, his deceased
wife, who is acknowledged in the dedication to *On Liberty* (1859). 'Like
all I have written for many years, it belongs as much to her as to me', he
writes there, and continues:

> Were I but capable of interpreting to the world one half of the great
> thoughts and noble feelings which are buried in her grave, I should
> be the medium of a greater benefit to it, than is ever likely to arise
> from anything that I can write, unprompted and unassisted by her
> all but unrivalled wisdom. (3)

The metonymic suggestion that it is her 'thoughts' and feelings' which
are 'in her grave' has the uncanny effect of presenting Taylor as almost
'buried (alive)', with Mill as a 'medium' (what we might call now a
'ghostwriter'), relaying her words to us from beyond the grave. If, as
Mill's editor Alan Ryan has suggested, *The Subjection of Women* is 'the
real dedication' to *On Liberty* (xviii), then it too contains the ghostly
traces of Taylor's voice, a 'phantom text' suggesting the 'civil death' of
women who cannot speak for themselves.

In the twentieth century, metaphors of burial, imprisonment and
spectrality proliferate in feminist theory, used by, among others,
Virginia Woolf, Hannah Gavron, Adrienne Rich, Luce Irigaray, Sarah
Kofman, Diana Fuss and Judith Butler, in ways which suggest that they
have a particular potency as theoretical 'tools'. There is, however, a
shift as they are no longer used to theorise women's 'subject' position
specifically within marriage but to analyse the repression of women's
'subjectivity' in a wider sense.

This can be seen in *A Room of One's Own* (1929) where Woolf famously invents the character of 'Judith Shakespeare' to demonstrate that no woman in the sixteenth century could have had the freedom of mind and body to write like Shakespeare during a period when she was liable to be 'locked up, beaten and flung about the room' (43). Judith's story of potential forced marriage, escape, seduction and suicide, her body 'buried at some cross-roads' (47), is a Gothic narrative in miniature. In the final pages of the essay Woolf returns to this ghostly figure in a passage which merges the spectral with the messianic in ways which anticipate Derrida's discussion of the 'messianic' as 'that other ghost' (168) in *Specters of Marx*. In the famous opening of Marx's *Communist Manifesto* (1848), 'A spectre is haunting Europe', as Derrida points out, the spectral is not what is past but what is 'to come' (37). Similarly, Woolf deploys the spectral figure of Judith Shakespeare to figure both women's vulnerable position as historical subjects in the past, and their messianic potential in the future. If certain conditions are met, Woolf suggests, 'the dead poet who was Shakespeare's sister will put on the body which she has so often laid down' (108). Here Judith Shakespeare is both a ghost, who has been repeatedly 'laid', and a messianic figure who 'would come if we worked for her' (108). Woolf's exploration of the potential of the spectral to figure repression anticipates Derrida's analysis. As he writes, 'Hegemony still organises the repression and thus the confirmation of a haunting. Haunting belongs to the structure of every hegemony' (37). The 'dead' Judith Shakespeare's attempts to 'return', to put on 'the body she has repeatedly laid aside', figure the hegemonic repression of women's consciousness and creative potential through history. Moreover, in Woolf's account of Judith Shakespeare 'who lives in you and in me' (107) there is a faint echo of Woolf's account of Mary Wollstonecraft (published in the same year as *A Room of One's Own*) which ends with the words 'we hear her voice and trace her influence even now among the living'.[25] To rephrase Marx, the spectre haunting patriarchy is feminist revolution.

It is perhaps not surprising that the emergence of second-wave feminism was characterised as 'the return of the repressed' by Elizabeth Wilson.[26] Each generation of women, Wilson argues, has had to 'make anew the effort to retrieve a past that continues to remain hidden' (195). Indeed, the development of second-wave feminist theory was closely connected to the (re-)reading of Gothic narratives and metaphors. The title of Hannah Gavron's sociological study, *The Captive Wife* (1966), for instance, might have been that of one of the modern Gothics written by Victoria Holt so hugely popular in the 1960s with their uncanny

repetition of a narrative of female imprisonment and death.[27] The metaphor of captivity echoes Wollstonecraft's comment that late eighteenth-
century women were like birds 'confined to their cages' which Gavron
quotes (21). It conveys the predicament of the young married mothers
Gavron interviewed in the 1960s, many of whom spoke of boredom
and frustration with their roles: 'I am haunted by a sense of wasted
time,' said one (115). It was the emotive title metaphor that newspaper
reviews picked up for their own Gothic headlines such as 'Prisoners in
their own Home' or 'Walled-in Wives' (xiii). The title also hints at what
we might call a 'phantom text' beneath Gavron's carefully scholarly
tone. In the text, as Elizabeth Wilson suggests, 'a half-suppressed understanding of the deeper springs of women's oppression kept breaking
through, yet was ultimately silenced or at least muffled by the reformist
framework from which she could not escape' (205). Here Gavron herself
becomes a kind of repressed Gothic heroine, only half aware of her own
captivity.

The close relationship between Gothic fiction and feminist theory
at this point, as with Wollstonecraft's work earlier, suggests a complex interchange between the two where each enables the other. Ellen
Moers's influential *Literary Women* (1976), which focused critical interest
on what she called 'female Gothic', came out of this 'new wave of feminism, called women's liberation' in the early and mid-1960s, as Moers
herself makes clear in the preface.[28] Indeed, the metaphor of 'liberation',
which presupposes captivity, is a direct descendant of Wollstonecraft's
Maria: 'Was not the world a vast prison, and women born slaves?' (64).
Metaphors of burial and death are particularly deployed to characterise the feminist literary critics' recovery of neglected writers, as in, for
instance, Adrienne Rich's assertion that feminist scholars were sharing
'the rediscovery of buried works by women...bringing literary history
and criticism back to life'.[29] Rich's important essay, 'When We Dead
Awaken: Writing as Re-Vision' (1971), takes its controlling metaphor of
the 'awakening of dead or sleeping consciousness' (34–5) from Ibsen's
eponymous play, but it is also very clearly in the tradition I have traced
back to Margaret Cavendish. Rich's interest, like Woolf's, is in the
repression of women's consciousness and creative potential. She uses
the metaphor of 'death' (as Gavron used that of the 'captive wife') to
express 'that female fatigue of suppressed anger and loss of contact with
my own being' (43), which came from living a traditional female life,
caring for a husband and small children.

At the end of the twentieth century, feminist theorists deployed
Gothic metaphors with particular vigour, often influenced by

Derridean deconstruction, to explore and challenge representations of femininity. With its roots in the Latin 'specere' (to look), the metaphor of the spectre has obvious appeal as a way of exploring representations of femininity within a symbolic based on visual difference. Thus Luce Irigaray, whose work offers one of the most systematic deconstructions of male systems of representation, uses the image of the 'speculum' to analyse the ways in which women have been 'rolled-up in metaphors, buried beneath carefully stylised figures'.[30] In such systems, particularly Freudian psychoanalysis, where men have attributed subjectivity only to themselves and reduced women to the status of object/other/nothing, she argues, the woman's sex organ 'represents *the horror of nothing to see*',[31] a phrase which recalls Freud's comment that some men find female genitalia 'uncanny' (368). Irigaray's work returns repeatedly to the erasure of maternal genealogies and a female divine within male systems of representation, arguing that our culture functions 'at a primal level...on the basis of a matricide' which results in, among other things, 'the burial of the madness of women – and the burial of women in madness'.[32] Lacking adequate symbolisation, women exist in a state of *'dereliction'* or abandonment (74). They are 'nowhere, touching everything, but never in touch with each other, lost in the air, like ghosts' (91). In the light of this, Irigaray sees redefining 'the right to civil identity' as 'one of the most urgent tasks of our time',[33] a comment which connects her work to that of Wollstonecraft.

In her reading of Freud's 'Femininity' and his comment that the psychical rigidity of the 30-year-old woman often 'frightens us', Sarah Kofman uses similarly Gothic language.[34] She argues that Freud 'immobilizes woman, imprisons her in her "nature" as in a yoke of iron' and that the lecture ends '*on a death sentence for woman*' (222). '[F]rozen with horror,' she continues, 'the psychoanalyst shrinks back in the face of this zombie he has just manufactured...as if he found himself face to face with Death itself' (223). She concludes, 'Psychoanalysis can never touch woman except to make a dead body of her' (223). Kofman's reading offers us Freud as a Gothic villain, a kind of Frankenstein in reverse, whose theories transform the living woman into a 'zombie'.

The final shift I want to note here is the use of Gothic metaphors to explore issues of lesbianism and homosexuality in the 1990s. As Paulina Palmer noted in 1999, 'the utilization of Gothic imagery and motifs as a vehicle for discussing lesbian/homosexual theoretical issues is...by now sufficiently commonplace to have aroused comment'.[35] The trope of spectrality has been used, as Palmer points out, by theorists such as Diana Fuss and Judith Butler to explore the ways in which lesbianism/homosexuality are 'repressed' within phallocentric culture and can thus be said to 'haunt' it (12–13). In the introduction to *Inside/ Out: Lesbian Theories, Gay Theories* (1991), Diana Fuss comments that:

> A striking feature of many of the essays collected in the volume is a fascination with the specter of abjection, a certain preoccupation with the figure of the homosexual as specter and phantom, as spirit and revenant, as abject and undead.[36]

Drawing on post-structural theories of subjectivity itself as unfixed, fluid, fragmentary and contingent, Gothic metaphors are used here (as Buse and Stott suggest) as a tool to theorise and destabilise the symbolism of phallocentric culture. The close inter-relationship of feminist theory and fiction is again crucial: Palmer suggests that the utilisation of Gothic imagery by contemporary theorists is in itself '[o]ne of the strongest encouragements to writers of lesbian fiction to experiment with the Gothic mode' (12). Not surprisingly, the metaphor of lesbianism/homosexuality as spectrality has proven a particularly useful tool with which to analyse fiction, most notably in Terry Castle's *The Apparitional Lesbian* (1993), which discusses fiction from the early twentieth century, and Palmer's *Lesbian Gothic* which focuses on the 1970s–90s. My purpose here is not to rehearse such theories and readings (which have been widely discussed) but place them as the most recent twist in a particular tradition. They might, however, encourage us to take another look at Margaret Cavendish's oration and note that her specific argument is that 'men' do 'not suffer us freely to associate amongst our own sex, but would fain bury us ...' (248), suggesting that it is the radical potential of relationships with other women (whether genealogical, political or sexual) which has always been most strongly repressed.

Feminist theory, then, has been 'haunted' by Gothic metaphors for several centuries, although their meanings shift over time. As their ubiquity suggests, what I have here called female Gothic metaphors have enormous power to convey women's experience of living in a culture which historically denied them legal status as 'subjects' within marriage, and which has continued to make women feel that they are denied a full subjectivity. Such metaphors offer an emotive and compelling way of challenging established and 'rational' hegemonies and 'theorising' alternative truths which may be difficult to express in other ways. However, as Terence Hawkes has argued, metaphors have a ' "normative" and reinforcing aspect, as well as an "exploratory" one', so that they 'affirm, in the end, as much as they challenge'.[37] Although she may seem at times to be edging towards an anti-feminist rhetoric, Mary Beard is right to remind us to be wary of such metaphors, which run the risk of reinforcing those enshrined in the work of Blackstone and others, and reducing living women to dead figures.

Notes

1. Mary R. Beard, *Woman as Force in History* (New York: Macmillan, 1946), 77. All subsequent references are to this edition and are given in the text.
2. Meredith Miller, '"I Don't Want to be A [White] Girl": Gender, Race and Resistance in the Southern Gothic', 137.
3. Eve Kosofsky Sedgwick, *The Coherence of Gothic Conventions* (New York and London: Methuen [1980], 1986), 166, 7. All subsequent references are to this edition and are given in the text.
4. David Punter, *Metaphor* (London: Routledge, 2007), 29. All subsequent references are to this edition and are given in the text.
5. Peter Buse and Andrew Stott, eds, *Ghosts: Deconstruction, Psychoanalysis, History* (London and Basingstoke: Palgrave Macmillan, 1999), 3. All subsequent references are to this edition and are given in the text.
6. Jacques Derrida, *Specters of Marx: The State of the Debt, the Work of Mourning, and the New International*, trans. Peggy Kamuf (New York and London: Routledge [1993], 1994). All subsequent references are to this edition and are given in the text.
7. Nicholas Royle, *The Uncanny* (Manchester: Manchester University Press, 2003), 280.
8. Ros Ballaster's discussion of sexuality as the 'unconscious' of feminist criticism also suggests the central place of the Gothic in feminist literary history, although she does not directly address these metaphors. Ros Ballaster, 'Wild Nights and Buried Letters: The Gothic "Unconscious" of Feminist Criticism', *Modern Gothic: A Reader*, eds Victor Sage and Allan Lloyd Smith (Manchester: Manchester University Press, 1996), 58–70.
9. Margaret Cavendish, 'Female Orations', *Political Writings*, ed. Susan James (Cambridge: Cambridge University Press), 248–51, 248, emphasis added. All subsequent references are to this edition and are given in the text. Susan James makes the important point that these orations 'rehearse a set of arguments which were debated in the so-called *querelle des femmes*' (fn, 248).
10. Sigmund Freud, 'The "Uncanny"', *Art and Literature*, The Penguin Freud Library, vol. 14, (London: Penguin [1985], 1990), 339–76, 366. All subsequent references are to this edition and are given in the text.
11. In Elaine Hobby, *Virtue of Necessity: English Women's Writing 1649–88* (Ann Arbor, MI: University of Michigan Press, 1989), 82. All subsequent references are to this edition and are given in the text.
12. Virginia Woolf, *A Room of One's Own* (London: Granada [1929], 1977), 59. All subsequent references are to this edition and are given in the text.
13. Frances E. Dolan, *Marriage and Violence: The Early Modern Legacy* (Philadelphia, PA: University of Philadelphia Press, 2008), 3. All subsequent references are to this edition and are given in the text.
14. Quoted in Beard, *Woman*, 78–9.

15. Civil death: 'ceasing to have a citizen's privileges, through outlawry, banishment etc.' (*OED*).

16. Dolan makes the same point, 76.

17. 'Sir William Blackstone', *Oxford Dictionary of National Biography*, <www.oxfordnb.com/view/printable/2536> Accessed 17/12/2008, 7.

18. Mary Wollstonecraft, *A Vindication of the Rights of Woman* (London: Penguin [1792], 1985), 87, emphasis added. All subsequent references are to this edition and are given in the text.

19. Diane Long Hoeveler, 'The Construction of the Female Gothic Posture: Wollstonecroft's *Mary* and Gothic feminism', *Gothic Studies* 6/1 (May 2004), 30–44, 31.

20. Mary Wollstonecraft, *Mary and Maria* and Mary Shelley, *Matilda* (London: Penguin, 1992), 61. All subsequent references are to this edition and are given in the text.

21. Markman Ellis, *The History of Gothic Fiction* (Edinburgh: Edinburgh University Press, 2000), 71.

22. Gavin Edwards has drawn attention to the revivification of this dead metaphor after 1789 and connects Wollstoncraft's use of it to Thomas Paine's argument that we can be 'imprison'd within the bastille of a word'. Gavin Edwards, *Narrative Order, 1789–1819: Life and Story in an Age of Revolution* (Basingstoke: Palgrave, 2006), 154.

23. Barbara Caine, *English Feminism, 1780–1980* (Oxford: Oxford University Press, 1997), 96–7. All subsequent references are to this edition and are given in the text.

24. John Stuart Mill, *On Liberty and The Subjection of Women* (London: Penguin, 2006), 133. All subsequent references are to this edition and are given in the text.

25. Virginia Woolf, 'Mary Wollstonecraft', *On Women and Writing: Her Essays, Assessments and Arguments*, ed. Michèle Barrett (London: The Women's Press, 1979), 96–103, 103.

26. Elizabeth Wilson, *Only Halfway to Paradise: Women in Postwar Britain: 1945–1968* (London and New York: Tavistock, 1980), 176. All subsequent references are to this edition and are given in the text.

27. Hannah Gavron, *The Captive Wife: Conflicts of Housebound Mothers* (London: Routledge and Kegan Paul [1966], 1983). All subsequent references are to this edition and are given in the text.

28. Ellen Moers, *Literary Women* (London: The Women's Press, [1976], 1978), 90, xiii. All subsequent references are to this edition and are given in the text.

29. Adrienne Rich, 'When We Dead Awaken: Writing as Re-Vision', *On Lies, Secrets and Silence: Selected Prose 1966–1978* (London: Virago [1979], 1980), 33–49, 33. All subsequent references are to this edition and are given in the text.

30. Luce Irigaray, *Speculum of the Other Woman*, trans. Gillian C. Gill (Ithaca, NY: Cornell University Press [1974], 1985), 144.

31. Luce Irigaray, *This Sex Which is Not One*, trans. Catherine Porter (Ithaca, NY: Cornell University Press [1977], 1985), 26.

32. Luce Irigaray, 'The Bodily Encounter with the Mother', *The Irigaray Reader*, ed. Margaret Whitford (Oxford: Blackwell, 1991), 34–46, 36, 37. All subsequent references are to this edition and are given in the text.

33. Luce Irigaray, *Thinking the Difference: For a Peaceful Revolution*, trans. Karin, Montin (London: Athlone, [1989], 1994), xvii.
34. Sarah Kofman, *The Enigma of Woman: Woman in Freud's Writings*, trans. Catherine Porter (Ithaca and London: Cornell University Press, 1985), 223. All subsequent references are to this edition and are given in the text.
35. Paulina Palmer, *Lesbian Gothic* (London: Cassell, 1999), 13. All subsequent references are to this edition and are given in the text.
36. Diana Fuss, ed., *Inside/Out: Lesbian Theories, Gay Theories* (London: Routledge, 1991), 3.
37. Terence Hawkes, *Metaphor* (London: Methuen, 1972), 88, 89.

3
'Mother Radcliff': Ann Radcliffe and the Female Gothic

Robert Miles

> I shall send you the Pot of Basil, St. Agnes eve, and if I should
> have finished it a little thing call'd the 'eve of St. Mark' you see
> what fine Mother Radcliff names I have – it is not my fault –
> I do not search for them...
>
> John Keats, Letter to George and Georgiana Keats,
> 14 February–3 May 1819[1]

In his essay on Walpole Walter Scott proves once again that he is the
master of the even-handed insult. He acknowledges that 'Mrs. Radcliffe'
was 'a name not to be mentioned without the high respect due to genius',
but then observes that she adopted the wrong solution to the problem posed by the supernatural in fiction. Walpole 'details supernatural
incidents as they would have been readily believed and received in the
eleventh and twelfth century'. Radcliffe rejected this simple expedient
in favour of explanation: 'the precaution of relieving our spirits from
the influence of supposed supernatural terror, seems as unnecessary
in a work of professed fiction, as that of the prudent Bottom' reassur-
ing the ladies that he is not really a lion.[2] Even as he praises Radcliffe,
Scott eroded the foundations of her literary reputation. When he comes
to write about her, for his *Lives of the Novelists* (1821–1824), he returns
to his task. He simultaneously praises her as the founder of her own
'class or school' (she is the 'first poetess of romantic fiction' [103]), and
then defends her against a charge that he admits ought not to be levelled against her: that she should be tarred with the same critical brush
that blackened 'the crowd of copyists who came forward in imitation
of Mrs. Radcliffe', assuming 'her magic wand, without the power...'
(111). If the tar sticks, it is because of her incautious wish to make like
Bottom, and reassure her readers 'that all the circumstances of her

42

narrative, however mysterious, and apparently superhuman, were to be accounted for on natural principles...' (115). If he built her up as a 'mighty enchantress' (105) who founded her own school of fiction – and for Scott, there was no higher praise – he also pulled her down as an earnest simpleton, in the process shaping the critical debate that by the end of the century would succeed in relegating Radcliffe to someone at the head of a second-division genre: the Gothic.

It was against this prejudice that Ellen Moers intervened with her strategic coinage, 'the Female Gothic'. Moers's definition is deceptively simple: 'the work that women writers have done in the literary mode that, since the eighteenth century, we have called the Gothic'.[3] Deceptive, because Moers links the mode to female subjectivity; she speaks of the 'long and complex traditions of the Female Gothic, where woman is examined with a woman's eye, woman as girl, as sister, as mother, as self' (109). 'Fear' and 'self-disgust' dominate these representations (90, 107); accordingly Moers opens the door to the school of feminist criticism that understands women's writing as a kind of mirror for the misogynistic distortions that inhere structurally within patriarchy.[4] This school achieved its apogee in the *Madwoman in the Attic*, a work that enjoyed a stately decline before its eventual eclipse by the historicising work of the 1990s, where the picture that emerged contradicted the one implied by Scott and Moers, and explicitly argued by Gilbert and Gubar; namely, that the Female Gothic was a species of writing peculiarly produced and consumed by women.[5] Scott's condescending reference to Radcliffe's 'crowd of copyists' need not be glossed as Hawthorne's later, specific, 'damned mob of scribbling women', for the simple reason that the gendering was sufficiently obvious to render the gloss otiose. For very different reasons, those picking up Moers's cudgel agreed with the 1790s cliché, that the Gothic was, virtually, an exclusive province of women writers and readers, the difference being that whereas the Gothic's critics viewed this with alarm, in the classic scenario of scullery maids having their minds turned by the reading material left lying around by their equally addled mistresses, 1970s feminism saw it as a burgeoning movement in grassroots literacy and consciousness-raising. Rendered monstrous by patriarchy, it stood to reason that the female psyche would evince its distorted provenance, once permitted expression, or once expression was seized. But that was not how the women writers of the period saw things. Riding the cresting wave of the bourgeois public sphere, women writers of the late eighteenth century understood themselves to be equal members of the republic of letters, rationally engaged in matters of public moment, not nursing grudges for the systemic violence done to their sex.[6] Macaulay, Barbauld, Baillie and Smith, let alone Wollstonecraft, did not self-identify as desperadoes breaking into the citadels of culture in order to send out encrypted messages about the horrors of patriarchy; rather they regarded themselves as equals in the literary public sphere, engaged in debating matters of overt substance, including, in Wollstonecraft's case, the evils of patriarchy. Just as critics such as Ann Mellor and E. J. Clery have sought to reclaim Gothic women writers as public intellectuals – as self-conscious activists seizing the key role of 'mothers of the nation', or as professional writers – bibliographers and book historians such as James Raven, Peter Garside and William St. Clair have undermined the view that the Gothic was somehow the peculiar province of women, either as writers or readers. As the publishing craze of the 1790s, the Gothic swept all before it; and while men may have been more reticent then women about putting their names on title pages, they seem to have been equally caught up in the fervour to produce or consume novels of the terrorist school.[7]

Once stripped of its twin assertions (a genre enabling the subjective exploration of the female condition exclusively aimed at women readers), what is left of Moers's category? It is all fine and well to define the Female Gothic as the work women have done in the Gothic mode, but for the category to have any point beyond the kind that excites librarians, there must be generic differences or features that set the Female Gothic text off from other kinds of Gothic writing, otherwise it is a case of a distinction without a difference. If those differences are not to be found in the subject matter (the female psyche), form ('encrypted') or readership (scullery maids and their mistresses), where are they to be located? Indeed, where could they be?

I would like to take advantage of the opportunity afforded by this collection to ask what remains viable from a category that shall shortly enjoy its first half-century, and which has undergone such stringent revision. By a viable category I mean one that is still capable of critical work. My argument will be that if the Female Gothic works still, it is because of Radcliffe's aesthetic legacy. The key to this legacy – a legacy amounting to an alteration in the generic DNA of the romance form – was first summed up by Norman Holland and Leona Sherman in a formulation arguably as influential as Moers's own, 'The image of the woman-plus-habitation and the plot of mysterious sexual and supernatural threats in an atmosphere of dynastic mysteries within the habitation has changed little since the eighteenth century.'[8] Boiled down like this, the formula would seem as applicable to Walpole's *Otranto* (1764) as to the romances of Radcliffe; even so I want to persist in arguing that Radcliffe is its proper matrix; or, to put it another way, between Walpole and Radcliffe the formula did materially change.

The implication in the epigraph from John Keats is that Radcliffe's fictional world is more than just that: it is a gestalt, an ecology of names and places, words and things, such that, once entered into, the subject becomes powerless as the logic of the gestalt works itself out in and through the receptive imagination. Under the sway of Mother Radcliff, one need not search, nor is it one's fault; the names come as naturally as leaves to a tree.

I will return to this sense of 'Mother Radcliff', that is, of Radcliffe as matrix, but before I do so I want to elaborate on how it is that the formulation of Holland and Sherman provides a key to Radcliffe's aesthetic legacy. Holland and Sherman appear to be spelling out the subjective, unconscious dimensions of the Female Gothic in a manner virtually identical to Moers, which is hardly surprising given their psychoanalytic background and training: in both the residues of patriarchal violence done to the female psyche are expressed in Gothic texts through the encrypted tale of 'woman-plus-habitation' combined with menacing males and threatened property. In fact there is nothing cryptic about Holland's and Sherman's formula. It includes generic features that are all on the surface: a heroine, a plot that includes threatened abduction, confusions over identity, and therefore mysteries of inheritance and property. One might say that this simply takes us back to Moers's argument, shorn of its later, psychoanalytic accretions, as her own criticism is focused on heroines and the quiddity of the plot structures favoured by women writers, such as, in Radcliffe's case, travelling. Indeed, Holland and Sherman seem prone to the same critique as the one afflicting Moers: they are guilty of extracting a formula that encodes concerns far removed from those appearing to motivate the writers themselves. Of course there is nothing wrong with such anti-intentional readings, but they do concede the case that the Female Gothic is a largely retrospective category (and if it is retrospective it cannot also claim to be referencing the interior realities of the female psyche, as true then, as they are now, other than by denying the historicity originally claimed for the Female Gothic). Holland and Sherman appear to be identifying a 'mythos', as Northrop Frye would put it, a recurring narrative structure universally embedded in the human imagination (hence its unchanging nature over two hundred years). As such they court the historicist critique that bedevils Moers. The very generality of their formulation, and the ubiquity of the plot elements in a genre that is famously capacious, would seem to undermine it: out of the vast soup of promiscuously mixed cliché, one can always find one's favoured letters and tropes, and doubtless they will also arrange themselves into a 'formula' such as Holland's and Sherman's.

In my first attempt to deal with these issues I suggested that for the category of the Female Gothic to perform critical work there must also be a Male Gothic (because if there is no difference one hardly needs a distinction). I further suggested a quasi-formal approach to the matter, where the category was determined, not by the gender of the producer, but by recurring structures. In particular I suggested that the Female Gothic was distinguished by problems inhering within the sublime, and in Male Gothic, by those inhering within the gaze. These were, moreover, discursive problems as they related to how fictional subjects were gendered, that is to say, constructed and known. Female writers might therefore intervene in Male Gothic (think of Charlotte Dacre), and vice versa (think of Francis Lathom or James Boaden).[9] I now want to take this position further and suggest that the Female Gothic will perform its most effective critical work if we approach it as a category determined by recurring formal elements that have a specific historical valence. In other words, it is not a matter of choosing between Moers's definition and the historical correction, between Female Gothicists as feminists spilling the beans about patriarchy in a manner encrypted even from themselves, and civic humanists engaged in the performative activity Jürgen Habermas terms 'public sphering'.[10] We can, in fact, have it both ways: the Female Gothicists were self-conscious agents intervening in the historical construction of gender, which they understood as a task authorised by their membership of the republic of letters. These writers worked within a code whose meaning was self-evident to all, a code ably adumbrated by Holland and Sherman in their defining formula.

I earlier said that Holland and Sherman's formulation might as easily describe Walpole as Radcliffe, but that something happened between *Otranto* and *The Italian* (1797) that entitled Radcliffe to the status of chief progenitor. This difference is delicately handled by Scott:

> Her heroines voluntarily expose themselves to situations, which in nature a lonely female would certainly have avoided. They are too apt to choose the midnight hour for investigating the mysteries of a deserted chamber or secret passage, and generally are only supplied with an expiring lamp, when about to read the most interesting documents. (115)

Some of the reviews were less delicate, scolding Radcliffe for the incongruous masculinity of her heroines. The point is closely associated with Moers's, when she says that travelling was the device Radcliffe expediently adopted for exposing her heroines to adventures while rescuing them from censure (126). Isabella wandering the crypts of Otranto, pursued, she fears, by Manfred, is, indeed, literally, an 'image of the woman-plus-habitation' beset by a plot thickened by 'mysterious sexual and supernatural threats in an atmosphere of dynastic mysteries', but she is not the story's focalising point despite Walpole's pioneering use of free indirect discourse in representing her plight.[11] The difference, at its simplest, is that Isabella is not the heroine of the work, more a convenient prop, at least in comparison with the full Radcliffe where the heroine is the candlelight around which the etch-marks of the burnished mirror appear to revolve. At its most complex the difference is a matter of the gestalt suggested by Keats.

In doing so Keats was not alone. For Scott, Radcliffe's genius principally lay in the potent wand she wielded as the 'mighty enchantress' (105). The figure is a mainstay of Radcliffe's contemporary reception, from Nathan Drake, to Scott, Coleridge and the many anonymous reviewers of her work.[12] Hazlitt may speak for them all when he asserts that Otranto was dry and meagre stuff compared to the reverie-engine that was a Radcliffe text.[13] To put matters differently, applying Holland and Sherman to Walpole's text really is an instance of the hermeneutic circle leading us astray, for while one can find the formula in Otranto, the discovery misleads as much as it informs. The Female Gothic always has something to say about the woman question, whereas Otranto tells us very little, even as it has much to offer regarding the Reformation, the Glorious revolution, Whig politics, and the matters of legitimacy these matters raised. The incidental nature of Walpole's feminism becomes apparent when placed next to Radcliffe's, where numerous textual decisions attest to Radcliffe's self-conscious interventions.

In relation to Walpole, Holland and Sherman's list specifies some accidental ingredients, whereas in Radcliffe it is a syntactic unit. Her mature works of Female Gothic (A Sicilian Romance [1790], The Romance of the Forest [1791] and The Mysteries of Udolpho [1794]) begin, not with the snuffing out of the male heir, and the rage of one of the Byronic hero's early avatars, but with a heroine-plus-habitation whose mysteries are both sexual and dynastic, where every unit is tightly linked with the next, in accordance with an underlying, discursive grammar. In A Sicilian Romance Julia Mazzini and her sister Emilia live in one wing of the ancestral mansion while their mother is secretly imprisoned in another after her husband had staged her death and funeral in order to clear the way for a marriage to his inamorata, the lubricious, and treacherous, Maria de Vellorno. As Lauren Fitzgerald argues, Radcliffe's plots turn on women's property and its threatened alienation.[14] Thus, it is not so much that Julia is threatened with being auctioned off to her father's creepy, elderly friend, the Duke de Luovo, like so much disposable property; it is that her property rights are placed in jeopardy by her father's scheme, should Vellorno conceive a bigamous male heir. Julia's history is a tissue of hair-breadth escapes from actual rape (by banditti) and virtual, through forced marriage, played out against a backdrop of paternal threats to disinherit, either through legal acts (writing her out), or illegal ones (the bigamous marriage). In *The Romance of the Forest* the screw is tightened. Adeline finds herself fortuitously encamped in the ruins of the paternal mansion, one ostensibly haunted by the ghost of her usurped and murdered father, and literally so by his writing, discovered in a chamber hidden behind the arras. Her protector, the weak Pierre La Motte, connives to turn her over to the Marquis Montalt, Adeline's as yet undiscovered uncle, and intending seducer/ravisher. It is only through the providential unwinding of the romance's crimes that Adeline's alienated property – including her name – is returned to her.

The internal logic of Radcliffe's plotting thickens once again in *The Mysteries of Udolpho*. At the centre of the plotting is the triadic structure of Emily's family home, a modest chateau dubbed 'La Vallée';[15] the castle of Udolpho in the Italian Pennines; and the Chateau-le-Blanc, where she comes to rest as the mysteries unravel. La Vallée and Udolpho are antithetical structures. The one is a pastoral retreat of bourgeois restraint and discipline, the other a medieval fortress located in the middle of bandit country (a holdover of what Matthew Arnold will later style England's 'barbarian' aristocracy). The former is a safe house where Emily's property and name are secure, guarded by St Aubert, an ideal paternal imago, whereas Udolpho is a structure of lawlessness, one of threat to both Emily's virginity and property, presided over by the inverse of the paternal ideal (the careless, rapacious and possibly homicidal Montoni, her erstwhile uncle, by marriage, and legal guardian). The ideal is a ghost (the phantasmagorical appearance of Emily's dead father), while its inverse is all too real, and physical. The tension between them is heightened by the fact that each includes an image of a 'dead' female that threatens their difference. In the Aubert family mansion it is the picture of the Marchioness de Villeroi, the mysterious woman over whose image Emily's father sighs, secretively, whose story appears to be recorded in the secret papers Emily is enjoined to burn without reading, where she catches a glimpse (the purport of which we are never told) that galvanises her soul, precipitating the phantas-magoric visitation of St Aubert's imago. When she ventures into his library to burn his papers, as she has been enjoined to do through her paternal promise, 'the countenance of her dead father' floats before her in his familiar armchair (103). The novel is structured so that we specu-late that the Marchioness is her father's secret lover, possibly the adul-terous mother of an illegitimate Emily.[16] What is worse, she seems to have some connection with the mysterious Laurentini, erstwhile heir-ess of Udolpho, and a woman of deeply suspect morals. Udolpho also conceals the image of a dead female, at least it does in Emily's fever-ish imagination: behind the coma-inducing black veil, as Emily and Catherine Morland alike project,[17] is the petrified corpse of Laurentini. The consequence of this secret 'wormhole' connecting what are other-wise antithetical universes, is the effacement of difference. Emily's elec-tric fear, in catching a glimpse of her father's secret manuscript, is that she is illegitimate, without title to the property Montoni will attempt to extort from her, and what is more, unsuccoured by a paternal image that would otherwise nourish her identity, feeding her resolve. As Herman Melville explains, in his elaborate borrowing of the device, in *Pierre, or the Ambiguities* (1852), once the paternal imago is sullied by suspicion, the heroine's world collapses into ambiguity. A consequence of the glimpse is that the difference between Udolpho and Emily's paternal home is effaced, with both presided over by sexually suspect paternal imagos, and both overtly hedged with threats to her property rights. The appropriately named Chateau-le-Blanc – the white house on which meaning shall be inscribed – is the mediating term between the antith-eses, between the paternal ideal, as dream-like pastoral haven, and its nightmarish opposite, Udolpho, replete with the differentially-locking door and complement of randy, roistering banditti. Chateau-le-Blanc subsists on a quotidian plane between these antithetical dream images, with links to both (not least through its positioning over the banditti-infested cavern which serves as a portal to the romance worlds of the other houses even as these supernatural irruptions are resolved in favour of the 'natural': in the end, the apparitions are, simply, banditti). It is while Emily resides at Chateau-le-Blanc that the mysteries are resolved: the woman in the picture is not Emily's adulterous mother, but Aubert's murdered sister (by the jealous Laurentini); nor is Udolpho's veiled fig-ure the disgraced nun, but a wax effigy. One might argue that at the Chateau-le-Blanc the connections between the ideal paternal residence, and its sinister obverse, are uncoupled; but by the same token one may observe that the quotidian world of the white house is forever troubled by the possibilities raised by the traffic it enjoys (in the movement of persons and information) with the dialectical extremes it synthesises.

Compared to *Udolpho*, *Otranto* is an accidental assemblage of the materials Radcliffe transforms into a deeply meditated narrative structure. While one can easily translate this narrative into Freudian terms, the temptation is best resisted: it is when we do so, that we lose our purchase on the contemporary ideological work Radcliffe's Female Gothic was meant to do. If we are attentive to Radcliffe's plots we'll see that the threats that motivate them, are not the Freudian formula of 'desire/prohibition/anxiety/fear of lost virginity', or its 1970s elaboration through Lacanian critiques of phallocentrism, but a 1790s agenda of lost genius and property. Radcliffe has her heroines travel, less to put them in the way of adventures, or temptations, and more to put them in situations of isolation and scenery where sublimity and other expressions of genius come naturally – indeed, spontaneously – to the heroine.

One of Radcliffe's great successes – perhaps her principal success – was to raise the cultural capital of (and here no other phrase will do) the Radcliffean matrix. For Scott, Radcliffe was the first poetess of Romantic fiction (103), or, as Nathan Drake put it, the 'Shakespeare of Romance writers'.[18] The signal fact, though, was the recognition commanded by Radcliffe that her style of romance constituted the beginning of a new school. The narrative bones of this new form are much as Holland and Sherman describe, plus the explained supernatural, but to that we must add numerous other innovations, which, if not entirely original in Radcliffe, were certainly *au courant*: the inclusion of chapter epigraphs;[19] the canny mix in quoted poets and dramatists, from notable Elizabethans (with Shakespeare the obvious principal), to fashionable pre-Romantics; the poems within the novel, usually produced by, or associated with, the heroine;[20] the systematic inclusion of the sublime and picturesque, as the systole and diastole of her narrative rhythms; poetic scenery-painting, done with such effect that her contemporaries read her through, not just Claude-, but Rosa- and Poussin-glasses; a structural historicity, so that the plots always turn on an implicit contrast between the medieval and the modern; and a romantic reinvention of the Mediterranean littoral, the troubadour world that stretches from the hill towns of the Languedoc, across Provence, through to those running down the spine of the two kingdoms (modern Southern Italy). One might sneer at this, as the fashionable, coffee-table culture of her Uncle Bentley's Chelsea house (Thomas Bentley was Wedgewood's design partner and a key member of the Dissenting intelligentsia with strong links to the Warrington academy).[21] But as Keats's comments attest, this was not, simply, the travel-brochure culture of an aspiring middle class, but a highly successful assemblage of cultural references, eagerly consumed by her audience, that had the effect of significantly raising the status of the culture to which a non-Classically trained woman (or man) might aspire.

This cultural capital, then, is put at the disposal of the heroine, who is represented as its principal conduit. At the same time, the heroine doubles the author, not by virtue of her personality, but as a cipher for the cultural capital to which the woman writer now has access.[22] Just as Radcliffe's status is reflected in her heroines, as they fall into reverie, poetry, or scenery appreciation, so does Radcliffe's own status rise, as her matrix finds critical acceptance. In this subtle manner, the heroine comes to stand in the place of the male role of genius. Radcliffe's heroines are irrepressible: no matter the horrors that befall them, or rather, as Austen understood, because of them, their genius flourishes. Lock them into a castle turret, and their imaginations soar with the sublimity of the scenery without; leave them camping out in a forested ruin, and they will probe behind the arras to discover blood-curdling mysteries. The true risks posed by Radcliffe's plots are not the rapes threatened with a surprising frequency in such a proper writer, but the alienation of property and place, for these are the enabling conditions of female creativity, and therefore genius. The convent thus has a double valence in Radcliffe: as a place of refuge it sustains the heroine's genius (so long as the fate of her property still hangs in the balance); as a final destination (with property lost), it is the cemetery of the living, a patriarchal Bastille where females are shorn of their expressive properties, beginning, literally, with Julia's mother in *A Sicilian Romance*, and echoed in *The Italian*, through Olivia's lot before the discovery of her daughter, Ellena (which with a nod to *A Winter's Tale* signals her return from petrifaction).

Keats's canniness as a commentator on Radcliffe is especially evident if we focus, not on the problematic *Eve of St Agnes* (1820) (although the heroine's active/passive position is distinctly Radcliffean), and more on the *Eve of St Mark* (1819), and *Isabella; or the Pot of Basil* (1818). The latter is straightforwardly Gothic in the violence of the brothers, who represent an unalloyed patriarchal principle, but it is especially Radcliffean in the stubborn persistence of Isabella, whose pot of basil is a memorial of her lost love as well as a token of her undying, unyielding, expressive talents. But in the *Eve of St Mark* Keats comes closest to the spirit of Radcliffe's Female Gothic through his figuration of the heroine whose devotion is also a mask for her creative participation in the imaginative realisation of the Radcliffean matrix (so that she is both passive conduit and productive centre), here represented as a Medieval church interior rendered sublime through the terrifying prospect of discovering oneself apprised of who among the parade of worshippers is marked for death.

In her important article on *Udolpho* and ideology Mary Poovey underlines the central contradiction that structures Radcliffe's narratives. The heroines subscribe to the cult of sensibility, or rather to a belated version that allots to women a special, empowering influence, whereby they are – through the gendered peculiarities of their genius – the principal engines of the modern, civilising process. At the same time a material reality is disclosed that is masculine in character, and utterly impervious to this idealised version of feminine influence (essentially Emily's situation, when caught in Montoni's implacable grip).[23] While I think Poovey is essentially right, matters look significantly different when we recall that her analysis is implicitly retrospective, in so far as it is filtered through the subsequent rise during the Victorian period of the ideology that empowered women only to lock them more securely in the domestic sphere. Radcliffe belonged to an earlier generation where the apparent reality of a republic of letters seemed to vouchsafe the possibility of a glorious equality of genius, regardless of gender. In other words, there is an optative character to Radcliffe's works that is bound to seem naive, given what came shortly after. Nevertheless, the optimistic mood is important for grasping Radcliffe's Female Gothic.

I think this is the essential correction that needs to be made to Holland and Sherman's formulation. 'The plot of mysterious sexual and supernatural threats in an atmosphere of dynastic mysteries' nicely captures the balance between the promise of inheritance and its possible curtailment. But we need to supplement 'the image of the woman-plus-habitation' with the recognition of what kind of 'habitations' Radcliffe's heroines inhabit: forest clearings, ruins, castle turrets; places where their genius flourishes. Of course, in these places where the heroine's genius is permitted to run free there is – always already – a corresponding threat.

It is for this reason that the sublime is the necessary aesthetic structure for the mediation of female aspirations. Through its obvious gendering the sublime encodes the patriarchal principle that must always be transcended if the Female Gothic is to realise its promise. The point is rendered palpable in an early work of proto-Female Gothic, Anna Letitia Barbauld's *A Summer Evening's Meditation* (1773). Barbauld belonged to the same dissenting circles as Radcliffe's uncle, Thomas Bentley, and was even closer to the progressive Enlightenment culture that also nurtured the young Ann Ward. Barbauld's poem is a secular – or perhaps, simply modernised – version of Isaac Watts's *The Adventurous Muse* (1709), both being paeans to Urania, the muse of astronomy. Watts was the dominant hymn writer prior to the Wesleys and one of the grandsires of the Dissenting community (the definitive collection of his poems and hymns was edited by Barbauld's grandfather, Philip Doddridge, also a pillar of the dissenting establishment). *A Summer Evening's Meditation* is one of the most audacious poems of its age. Published under Barbauld's own name, it represents an implicitly feminine soul reconnoitring the heavens in Miltonic blank verse, sounding ultimate mysteries, as if an unfallen Lucifera. But the most audacious stroke of all is to represent the soul falling back before the sublime prospect in explicit recoil against penetrating, patriarchal knowledge (thereby implicitly critiquing the scientific project of Joseph Priestley and other fathers of the Warrington Academy). The poem is at once a transcendent representation of female genius, of female genius unbound, and a rejection of the sublime as a power structure that would ultimately enslave it.[24]

At the moment of sublime dilation, the speaker asks:

What hand unseen
Impels me onward through the glowing orbs
Of inhabitable nature far remote,
To the dread confines of eternal night,
To solitudes of vast unpeopled space,
The deserts of creation, wide and wild;
Where embryo systems and unkindled suns
Sleep in the womb of chaos?
Fancy droops,
And thought astonished stops her bold career;[25]

Pulled up short, the speaker explains the change in tack, by directly addressing the lord:

Oh, look with pity down
On erring, guilty man – not in thy names
Of terror clad; not with those thunders armed
That conscious Sinai felt, when fear appalled
The scattered tribes; Thou hast a gentler voice,
That whispers comfort to the swelling heart,
Abashed, yet longing to behold her maker. (l. 107–113)

The antinomy in Barbauld's thought hinges on a near homophony, between the 'abashed' of the final line, and 'abased'. Barbauld amplifies her thinking in her essay, 'Thoughts on the Devotional Taste, on Sects, and on Establishments', published two years after her poem (1775):

> When we trace the footsteps of creative energy through regions of unmeasured space, and still find new wonders disclosed and pressing upon the view – we grow giddy with the prospect; the mind is astonished, confounded at its own insignificance; we think it almost impiety for a worm to lift its head from the dust, and address the Lord of so stupendous a universe; the idea of communion with our Maker seems shocking, and the only feeling the soul is capable of in such a moment is a deep and painful sense of its own abasement.[26]

The Burkean sublime – in which we fall back in astonishment at a pre-potent masculine power – is rejected as a form of abasement, where the subject is reduced to the status of a mute, wondering, abject worm. For Barbauld this was the terminus of the highly competitive practice of the Warrington scientific community, with its whiff of masculine vain-gloriousness. In its place the 'abash'd' soul (the gendering of the term is calculated) is balanced between sublime yearning ('swelling', line 112) and deferential openness ('abashed', line 113). Barbauld's poem is not Gothic, but only because being abashed, rather than abasement, is an option extended by a beneficent deity. Should the sublime prove to be pre-potent the Gothic would surely follow. The sublime, then, is central to the Female Gothic – to the Female Gothic as Radcliffe fashioned it – because it simultaneously uplifts the female soul (thus representing genius) while threatening to render the female soul 'abject' through self-abasement before the masculine principle. As such, in itself it encodes the contradiction analysed by Poovey, of uplifting the female self only to enslave it further. Radcliffe's trick is to find a balanced middle ground, in Barbauld's manner.

There are, then, four necessary and sufficient conditions for Radcliffe's Female Gothic. There must be figurations of female genius; the possible expression of genius is tied to property, to both its presence and threatened alienation; the threat is explicitly tied to the patriarchal principle – most generally, through the sublime; and finally, the mother's absence is not a token of her irrelevance but of her supreme importance as a deferred object of the heroine's unconscious search. I earlier argued that if the phrase 'Female Gothic' is to perform useful critical work it requires a difference. While I do not have space to delineate what the

Male Gothic might be, in any depth, it does seem to be the case that the gaze (by which I also mean scopophilia, the ocularcentric, and the ocularphobic) is indeed material to it. While Wordsworth's *Prelude* is not a Gothic poem, it does have its moments when its tone Gothically darkens, most of which revolve around Wordsworth's rejection of the 'despotic eye',[27] in favour of a visionary – metaphysical – third eye. Wordsworth's famous 'spots of time' passages narrate just such moments of transcendence, but in so far as they are recollected with a sense of foreboding, they hint at Gothic terrors (think of the 'visionary dreariness' or the spot of grass forever blasted by hanging).[28] The troubled gaze readily links a work like Lewis's *The Monk* (1796) with Hawthorne's *The Blithedale Romance* (1852), both works turning on the arrested development of scopophiliacs.

With this in mind one can see that in *The Italian* Radcliffe plays with both the Female and Male Gothic, which work against each other in contrapuntal fashion. Ellena d'Rosalba's story follows the contours mapped out by Holland and Sherman: we encounter Ellena in her cottage where her fate of impoverished gentility – complete with forced stints of menial piecework – is in stark contrasts with the hints of something better, in her body and manners. If Vivaldi's courtship provides the sexual interest, the Marquise's machinations, via her tool, Schedoni, provides the supernatural threats. As Ellena's usurping uncle – that is, as her father's murderer and mother's rapist – he also introduces the dynastic mysteries and, symbolically at least, the sexual threat. Ellena's forced travels and unconscious search for Olivia, her mother (coyly hinted at through the epigraph from *Twelfth Night* which puns on Viola's professed desire for another Olivia)[29] completes the narrative pattern of the Female Gothic. Her imprisonment in the turret of the convent of San Stefano is a late example of the Radcliffean sublime, and, like late style generally, is self-reflexive about Radcliffe's narrative practice. On the one hand Ellena has unwittingly made contact with her mother, the nun Olivia; fortified by her presence, Ellena's genius flourishes, as her imagination projects outwards in a bravura piece of Burkean sublimity. At the same time, her imagination's limit is the patriarchal principle itself, the male deity as grand architect.

> To Ellena, whose mind was capable of being highly elevated, or sweetly soothed, by scenes of nature, the discovery of this little turret was an important circumstance. Hither she could come, and her soul, refreshed by the views it afforded, would acquire strength to bear her, with equanimity, through the persecutions that might

await her. Here, gazing upon the stupendous imagery around her, looking, as it were, beyond the awful veil which obscures the features of the Deity, and conceals Him from the eyes of his creatures, dwelling as with a present God in the midst of his sublime works; with a mind thus elevated, how insignificant would appear to her the transactions, and the sufferings of this world! How poor the boasted power of man, when the fall of a single cliff from these mountains would with ease destroy thousands of his race assembled on the plains below! How would it avail them, that they were accoutred for battle, armed with all the instruments of destruction that human invention ever fashioned? Thus man, the giant who now held her in captivity, would shrink to the diminutiveness of a fairy; and she would experience, that his utmost force was unable to enchain her soul, or compel her to fear him, while he was destitute of virtue.[30]

The usual way of interpreting this passage is to say that it acknowledges Ellena's credentials, as the embodiment of sensibility, as she withdraws from potential hubris into due appreciation of a proper religious modesty. Alternatively, it is yet another recoil against the masculine principle, as the vaulting ambition she repudiates is, indeed, 'man's'. In this respect her treatment of the sublime doubles Barbauld's, as it negotiates a balance between the abasement encoded within Burke's sublime (one especially perilous for female subjectivity) and an equally suspect vaingloriousness.

Vivaldi's complementary male-Gothic story turns on the perils of seeing, from his initial scopophilia, when he pushes at the boundaries of propriety as he probes Ellena's veil, to his scopophobia, when, with the tables turned, he finds himself the object of the Inquisition's invasive, institutional gaze. I mention this, as a way of making the point that Radcliffe's Female Gothic is less a formula and more a narrative grammar with deep roots in the ideological circumstances of her time. There is a Male Gothic grammar for Radcliffe to explore, not because, if there is a Female Gothic, there must be a Male, but because the period has its own gender-political 'unconscious' (I mean this in the Jamesonian sense) constraining and shaping the narrative imagination. If the linguistic metaphor is to work (where I speak of a 'narrative grammar') it must also be shareable, something understood and reproduced by others. Radcliffe's Female Gothic survives – is a narrative enterprise we can index – because others understood and 'spoke' it. In a general way this is the point of the epigraph from Keats: if his phrase designates a matrix ('Mother Radcliff'), it is, in narrative terms, a deep grammatical one, at once productive and transformative.

Notes

1. John Keats, *Letters Of John Keats: A Selection*, Robert Gittings, ed. (Oxford: Oxford University Press, 1970), 214.
2. Walter Scott, *Sir Walter Scott on Novelists and Fiction*, Ioan M. Williams, ed. (London: Routledge & Kegan Paul, 1968), 89. All subsequent references are to this edition and are given in the text.
3. Ellen Moers, *Literary Women* (New York: Doubleday, 1976), 90. All subsequent references are to this edition and are given in the text.
4. For Gothic as a patriarchal mirror, see Clare Kahane, 'Gothic Mirrors and Feminine Identity', *Centennial Review* 24 (1980): 43–64.
5. For an example of historicist critique of Gilbert and Grubar, see Jacqueline Howard, *Reading Gothic Fiction: A Bakhtinian Approach* (Oxford: Clarendon Press, 1994), 63–5.
6. For instance, a contemporary of Mrs Barbauld's comments that for her 'the republic of letters was real, and she was a firm believer in the equality of man and state of freedom. All her writings prove her reasonable hope and belief in human progress, and manifest a great degree of modesty.' Quoted in Grace A. Ellis, *A Memoir of Mrs. Anna Laetitia Barbauld with Many of Her Letters*, 2 vols (Boston, MA: James R. Osgood and Company, 1874), I, 250.
7. For the market dominance of the Gothic, see my '1790s: The Effulgence of Gothic', *The Cambridge Companion to Gothic Fiction*, ed. Jerrold E. Hogle (Cambridge: Cambridge University Press, 2002), 41–62, see 42–5. For the gender distribution, see Peter Garside, 'The English Novel in the Romantic era: Consolidation and Dispersal', *The English Novel, 1770–1829: A Bibliographical Survey of Prose Fiction Published in the British Isles*, eds, Peter Garside, James Raven, and Rainer Schöwerling, 2 vols (Oxford: Oxford University Press, 2000), 15–103. Garside supplies a table ('Figure 2. Authorship of New Novels, 1800–1829: Gender Breakdown', 74) showing the total number of novels published during the period by gender, with a third line registering the percentage of anonymous publications. Although the numbers of Gothic novels steadily declined after the first decade of the century its market share was frequently as high as 33 per cent during this ten-year period. The period coincided with a surge in male authorship, where men several times eclipsed the production of women authors. Moreover, the lines for identified male authors, and anonymous, are inversely related, strongly suggesting that male authorship declines, not because fewer men are writing, but because fewer are declaring their authorship. Given that only up to a third of the whole were Gothic, it does not follow that male Gothic production matched female. However, the salient point is that the available information fails to support the long-held assumption that the Gothic novel was dominated by women writers.
8. Norman Holland and Leona Sherman, 'Gothic Possibilities', *New Literary History* 8/2 (1977), 279–94, 279.
9. Robert Miles, *Gothic Writing 1750–1820: A Genealogy*, 2nd edition (Manchester: Manchester Press, 2002), 46–7.

10. Jürgen Habermas, *The Structural Transformation of the Public Sphere: An Inquiry into a Category of Bourgeois Society*, trans. Thomas Burger with the assistance of Frederick Lawrence (Cambridge, MA: MIT Press, 1990). For the performative aspect of Habermas's public sphere theory, see my *Romantic Misfits* (Basingstoke and New York: Palgrave Macmillan, 2008), 13–18.
11. Marshall Brown, *The Gothic Text* (Stanford, CA: Stanford University Press, 2005), 31.
12. For details see my *Ann Radcliffe: The Great Enchantress* (Manchester: Manchester University Press, 1995), 7, 14.
13. William Hazlitt, *Lectures on the English Comic Writers* (London, New York and Toronto: Oxford University Press [1819], 1907), 165.
14. Lauren Fitzgerald, 'Gothic Properties: Radcliffe, Lewis, and the Critics', *The Wordsworth Circle* 24/3 (Summer 1993), 167–70.
15. 'La Vallée' is a 'small estate in Gascony', its main building 'merely a summer cottage', albeit one with a library occupying 'the west side of the chateau' – Ann Radcliffe, *The Mysteries of Udolpho*, Bonamy Dobrée, ed. (Oxford: World's Classics [1794], 1966), 2. All subsequent references are to this edition and are given in the text.
16. The point is explicitly made in the romance's denouement (*Udolpho*, 663).
17. When Isabella Thorpe asks 'Are not you wild to know?' what lies behind the black veil, Catherine replies, 'I am sure it is Laurentina's skeleton.' Jane Austen, *Northanger Abbey*, Marilyn Butler, ed. (Harmondsworth, Middlesex: Penguin, 1995), 36.
18. Nathan Drake, *Literary Hours, or Sketches Critical and Narrative*, 2nd edition, 2 vols (New York: Garland [1800], 1970), 359.
19. According to Leah Price, Radcliffe was the first to include epigraphs at the head of chapters: *The Anthology and the Rise of the Novel: From Richardson to George Eliot* (Cambridge: Cambridge University Press, 2000).
20. In the history of the English novel the mixing of prose and poetry is largely restricted to the Romantic period, a movement in which Radcliffe's example was not the first, but certainly among the most popular. See Marshall Brown, 'Poetry and the Novel', *Cambridge Companion to Fiction in the Romantic Period*, Richard Maxwell and Katie Trumpener, eds (Cambridge: Cambridge University Press, 2008), 107–28, 109.
21. See Alison Kelly, 'Bentley, Thomas (1731–1780)', *Oxford Dictionary of National Biography*, H. C. G. Matthew and Brian Harrison, eds, (Oxford: Oxford University Press, 2004), http://www.oxforddnb.com.ezproxy.library.uvic.ca/view/article/2175. Accessed 17 March 2009.
22. According to Marshall Brown, such self-reflexivity is a defining feature of the German novel during the period, but a rare one among English novels – Marshall Brown, 'Theory of the Novel', *The Cambridge History of Literary Criticism: Volume V, Romanticism*, ed. Marshall Brown (Cambridge: Cambridge University Press, 2000), 250–71, 256.
23. Mary Poovey, 'Ideology and the Mysteries of Udolpho', *Criticism: A Quarterly for Literature and the Arts* 21 (1979), 307–30.
24. I develop this point at greater length in *Romantic Misfits: Palgrave Studies in the Enlightenment, Romanticism and the Cultures of Print* (Basingstoke and New York: Palgrave Macmillan, 2008), 185–6.

25. Anna Laetitia Barbauld, 'A Summer Evening's Meditation', lines 91–100, *Romanticism: An Anthology*, 3rd edition, Duncan Wu, ed. (Oxford: Blackwell, 2006), 35–7. All subsequent references are to this edition and are given in the text.

26. Anna Laetitia Barbauld, *Anna Letitia Barbauld: Selected Poetry and Prose*, Elizabeth Kraft and William McCarthy, eds (Peterborough, Ontario: Broadview, 2002), 215–16.

27. J. C. Maxwell, *William Wordsworth: The Prelude: A Parallel Text* (Harmondsworth: Penguin, 1971).

28. William Wordsworth, *The Prelude*, Book XI, lines 295 and 311.

29. Ann Radcliffe, *The Italian*, Robert Miles, ed. (Harmondsworth, Middlesex: Penguin, [1794] 2000), 33.

30. Radcliffe, *The Italian*, 106–7.

4
Disturbing the Female Gothic: An Excavation of the *Northanger* Novels

Angela Wright

'...my dearest Catherine, what have you been doing with yourself all this morning? – Have you gone on with Udolpho?'

'Yes, I have been reading it ever since I woke; and I am got to the black veil.'

'Are you, indeed? How delightful! Oh! I would not tell you what is behind the black veil for the world! Are you not wild to know?'

'Oh! yes, quite; what can it be? – But do not tell me – I would not be told upon any account. I know it must be a skeleton, I am sure it is Laurentina's skeleton. Oh! I am delighted with the book! I should like to spend my whole life in reading it. I assure you, if it had not been to meet you, I would not have come away from it for all the world.'

'Dear creature! how much I am obliged to you; and when you have finished Udolpho, we will read the Italian together; and I have made out a list of ten or twelve more of the same kind for you.'

'Have you, indeed! How glad I am! – What are they all?'

'I will read you their names directly; here they are, in my pocket-book. Castle of Wolfenbach, Clermont, Mysterious Warning, Necromancer of the Black Forest, Midnight Bell, Orphan of the Rhine, and Horrid Mysteries. Those will last us some time.'

'Yes, pretty well; but are they all horrid, are you sure they are all horrid?'

Jane Austen, *Northanger Abbey*[1]

Whatever else it may have contained, Isabella Thorpe's pocket-book does not register, record or establish a 'Female Gothic'. It contains the titles of seven novels, not their authors. Consequently, this pocket-book reading list conveys no information about the gender of the authors. By contrast, John Thorpe responds to Catherine Morland's query 'Have you ever read Udolpho, Mr Thorpe?' with 'Not I, faith! No, if I read any it shall be Mrs. Radcliff's [*sic*];' (45), and Henry Tilney praises the 'hair-raising' prose of 'Mrs. Radcliffe' (95). It is the reading minds of John and Henry, not those of Isabella and Catherine, which respond to author-ship, and the gendering of a text through authorship.

Ellen Moers first established the term 'Female Gothic' in 1976 with her 'easily defined' assumption that it is 'the work that women writers have done in the literary mode that, since the eighteenth century, we have called the Gothic'.[2] Moers almost immediately eroded her seemingly straightforward definition, however, by shifting her focus from author-ship to thematics. She argued that Ann Radcliffe's foregrounding of 'a young woman who is simultaneously persecuted victim and courageous heroine' established a crucial Gothic trope (91). In 1993 Jacqueline Howard rightly challenged the assumption that 'male' and 'female' authorship inevitably carries 'necessary psychological consequences' to the texts that they produce.[3] In 1994, E. J. Clery also interrogated the 'common-sense category' of 'Female Gothic' by revisiting the long-established lin-eage of heroine-centred novels by both male and female authors from which Radcliffe undoubtedly drew inspiration.[4] These and many other fruitful interventions have usefully promoted a critical wariness of the term 'Female Gothic' that is recognised by the editors of special issues upon the topic. In a double issue of *Women's Writing* on 'Female Gothic' in 1994, Robert Miles warned against regarding 'Female Gothic' as a 'self-evident literary classification', and in 2004 Andrew Smith and Diana Wallace introduced a new 'Female Gothic' collection in *Gothic Studies* by acknowledging that the term is 'possibly, too essentialising'.[5] The fragile critical taxonomy inaugurated by Moers has proved to be of value less for its argument than for the debates that it continues to provoke.

Following Ellen Moers, my critical intervention commences in the 1790s, and also invokes the problematic spectre of Jane Austen's *Northanger Abbey* (1818). At the beginning of 'Female Gothic' Moers fol-lows the lead of Austen's Henry Tilney. The first (and only) example that Moers pulls from Jane Austen's *Northanger Abbey* places him centre-stage: 'Jane Austen has Henry Tilney, in *Northanger Abbey*, say that he could not put down Mrs. Radcliffe's *Mysteries of Udolpho*: "I remember finishing it in two days – my hair standing on end the whole time"' (91). Moers wishes to highlight first and foremost the physiological effects of reading Gothic novels, but she relies predominantly upon accounts of men reading Gothic fiction (91).[6] In itself, this reliance need not be problematic, but it does undermine the argument for a female-centred tradition which Moers wishes to propose. This is because Austen's *Northanger Abbey*, first composed in 1798, problematises assumptions about gendered reading habits that were already prevalent in the 1790s. As I will argue, it executes this problematisation on two levels. First, *Northanger Abbey* foregrounds acts of reading and debating Gothic novels that involve both men and women. Second, through its evocation of what we now recognise as the 'Northanger Novels', the novel fleetingly resurrects a neglected tradition of Gothic writing in the 1790s that was remarkable for its equality of gender at the level of authorship, themes and reciprocity.

Besides Henry Tilney, at least two other characters know how to read fiction in *Northanger Abbey*. Catherine Morland and Isabella Thorpe's Gothic reading syllabus from the absent Miss Andrews may well be a subject of mirth, but their volatile vision nonetheless conveys an excitement about reading that distinguishes them from the comparatively detached Henry Tilney. Catherine's assured declaration that she 'should like to spend [her] whole life' in reading *The Mysteries of Udolpho* (1794), Isabella's promise that next they 'will read the Italian together', the thrilled anticipation in Catherine's interrogation of Isabella's other proposed titles, 'are you sure they are all horrid?': together, these phrases suggest an absorption in reading that is collective, imaginative and excited.

Acts of reading and debating Gothic fiction lie unapologetically at the heart of *Northanger Abbey*. The vigorous and animated ways in which reading is debated between both men and women are no doubt a reflection of Austen's own familial experiences. When, for example, the Austens were invited to subscribe to a new library run by one Mrs Martin, who took the pains to emphasise that 'her Collection is not to consist only of Novels', Austen noted dryly in a letter to her sister Cassandra that '[Mrs Martin] might have spared this pretension to *our* family, who are great novel readers and not ashamed of being so'.[7] Austen did not perceive the need to excuse her family for their unapologetic novel-reading habits. An earlier letter observes without judgement that 'My father is now reading the "Midnight Bell", which he has got from the library'.[8] Her note of her father's consumption of one of the titles that appears in *Northanger Abbey* – the anonymously published *The Midnight Bell* (1798) by Francis Lathom – is significant precisely because of the lack of importance that Austen attaches to it. No value judgement accompanies this rare picture of a man reading a Gothic

romance and thus it becomes difficult to argue that Austen's simultaneously composed *Northanger Abbey* can be a straightforward critique of
women's consumption of Gothic fiction.[9]

Austen brilliantly evokes the pleasure and the debates that 'Gothic'
works stimulate in *Northanger Abbey*. She also takes pains to illustrate that
it is not only women who read and respond to Gothic fiction. When, for
example, Catherine registers surprise at Henry's eager consumption of
The Mysteries of Udolpho, saying 'But I really thought before, young men
despised novels amazingly', Henry is proud to declare, 'I myself have
read hundreds and hundreds' (96). There then ensues a debate on the
relative merits of novels and history between Henry, his sister Eleanor
and Catherine as they walk on Beechen Cliff. Catherine complains that
history 'tells me nothing that does not either vex or weary me. The quar-
rels of popes and kings, with wars or pestilences, in every page; the men
all so good for nothing, and hardly any women at all – it is very tire-
some' (97). While at first glance this observation seems laughably naive,
Catherine's observation echoes a more seriously argued complaint by
one of the first women to write in the Gothic mode. Austen takes inspiration for the Beechen Cliff debate from Clara Reeve.[10]

Reeve's preface to her defence of novels entitled *The Progress of
Romance* (1785) foregrounds the occlusion of women from the history of literature, and seeks to reposition them at the heart of a literary tradition, the romance: 'The learned men of our own country,
have in general affected a contempt for this kind of writing, and looked
upon Romances, as proper furniture only for a lady's library.'[11] Reeve
then presents a Socratic dialogue between two women, Sophronia and
Euphrasia, and a man, Hortensius. Euphrasia leads the debate, aiming to
trace 'Romance to its origin' in order to prove its ancient, Latinate roots
and thus its credibility as a genre. However, while Reeve's Euphrasia has
an uphill struggle to persuade Hortensius of the validity of Romance,
Austen's Catherine finds a much more receptive audience in Henry
Tilney. Austen adopts the model of Reeve's debate, with two women
and one man debating the relative merits of history and fiction, but it
is more difficult to determine who exactly the leader in her later debate
is, and whether that matters. Henry warns Catherine,

> Do not imagine that you can cope with me in a knowledge of
> Julias and Louisas. If we proceed to particulars, and engage in the
> never-ceasing inquiry of 'Have you read this?' and 'Have you read
> that?' I shall soon leave you as far behind me as – what shall I say? – I
> want an appropriate simile; as far as your friend Emily herself left

poor Valancourt when she went with her aunt into Italy. Consider how many years I have had the start of you. I had entered on my studies at Oxford, while you were a good little girl working your sampler at home! (96)

The question of whether Henry's 'studies' at Oxford centre upon his classical education or his copious romance-reading is left deliberately ambiguous and thus undermines the arbitrary division forged between romance and 'works of genius' by Reeve's earlier male protagonist, Hortensius. Henry's search for an appropriate paradigm of his reading knowledge leads him to Radcliffe's *Mysteries of Udolpho*, where he then compares himself to the heroine, Emily, and Catherine with Valancourt, the hero. Henry's gender inversion is illustrative of both the pervasive influence of Gothic romance in the 1790s and Austen's relative indifference to the gendered identity of its readership.

Northanger Abbey has long been read as a parody of Gothic fiction.[12] Due to its earlier composition date it at first glance appears to participate in the spate of satirical open letters that began to criticise Gothic fiction in the late 1790s. 'Anti-Ghost', for example, who 'sent' the open letter 'On the New Method of Inculcating Morality' to *Walker's Hibernian Magazine* in 1798, complained about the novel's inability to impart knowledge and facts: 'So much for the *instruction* to be derived, if it *really* wanted in this enlightened age. But what is the *information* we learn?'[13] Austen's novel in many ways illustrates similar anxieties about the uncritical consumption of large amounts of Gothic fiction, but she cleverly inverts such satirical responses to the novel when she has Catherine Morland complain that learning *history* is a torment for children, and that 'to *torment* and to *instruct* might sometimes be used as synonymous words' (98).

During the very years in which Austen first composed *Northanger Abbey*, the Gothic novel and its perceived 'female' readership attracted an unprecedented level of opprobrium across the political spectrum of the periodical press. The *Monthly Mirror*, for example, published an anonymous letter with the sensation title 'Novel Reading a Cause of Female Depravity', and even the anonymous 'Jacobin Novelist' who penned 'The Terrorist System of Novel-Writing' in *The Monthly Magazine* complained about his daughters' consumption of Gothic fiction, stating that they 'would read [Gothic romances] whether I pleased or not'.[14] The reasons for such disapproval were due in large part to the sheer volume of Gothic romances that were being published, many (but by no means all) of them by women writers. While Radcliffe usually escaped the disapproval of such critics her imitators did not. In 1796, for example, one reviewer of the newly published *Austenburn Castle* by an 'unpatronized female' noted with despair that 'Since Mrs Radcliffe's justly admired and successful romances, the press has teemed with stories of haunted castles and visionary terrors; the incidents of which are so little diversified, that criticism is at a loss to vary its remarks.'[15] The critical anxiety generated by this lack of originality was undoubtedly exacerbated by publishers such as William Lane of the Minerva press who actively encouraged female authors to come forward with romances composed in the same vein as Radcliffe.[16]

Isabella's pocket-book list undoubtedly contains material that can be deemed to be repetitive. Founded upon Austen's own careful reading, however, this list is deliberately eclectic. It is neither determined by the gender of its author, nor by the gender of its readership. The deliberate anonymisation of the list's titles (of which only one was published anonymously) and the pains that Austen takes to portray Henry also reading this fiction: taken together, these factors suggest that she wishes to unsettle the easy and repetitive complaints circulated in the periodical press concerning both female authorship and the uncritical female readership of the Gothic novel. The collation of the 'Northanger Novels', I think, is where it becomes difficult to argue for a 'Female Gothic' aesthetic in the 1790s that is predicated upon either the gender of the author or the gender of the reader.

If Austen's response to the contemporaneous periodical satires on the Gothic seems at best equivocal, one wonders what she would have made of early twentieth-century critical assessments of Isabella's reading list. J. M. S. Tompkins, for example, dismissed Austen's 'forgotten predecessors' as 'the leaf-mould in which that exquisite and thriving plant [Austen] was rooted'.[17] Michael Sadleir, the ardent bibliographer of the Gothic novel who confirmed the very existence of the 'Northanger Novels', went further in presuming to speak for Austen's opinion of these productions, 'for whose lack of restraint and very miscellaneous talent [she] could have felt neither respect nor tenderness'.[18] This conjecture is not supported by the textual evidence which comes from Austen's fiction. Throughout her works, we find that the characters who openly deride novels and romances are in fact the ones we are encouraged to dislike. John Thorpe in *Northanger Abbey*, Isabella's pushy brother who cannot recognise the title of a Radcliffe novel (*The Mysteries of Udolpho*) but presumes to speak for the quality of her fiction, is only matched in levels of inflated self-consequence by the opinionated Mr Collins in *Pride and Prejudice* (1813), who also affects to despise novels.

The 'Northanger Novels' – those anonymised titles that Austen so tantalisingly evokes in Isabella's pocket-book – raise the spectre of a Gothic tradition that is remarkable for its reciprocity and equality. This tradition is conceptualised quite differently from what we now know as the 'Female Gothic'. Besides the references to Radcliffe's two best-known novels, *The Mysteries of Udolpho* and *The Italian* (1797), the other titles cited by Isabella are bona fide Gothic romances: Eliza Parsons published *Castle of Wolfenbach* in 1793 and *The Mysterious Warning* in 1796; Regina Maria Roche published *Clermont* in 1798; Peter Teuthold translated *The Necromancer: Or the Tale of the Black Forest* from the German of Lawrence Flammenberg in 1794; Francis Lathom published *The Midnight Bell* anonymously in 1798; Eleanor Sleath *The Orphan of the Rhine* in 1798; and Peter Will adapted *Horrid Mysteries* from the German of the Marquis of Grosse in 1796. These novels were unashamedly inspired by the continental tradition of romance-writing.[19]

It is impossible to render justice to all seven 'Northanger' titles, but from an examination of two popular titles (one by a woman, and one by a man) we can discern some interesting shared themes that illustrate that Austen's selection of them was far from random. Each novel contains a murder or attempted murder of one family member by another. Discarded, spectral mothers loom large, confirming the Gothic's persistent anxiety with the relegation of the maternal figure. This tradition permeates the Gothic from Sophia Lee's fictionalisation of the imprisoned Mary, Queen of Scots as a mother in *The Recess* (1783–4), through Radcliffe's fiction and the 'Northanger Novels'.

Eliza Parsons's *Castle of Wolfenbach* (1793) is chronologically the first of the 'Northanger Novels'. Its comparatively early date marks it out, for it is difficult to argue (as many critics did and do) that Austen could have used this particular title as part of a wider critical point about repetition and imitation.[20] The novel roughly divides its two volumes between a tale of terror and a sentimental tale of conduct as did other Gothic-sentimental novels such as Regina Maria Roche's *The Children of the Abbey* (1796). The *Critical Review* noted of *Wolfenbach* that the two stories 'are not sufficiently interwoven with one another' to form a coherent narrative, but the 'terrible' in the end 'prevails'.[21] A similar criticism was levelled at *Northanger Abbey* for its uneasy movement between the spheres of Bath and the eponymous abbey. Austen's own division between Gothic narrative and novel of manners was picked up by the *British Critic*, which noted that '*Northanger Abbey* ... is simply, the history of a young girl' which moved unevenly between Catherine's education and the 'rather improbable' incidents and 'characterization of General Tilney'.[22] Austen's own dual structure is clearly indebted to such earlier works as *Castle of Wolfenbach*.

Castle of Wolfenbach begins, unsurprisingly, with reports of the eponymous castle being haunted. A young unprotected woman seeks shelter in the castle and is told by the servant Jacqueline, 'O! dear madam, why it is haunted; there are bloody floors, prison rooms, and scriptions, they say, on the windows, to make a body's hair stand on end.'[23] *Wolfenbach* pays homage to Radcliffe's second published novel, *A Sicilian Romance* (1790), which uses a line from Shakespeare's *Hamlet* on its title-page: 'I could a tale unfold!' The natural continuation of this speech from *Hamlet's* ghost, 'whose lightest word/Would harrow up thy soul', clearly connects Radcliffe's and Parson's shared aims of evoking terror through the narration of a hidden history. In *Castle of Wolfenbach*, the heroine Matilda notices 'a light glide by from an opposite wing' (7). Again this clearly connects this narrative to that of Radcliffe's second novel, *A Sicilian Romance*, where the heroine Julia also first notices a light in the opposite wing of the castle which, it later transpires, emanates from the hidden chamber of her long-believed-dead mother.

Where Parsons deviates from the Radcliffean model, however, is in the far more explicitly violent depiction of marital conflict. The intrepid heroine Matilda discovers that the light comes not from a ghost (as, predictably, the servants believe) but from the long-incarcerated Countess of Wolfenbach, who has been rendered a prisoner in her own home by her jealous husband. Almost immediately after Matilda has made her acquaintance, the Countess is abducted and Matilda discovers her servant 'on the bed weltering in blood!' (24). She further discovers that 'On the floor was plain mark'd the shape of a hand and fingers traced in blood, which seemed to have flowed in great quantities' (27). We later discover that the Countess has escaped safely but this is only secondary to the bloody scenes that Parsons chooses to depict at the opening of her novel. The lack of initial explanation for the Countess's disappearance and the immediate scenes of violence distinguish this from Radcliffe's model. Furthermore, they transform this into a novel about marital violence. Parsons splices this intelligently with moments of comedy in her later depictions of Parisian and London mores and her critique of Matilda's indulgence in sentiment, but the 'terrible' dominates this second narrative as the Countess must wait for her husband's death in order to be released from her marriage vows and reunited with the son taken from her at birth. Sadleir criticised Parsons for her 'cold and violent…scenes of almost sadistic cruelty', but it could be argued conversely that Parsons in fact exposes much more effectively than either

Radcliffe or Maria Regina Roche (with whom Sadleir compared Parsons unfavourably) the bloody consequences of a forced, loveless marriage.[24] After the Countess has been abducted, Matilda discovers the following lines etched upon the window panes of the Countess's cell:

> 'I am dumb, as solemn sorrow ought to be;
> Could my griefs speak, my tale I'd tell to thee.'

> 'A wife, a mother – sweet endearing ties!
> Torn from my arms, and heedless of my cries;
> Here I am doomed to waste my wretched life,
> No more a mother – a discarded wife.' (29)

The Countess's enforced silence forges an arbitrary division between herself as a living subject, and her 'griefs'. These ('griefs') are all that remain and they must tell her tale of becoming 'No more a mother – a discarded wife'. Her husband forces her to haunt the gallery every night with her lamp in order to scare off would-be intruders with the belief that there is a ghost. In effect, this is precisely what the Countess of Wolfenbach has become. Her spectral existence interrogates the eighteenth century's legal limitation of the roles of wife and mother.

The arbitrary tyranny of husbands and would-be suitors is laid uncomfortably bare in *Castle of Wolfenbach*. Matilda's lascivious uncle 'Count Weimar' wishes to seduce her. To this purpose he pursues Matilda across Europe and in France has a *lettre de cachet* issued against her in order that she remain within his power. Once in England, safely reunited with her friends and the now-safe Countess of Wolfenbach, her uncle persists. However, in a conversation which accords with Diane Long Hoeveler's point that Parsons is 'blatantly nationalistic in her celebration of British superiority', Matilda is reassured about her safety in England by Mrs Courtney:[25]

> Fear nothing, (said Mrs Courtney;) you are in the power of your friends; he must prove his right to you before he can take you from us: here are no lettres de cachet, the laws will protect you from injury; compose yourself, therefore, my dear girl – in England no violence can be offered to you in any shape. (107)

Mrs Courtney's complacent observation upon the superiority of England is not truly challenged within the textual world of *Wolfenbach*, but Austen's renegotiation of this in *Northanger Abbey* is more ambivalent.

The protracted rebuke that Henry serves to Catherine after her romance-fuelled erroneous assumption that General Tilney has in fact murdered his wife focuses upon both the 'preparation' of education and the 'connivance' of the law:

> Dear Miss Morland, consider the dreadful nature of the suspicions you have entertained. What have you been judging from? Remember the country and the age in which we live. Remember that we are English, that we are Christians. Consult your own understanding, your own observations of what is passing around you – Does our education prepare us for such atrocities? Do our laws connive at them? Could they be perpetrated without being known, in a country like this, where social and literary intercourse is on such a footing; where every man is surrounded by a neighbourhood of voluntary spies, and where roads and newspapers lay everything open? (172)

We know that Catherine's 'education' has prepared her for such atrocities because her female education has been cruelly deficient in certain areas. Likewise, while the law may not tolerate murder it does permit General Tilney to turn a young unprotected female out of his house without money in the middle of the night, once he has discovered that Catherine has no fortune. While Austen clearly took inspiration from Mrs Courtney's nationalistic observation in *Wolfenbach*, she was perhaps more struck by the theme of marital violence offered in the first volume of the novel, for we discover that General Tilney cruelly neglected his wife when she was alive.

The confident assertion by Moers that 'Female Gothic' foregrounds a heroine certainly holds true for *Castle of Wolfenbach*, both in terms of Matilda's brave confrontation of a seeming ghost (the Countess) and her own persecution by 'Count Weimar'.[26] Parsons's novel is fully aware of its participation in a tradition, however. When, for example, the Countess's brother-in-law explains his duty of protecting both the Countess and Matilda from their respective persecutors, his interlocutor, the German ambassador drily remarks, 'Upon my word, Marquis, ... you are quite a knight-errant, to protect distressed damsels.' The Marquis defends his 'very honourable employment' by observing that 'though these are not the days of romance, yet I have met with such extraordinary incidents lately as carry much the face of the wonderful stories we have heard of former times' (113). Through her character, Parsons takes pains to emphasise the continuing political and literary relevance of romance and chivalry in the 1790s. It reminds the reader both that eighteenth-century

Europe permits women to be incarcerated and abducted and that this tale participates willingly in what Clara Reeve took pains to establish as a strong, ancient and unashamed lineage of romance.

The self-conscious participation in the tradition of romance is a feature shared by all of the 'Northanger Novels'. Eleanor Sleath's *The Orphan of the Rhine* (1798), for example, has a heroine whose name Julie de Roubine is unashamedly taken from Henry MacKenzie's eponymous heroine who in her turn unashamedly took her name from Jean-Jacques Rousseau's *Julie, ou la Nouvelle Heloise* (1761). When Henry warns Catherine that she cannot improve upon his readerly knowledge of 'Julias and Louisas', he undoubtedly refers to this proud, unashamedly reciprocal tradition in romance.[27] While it is not my purpose to track down every single shared name, it is, nonetheless, important to note the participation of the 'Northanger Novels' in a mutual discourse of romance. Important, because Austen clearly recognised and celebrated that shared heritage in her own work.

Austen's challenge to the role of the heroine in *Northanger Abbey* begins with the opening words, 'No one who had ever seen Catherine Morland in her infancy, would have supposed her born to be an heroine' (13). Arguably, this is inspired by her readings of the 'Northanger Novels'. These novels both celebrate and trouble the assumption that a heroine must take centre-stage. Francis Lathom's *The Midnight Bell*, for example, instead shares the narrative perspective between the young hero Alphonsus and his wife Lauretta. Foregrounding a married couple in itself is unusual, but the way in which Lathom then shifts spontaneously between male and female perspectives is highly significant. David Punter and Alan Bissett have fruitfully interrogated the oddities of Lathom's narrative perspectives in relation to a queer aesthetic. Focusing upon the novel's intense portrayals of emotive friendships between men, they argue that Lathom's constant 'deferral of meaning' exposes a particular melancholy which 'it is possible to read...in terms of separation, loss: at which point the whole structure becomes enmeshed in the complexities of gender differentiation'.[28] Their reading of *The Midnight Bell* goes some way to accounting for the novel's constant deferral of Alphonsus and Lauretta's happiness and the ease with which Lathom oscillates between their gendered perspectives.

Lathom ventriloquises a heroine's perspective extremely well, portraying her emotions while locked in a cell overnight with warmth and sympathy. The abduction of Lauretta by the libertine chevalier Theodore, her voyage through deserted castles and her eventual refuge in a disused cavern is again undoubtedly informed again by Radcliffe's earlier titles *A Sicilian Romance* and *The Romance of the Forest* (1791). This, however, is not the most interesting aspect of the narrative. Of greater significance is Lathom's repositioning of his hero, Alphonsus, as a character so richly endowed with the characteristics of sympathy and sensibility that he comes across as lacking confidence in his own faculties of judgement. Alphonsus has been forced out of his ancestral home by a mother who refuses to tell him who has murdered his father. Of course, he has many questions which demand answers but the protracted portrayal of his self-doubt is highly suggestive:

> 'My uncle,' he said, 'my mother avows to be innocent, – why should I fear him? – but still, she conjures me not to see him: – some secret cause doubtless actuates her conduct, – why hide it from me? – Should she have leagued with him to murder my father! – have taken him to her bed, and driven me from the castle, that I might not be a witness of her shame!' The thought went nigh to madden him. 'She is not so base,' he cried: 'Would she, had this been so, have supplicated the count on her knees? – it could not have been done to deceive me, for she expected not my entrance. – What cause could there be for that mysterious conduct? – for her still more strange appearance on the morning she sent me from the castle? – for the blood that stained her hand?'[29]

The series of questions that Alphonsus poses to himself indicates a crisis of confidence in his own judgmental capacities for Alphonsus constantly defers settling upon one particular explanation of his mother's behaviour. This deferral haunts the novel, as Alphonsus wanders Europe in self-imposed exile taking a number of menial employments along the way. His marriage to Lauretta, her abduction and subsequent restoration to him, leave no narrative space to describe a happy marriage. Instead, when all the other narrative difficulties have been resolved, Alphonsus finally confronts his past and returns to the castle where the midnight bell tolls each night. Here, his first encounter with his spectral mother in the crypt of the chapel derails his senses:

> The tears stole down his cheek. – 'My mother was once kind, as you are now; and for one, one act of disobedience, though my rent heart could no longer exist in uncertainty, she has – Oh, had you seen her!' a sigh, drawn from the bottom of his heart, followed: – falling on his knees, he clasped Lauretta's hand, and pulled her down by him; – 'Pray with me; pray to my mother for her forgiveness.' [...] at length,

when he raised his eyelids, his eyes which had before betrayed the wildest frenzy, bespoke the most painful sorrow: he looked anxiously round the apartment, and discovering Lauretta, he beckoned eagerly to her; she flew to his side: she grasped her hand in his, – 'Do not leave me! Promise you will not leave me.' (195)

The repositioning of Alphonsus as the principal victim in Lathom's text is far from accidental. His temporary loss of reason is reminiscent of the only moment in *The Mysteries of Udolpho* when Emily St Aubert, weighed down by grief, loses her reason after mistaking the waxen figure for a corpse in Udolpho.

> With some difficulty, Annette led her to the bed, which Emily examined with an eager, frenzied eye, before she lay down, and then, pointing, turned with shuddering emotion, to Annette, who, now more terrified, went towards the door, that she might bring one of the female servants to pass the night with them; but Emily, observing her going, called her by name, and then in the naturally soft and plaintive tone of her voice, begged, that she, too, would not forsake her.[30]

Both Emily and Alphonsus respond to things that they imagine that they have seen. In Emily's case the waxen figure reminds her of her own familial losses; the case of Alphonsus is strikingly similar.

It is perfectly possible to argue that Lathom's Alphonsus is feminised by his over-heated imagination and thus that this novel participates in a 'feminine' tradition of Gothic. Indeed, Michael Sadleir argues for this in his own early excavation when he connects *The Midnight Bell* as a 'terror' narrative with the productions of Parsons and Roche.[31] One could further argue that Radcliffe's *The Italian*, which also affords its hero Vivaldi a level of interiority and uncertainty unusual at the time, also effectively 'feminises' its hero and thus continues to participate in a 'feminine' tradition of Gothic. While there is merit to this argument, Austen's inclusion of the anonymised *The Midnight Bell* uncovers questions about the centrality of the heroine and the author's gender to any conception of 'Female Gothic'. The wanderings of Alphonsus through Europe are narrated with such brevity as to make them of little consequence. More important is the later part of the story, which constantly shifts focus between hero and heroine. The effect of this permanent movement is to unsettle our expectations about the form of the Gothic romance. Undoubtedly, in the equality of values and debate that Austen offers alternately to Catherine and Henry she was influenced by

Lathom's repositioning of hero and heroine. This, I think, is why *The Midnight Bell*'s inclusion in Isabella's reading list is of such significance.

I have argued in this essay that Austen carefully challenges assumptions about gendered reading habits and authorship in *Northanger Abbey*. Through the construction of Isabella's list she also interrogates complacent equations between heroinism and the Gothic that were already in place by 1798. Austen provides a list of Gothic texts that are unafraid to tackle themes of marital conflict under the auspices of romance, happily participatory in the continental discourse of romance, composed both by men and women, and varied in terms of gendered perspectives.

The 'Northanger Novels' evade our current understanding of the label 'Female Gothic' almost completely. This evasion is rendered all the more forceful in *Northanger Abbey* by the centrality of Catherine Morland's reading experiences. While she and Henry debate Gothic romance with almost equal verve she attaches little significance to the question of gendered authorship, in contrast to her male counterparts. Whether a novel was composed by a male or female, or published anonymously, did not matter so much as whether it was 'truly horrid'.

Notes

1. Jane Austen, *Northanger Abbey*, ed. Marilyn Butler (Harmondsworth: Penguin [1818], 1995), 37. All subsequent references are to this edition and are given in the text.
2. Ellen Moers, *Literary Women*, introd. Helen Taylor (London: The Women's Press [1976], 1986), 91. All subsequent references are to this edition and are given in the text.
3. Jacqueline Howard, *Reading Gothic Fiction: A Bakhtinian Approach* (Oxford: Clarendon Press, 1993), 57.
4. E. J. Clery, 'Ann Radcliffe and D. A. F. de Sade: Thoughts on Heroinism' in 'Female Gothic', ed. Robert Miles, *Women's Writing*, 1/2 (1994), 203–14.
5. Robert Miles, ed. 'Introduction' to 'Female Gothic', *Women's Writing*, 1/2 (1994), 132; Andrew Smith and Diana Wallace, eds, 'Introduction' to 'Female Gothic', *Gothic Studies*, 6/1 (May 2004), 2.
6. The second example that Moers provides comes from William Hazlitt: 'According to Hazlitt, Ann Radcliffe had mastered "the art of freezing the blood"' (91). Only after these does Moers offer an example of a female reading with Mary Shelley.
7. Letter to Cassandra Austen, Tuesday 18 December 1798, in Deirdre Le Faye, ed. *Jane Austen's Letters* (Oxford: Oxford University Press, 1995), 26.
8. Letter to Cassandra Austen, Wednesday 24 October 1798 (Le Faye, 1995), 15.
9. For further debate on the incomplete nature of the records we have of men reading and responding to fiction, see E. J. Clery, 'Women, Luxury and the Sublime' in *The Rise of Supernatural Fiction, 1762–1800* (Cambridge: Cambridge

University Press, 1995), 98. Clery rightly takes issue with claims by J. M. S Tompkins, for one, that 'women were supposed to constitute three-quarters of the novel-reading public'. (J. M. S. Tompkins, *The Popular Novel in England, 1770–1800* (London: Methuen [1932], 1969), 120.

10. Marilyn Butler also makes this connection between Reeve and Austen, stating that the Beechen Cliff debate is 'an echo perhaps of Reeve's *Progress of Romance*', but she does not pursue it any further. Butler, ed., xx.

11. Clara Reeve, *The Progress of Romance*, vol. I (London, 1785), 6.

12. *Northanger Abbey* was first drafted under the title *Susan* between 1798 and 1799. Between these years and 1803 it was completed, and sold to the publisher Crosby, of Stationer's Hall Court. He announced it as being 'in the press' but, for some reason, did not publish it at this time. Austen's brothers bought back the ms from Crosby for the same price, and published it posthumously with *Persuasion* in 1818. For further information on this, derived from Austen's letters, see Deirdre Le Faye, *Jane Austen: A Family Record*, 2nd edition (Cambridge: Cambridge University Press, 2003) and Michael Sadleir, 'All Horrid? Jane Austen and the Gothic Romance' in *Things Past*, ed. Michael Sadleir (London: Constable, 1944), 167–200, 169.

13. 'On the New Method of Inculcating Morality', signed by 'Anti-Ghost' for *Walker's Hibernian Magazine* (January 1798), 10.

14. Anon, 'Novel Reading a Cause of Female Depravity', *Monthly Mirror*, 4 (November 1797), 277–9; Anon, 'The Terrorist System of Novel Writing', *Monthly Magazine*, 4/21 (August 1797), 102.

15. Anon, *The Critical Review*, 16 (February 1796), 222.

16. For further exploration of this, see Edward Jacobs, 'The Gothic Library' in his monograph *Accidental Migrations: An Archaeology of Gothic Discourse* (Lewisburg, PA: Bucknell University Press, 2000), 157–235.

17. Tompkins, vi.

18. Sadleir, 172. For a full account of Sadleir's excavation of the 'Northanger novels', and the collection in which they are now housed, see Frederick S. Frank, 'Gothic Gold: The Sadleir-Black Collection' *Studies in Eighteenth-Century Culture*, 26 (1998), 287–312.

19. Although the 'Northanger novels' were out of print for the majority of the twentieth century, Sadleir's painstaking excavation of them has guaranteed them some level of critical recognition, and they are now coming back into print. See Michael Sadleir, 'The Northanger Novels: A Footnote to Jane Austen', *English Association Pamphlet*, No. 68 (November 1927). Valancourt Books have now issued five out of seven of the Northanger titles, with the remaining two titles due in 2009.

20. Sadleir, for example, argues that '[Austen] is out after the Gothic Romance, and sets her snares with care and ingenuity' (180).

21. Anon, review of *Castle of Wolfenbach*, *Critical Review*, 10 (January 1794), 50.

22. Anon, review of *Northanger Abbey* and *Persuasion*, *British Critic*, IX (March 1818), 293–301, 300.

23. Eliza Parsons, *Castle of Wolfenbach: A German Story. In Two Volumes*, ed. Diane Long Hoeveler (Kansas City, MO: Valancourt [1793], 2006), 4. All subsequent references are to this edition and are given in the text.

24. Sadleir, 184.

25. Hoeveler, introd. to *Castle of Wolfenbach*, ix.

26. Moers, 91.
27. Sleath's novel *The Orphan of the Rhine* also has a libertine, murderous female character named Laurentina exactly after Radcliffe's fallen Signora Laurentini in *The Mysteries of Udolpho* (1794).
28. David Punter and Alan Bissett, 'Francis Lathom in the Eighteenth Century' *Gothic Studies*, 5/1 (May 2003), 55–70.
29. Francis Lathom, *The Midnight Bell*, introd. David Punter (Kansas City, MO: Valancourt [1798], 2007), 12. All subsequent references are to this edition and are given in the text.
30. Ann Radcliffe, *The Mysteries of Udolpho*, ed. Bonamy Dobree (Oxford: Oxford University Press [1794], 1986), 351.
31. Sadleir, 180.

5
Bleeding Nuns: A Genealogy of the Female Gothic Grotesque

Alison Milbank

Although the aesthetics of the sublime have received exhaustive treatment in relation to the Gothic novel, those of the grotesque have received scant attention, despite the fact that the whole concept of the grotesque as an artistic mode was under intense scrutiny during the period of the rise of the Gothic in the latter half of the eighteenth century, with another phase of debate and development in the writing of Hugo, Ruskin and Bagehot in the nineteenth century.[1] Given the way in which the monstrous, the hybrid and the disgusting are central to the Gothic genre, this neglect by recent critics is somewhat surprising. The Gothic grotesque, moreover, as this essay will demonstrate, comes to be associated with the female, in contrast to the sublime, which from Burke's *Enquiry* (1757) onwards, came to be conceived in specifically masculine terms.[2] Where the Female Gothic grotesque has received some study is in an article on the southern Gothic of Carson McCullers, by Sarah Gleeson-White, in which the unruliness and gigantism of the female body becomes a mode of escape from 'southern daintiness'.[3] Similarly, Mary Russo discussed the grotesque portrayal of femininity in twentieth-century Hollywood as an inherently liberatory mode for gesturing to feminist unease with 'normality' and the constraint of gender roles. What little discussion of the Gothic grotesque there is tends to use the theoretical formulation not of aestheticians contemporary with the Gothic writers themselves but that of Mikhail Bakhtin, whose interpretation of Rabelais as offering a reading of the porous, degraded grotesque body as socially transformatory has become highly influential, and indeed undergirds Russo's delineation of a female grotesque as 'incomplete, in motion, and at risk' and 'a hopeful point in between'.[4] Both Russo and Margaret Miles point out the lack of attention to gender in Bakhtin's delineation of the grotesque body.[5] While Russo has been criticised for stretching the concept of the grotesque to cover any female body from that of the acrobat to fetishised body parts, there is no doubt that Bakhtin himself states that a 'senile, pregnant hag' would be the epitome of the grotesque, and that the grotesque body is one of 'birth-giving death', in which a female anatomy is central.[6] The pregnant body in the Rabelaisian narrative on which Bakhtin builds his theory dies, however, in giving birth to a giant son who splits her apart. This does not matter for Bakhtin in the context of a cosmic body, which includes both birth and death in a massive act of becoming and renewal.

Although Bakhtin may ignore the specificity of the abjected and grotesque female body, his theory offers a drama of demystification, as the orthodox, the decorous and the authoritative is 'uncrowned' by the carnivalesque energies of the grotesque, and this conception is highly attractive to a generation of scholars nurtured in deconstructive modes of literary analysis, for it mimics their own critical procedures. It imitates also the gesture of the Gothic heroine herself, whose flight from tyrannical imprisonment defies patriarchal authority and decrowns the power of the supernatural. The Gothic critic imitates the heroine of Ann Radcliffe's *The Mysteries of Udolpho* (1794) who lifts the black veil to reveal the presence of nothing more than a wax image, by demystifying the terrors of the Gothic plot as no more than a series of gawkily arranged literary conventions. The very awkwardness of the tropes – their own grotesque character – is what enables the text to offer an unmasking of social anxieties.

One can draw parallels between Bakhtin's attempt to restore a revolutionary vision to Communism while under the tyranny of Stalinist rule and the Gothic novel's project of narrating an escape from the imprisoning structures of a past age as a way of challenging the social tyranny of its own time. In both cases, the past that is rejected – for Bakhtin and Gothic novelists alike the medieval social and religious order – is also attractive. For it is in pre-revolutionary Russia and France that the carnivalesque flourished and offered a model of social transformation. Similarly, the Gothic heroine both flees the tyranny of abbot and patriarch yet mediates the positive values they have traduced: she is both transgressive yet loyal in a double gesture by which she becomes the heir to the very castle from which she escapes, enabling its passage into modernity.

The energies of the Gothic novel are derived from this ambiguity at its heart; the novel creates a past from which it then proceeds to flee. But the problem with Bakhtin's grotesque body is that it has lost all sense of duality and ambiguity. Bakhtin does indeed state that the grotesque body is a double one, but he allows no tension between its deathly and fertile motions, since both are subsumed by the cosmic renewal of the material that he celebrates.[7] In seeking to argue that the grotesque degrades the spiritual in favour of a purely material reality, Bakhtin also removes the very authority and alterity that makes the image significant. Rabelais's original novels are comic in their degrading of church towers as phallic – causing childbirth by their very shadow – because the church was a significant social and symbolic presence. It has to remain significant to sustain the humour. To use a modern analogy, the highly grotesque British television comedy series, *The Vicar of Dibley* (1994–2007), works by presenting a Parochial Church Council meeting that is full of disgusting food and highly vulgar, bawdy talk, and a woman priest whose addiction to chocolate is Gargantuan in nature. Its humour is engendered – and rendered grotesque – by contrasting sacred and secular and putting them in contiguity. Yet the effect is not so much to 'uncrown' the sacred as to 'crown' the secular by means of the sacred, which protects and, indeed, embraces it by its own incarnational logic. For the quasi-Rabelaisian carol about Christ emerging from Mary's birth canal in one Christmas episode of the programme is strict Christian orthodoxy. If, as Bakhtin claims, the sacred is completely degraded by the grotesque in favour of a wholly materialist vision, then the grotesque is no longer monstrous: you cannot have the carnivalesque without the Christian Lent, or, in terms of the Gothic novel, a heroine without a castle from which to flee.

This chapter seeks to offer a somewhat different, more historical account of the grotesque mode in Gothic fiction, in which, rather than reading the texts against the grain, seeking meaning in the interstices of the writing, I shall seek to understand what deliberate use of the grotesque is made by writers from Horace Walpole to Charlotte Brontë, and argue that the grotesque has offered particular advantages for female writers. In so doing, I shall argue that it is the *active contradictions* of the grotesque mode which not only enable a productive model of female subjectivity and also authorship, but also form a starting point for metaphysical exploration. The figure of the bleeding nun is one figure in which these contradictions can be both displayed and also explored.

Eighteenth-century Gothic: Masculine freedom and limitation by the female

Although early practitioners of the Gothic such as Clara Reeve and Ann Radcliffe eschewed the excesses of hybridity and monstrosity that characterise the grotesque, and sought instead for a feminisation of the sublime, their male counterparts were quick to display the grotesque mode as a sign of their artistic freedom. In the mid-eighteenth century, the grotesque, according to Wolfgang Kayser, was primarily comic and satirical in character.[8] The gigantic enchanted helmet with its waving plumes that crushes Manfred's son's body as an agent of divine retribution in Walpole's *The Castle of Otranto* (1764) bears the marks of the comic grotesque in its absurd disproportion, as well as its prominent materiality.[9] Similarly, the fact that one prominent sign of a retributive supernatural force at work is that a statue bleeds from the nose mixes the horrific, the eerie and the comic in a manner specific to the grotesque mode. By the late eighteenth century, a substantial body of reflection on the grotesque had developed, particularly in Germany, in which a term that had originally been coined in the Renaissance, to describe the ornamental style of Roman frescoes at the so-called Palace of Titus, which showed enlaced and involved admixtures of plant, human and animal forms growing in and out of each other, was now applied to literary texts. It was used to describe particular *visual* effects: the contorted bodies of Dante's *Inferno*, the metamorphoses of Ovid's protagonists, and the bizarre effects of the fantastic tales of Hoffmann. In all these examples the grotesque is caused by the horrified reception of what one sees: Dante's soothsayers, whose faces are on their backs, disturb our sense of the body's decorum and form; Hoffmann's story 'The Sandman' (1816) orchestrates a number of grotesque images – such as the female automaton – to question the nature of the real.[10] Similarly, *The Castle of Otranto* offers a supernatural effect in the bleeding nose of Alonso's statue, which is an image that is visually comprehensible but difficult to categorise: is it meant to be a joke? Is it disgusting? Is it a satire of Catholic piety? To be grotesque images must not merely be horrifying: they must provoke epistemological dubiety. As Geoffrey Harpham puts it, 'they stand at the margin of consciousness between the known and the unknown, calling into question the adequacy of our ways of organising the world.'[11] The helmet, therefore, is disturbing because its size is disproportionate, and also because it is a piece of clanking metal and yet supernatural. It crosses and confuses mental categorisation. In that sense, the whole novel has this satirical grotesque quality, which deliberately puts characters of modern sensibility into medieval scenes, and is presented with a spoof piece of historicist framing as an early Renaissance printed book 'discovered' in the library of an ancient Catholic family in the north of England. As with Walpole's architectural *jeu d'esprit*, Strawberry Hill, *The Castle of Otranto* was an exercise in the omnipotence and free expression of the author's genius, to which the self-referential nature of the fiction bore witness. This was an aspect of the grotesque central to German Romanticism. Christophe Wieland, writing about caricature in 1775, divided it into three main classes: natural distortion faithfully described, artistic enhancement of an already monstrous original, and

> purely fantastic caricatures, or grotesques in the proper sense, where the painter, disregarding versimilitude, gives rein to the unchecked fancy (like the so-called Hell Bruegel) with the sole intention of provoking laughter, disgust, and surprise about the daring of his fantastic creations by the unnatural and absurd products of his imagination.[12]

The true grotesque here is quite unreal, and its fantastic quality reveals the power of the author's 'wild imagination'.[13]

Matthew Lewis in *The Monk* of 1796 shares his Whig predecessor's satiric edge and delight in deliberately 'grotesque attitudes' but he takes it one stage further by including a female grotesque in the form of the bleeding nun. One of his sources is a 1773 ballad by Gottfried Bürger, 'Lenore', in which a bereaved bride is taken off to a coffin bridal couch by her dead lover, whom she believes to be still alive. This celebrated ballad was translated by William Taylor in 1796, by Lewis's friend William Robert Spencer, and by Walter Scott, among others. Central to the poem's grotesque effect is the way in which blooming love and dead flesh are brought into propinquity:

> And when hee from his steede alytte,
>   His armour, black as cinder,
> Did moulder, moulder all awaye,
>   As were it made of tinder.

> His head became a naked skull;
>   Nor haire nor eyne had hee:
> His body grew a skeleton,
>   Whilome so blythe of blee.

> And att his dry and boney heele
>   No spur was left to be;
> And inn his witherde hande you might
>   The scythe and hour-glasse see.[14]

Matthew Lewis imitates Bürger's grotesque effect but reverses the gender of the protagonists, so that as Lenore takes a skeleton for a living man until this moment of revelation, Don Raymond takes a spectre for his beloved Agnes, who was supposed to don the bleeding nun disguise for their elopement. He clasps what he believes to be Agnes's body to his bosom, promising, 'In my veins while blood shall roll...I am thine!'[15] What renders both phantoms grotesque rather than merely uncanny is their visual and tactile presence: the one a skeleton with a scythe, the other white-robed, bloody, armed with rosary, lamp and dagger; the nun in particular has the added contradictory element of a corpse still able to bleed. The bleeding nun conjoins the opposite categories of death and life, physical and spiritual, natural and supernatural in a monstrous form that anticipates a later scene in the novel in which the monk Ambrosio has Antonia encoffined as deceased, so that he might re-animate the 'corpse' and ravish her in her sepulchre, where he will also stab her to death with a dagger. Antonia too, in the convent vault, will become a bleeding quasi-nun.

Critics such as David Morse interpret the grotesque female dualities of *The Monk* as evidence of unease with the social and psychic repression of female sexuality implicit in the cult of female chastity:

> The myth of the Bleeding Nun is built around a structural opposition between the fact that the nun is veiled and the fact that she is bleeding. The veil stands for the traditional chastity ascribed to women, the fact that their charms are traditionally covered, the belief that sex does not and need not concern them. The symbol of the veil is contradicted by the symbol of blood, which implies both the defloration of the virgin and the menstrual flow, which is a perpetual sign of a woman's capacity to have children.[16]

Like Bakhtin who detects in Rabelais's deaths a renewal of life, Morse here sees fertility in the dead nun. Lewis's novel does indeed conflate nuns with sexual intercourse, but hardly with female pleasure in mind and certainly not female life. Each act of penetrative coition leaves Ambrosio disgusted with the woman with whom it has been performed precisely because it does not transport him beyond himself. In Sadean fashion, the libertine monk seeks liberation from social and material constraint in coition, but here is always thrown back by a sense of disgust and shameful restraint. The bleeding nun is therefore not a figure of feminine sexual repression but materiality and mortality: the blood shed at virginal desecration is less an opening to female sexual flourishing than the stain of mortality itself, to which the spectre of the bleeding nun seeks to chain Don Raymond. She stands as a figure for the association of death with nearly all the women characters of the novel: Agnes perishes with her baby in the vault where Antonia will be murdered; Antonia's mother and servant are killed to facilitate her seduction; Matilda survives indeed, but she is not a woman at all but Lucifer's 'crafty spirit' (375).

The grotesque therefore has begun to lose some of its earlier association with artistic freedom and instead come to demonstrate limitation. The ascendancy of the author still survives in the arbitrary way in which the tone of the novel lurches from excited playfulness to drastic and violent judgement on Ambrosio, who ends up with his eyeballs pecked by eagles before he is hauled off to eternal damnation. But the central function of Lewis's grotesque has been to demarcate the limitations of masculine freedom, and the failure to achieve liberation from material constraints. The incest theme – Ambrosio unwittingly rapes his sister and murders both her and his own mother – is not a marker of subversion so much as this same failure of the libertine project. Again, one can compare this usage with that of contemporary German thought, most notably with Friedrich Schlegel's reflections upon the grotesque in the 1798 *Athenäum*, where he begins to align the grotesque not only with comedy but tragedy, and with alienation, something that Kayser also associates with the imaginative works of Jean Paul, and the tales of Georg Büchner.[17] The distance engendered by the grotesque that creates a sense of artistic freedom for Walpole is now a potential source of horror at a limit that resists the subject's attempt to transcend it.[18]

Mary Shelley's critique of the masculine grotesque

Mary Shelley, a careful reader of *The Monk*, which was a favourite with her husband, surely has the bleeding nun in mind when she describes the nightmare that follows Frankenstein's success in infusing life into his creature in her own Gothic novel:

> I thought I saw Elizabeth, in bloom of health, walking in the streets of Ingolstadt. Delighted and surprised, I embraced her, but as I imprinted the first kiss on her lips, they became livid with the hue of death, her features appeared to change, and I thought that I held the corpse of my dead mother in my arms; a shroud enveloped her form, and I saw the grave-worms crawling in the folds of the flannel.[19]

Like Raymond, Frankenstein embraces his bride, only to encounter a corpse: his Elizabeth is not herself, but another. Significantly, the dream comes immediately after Victor has successfully infused life in his creature but runs away from it after its eye opens. The proximity of the blooming health and the grave-worms in the dream-woman creates a grotesque effect equal in horror to that of the creature himself, who is a living being formed from the body parts of various corpses. Elizabeth, Victor's destined bride, becomes a literal barrier to the consummation of his sexual desires by her grotesque transformation, not only into his mother but into a corpse. Like Ambrosio, Victor Frankenstein had sought transgressive knowledge, and like Ambrosio he is baulked in his dream by the mortality of the body and by the confines of incest.

The creature too, whose quasi-divine creation should be a sign of Victor's victory over matter, is rather a marker of the end of his freedom of the will. He also is described in grotesque terms:

> His limbs were in proportion, and I had selected his features as beau-
> tiful. Beautiful! – Great God! His yellow skin scarcely covered the
> work of muscles and arteries beneath; his hair was of a lustrous black,
> and flowing; his teeth of a pearly whiteness; but these luxuriances
> only formed a more horrid contrast with his watery eyes, that seemed
> almost of the same colour as the dun white sockets in which they
> were set, his shrivelled complexion, and straight black lips. (85)

The creature is not only literally a physical and gender hybrid in his body parts that are taken from different corpses, but equally an aesthetic one in which harmony of proportion – a Pythagorean and Renaissance criterion for beauty – is at odds with the integrity of feature. There is also something feminine about his features being described as beautiful, since beauty had come to be associated with the female in eighteenth-century aesthetics. The luxuriance of teeth and hair is a bodily attribute that survives death, leading Edgar Allan Poe's deranged protagonist to attempt a post-mortem extraction on the teeth of the loathed Berenice. In contrast, the creature's eye, an organ long regarded as the window of the soul, fails to gleam and the black lips are those of a corpse. Again, as with Lewis's Ambrosio, an attempt to move beyond social and ethical limits rebounds, and the grotesque character of the creature is the marker of that limitation.

In a novel that engages Milton's *Paradise Lost* (1667) at every level, the characters which these two grotesques of Elizabeth and the creature call to mind are those of Sin and her son Death, in Book II of the poem. Sin, the offspring and later mate of Satan, is half-woman, half-coiled serpent, and the lower parts of her body are gnawed by hell hounds; the offspring she conceived is Death, who is derided as 'execrable shape', 'grieslie terror' and 'dreadful and deform' as Satan faces an attack by his son.[20] Shelley would have known Fuseli's painting of the scene made for the Milton Gallery in 1799 in which a noble (and beautiful) Lucifer is confronted by these two grotesques.[21] The trio form a demonic parody of the relations of the Trinity – Father Lucifer, Son Sin, begotten by the Father and the Spirit, Death proceeding from them both – and of God's creation of Adam first and then Eve from Adam's rib. This second analogy is that claimed by the creature in his encounter with Frankenstein in the Alps – 'Remember, that I am thy creature: I ought to be thy Adam; but I am rather the fallen angel, whom thou drivest from joy for no misdeed' (126). Since the creature has already murdered William and implicated the innocent Justine, he is more like Milton's Death than a fallen seraph, as his guilty progenitor had already intuited.

What Shelley appears to be demonstrating through her employment of Miltonic grotesques is the monstrously perverted nature of Frankenstein's creation. She does not simply criticise the attempt of the scientist to play God, but also the Romantic artist's assertion of complete freedom that was an important element in Walpole's satiric Gothic. Frankenstein is shown to be an Ambrosio, who seeks immortality and emancipation through the deaths of others – a claim rendered actual when he leaves Elizabeth on their wedding night, and she is killed by the creature in revenge for the destruction of his own bride. As with Ambrosio, however, for Frankenstein every attempt at self-transcendence is baulked by the grotesque.

Genius and originality of vision was a central tenet of Romanticism, as if the imagination created *ex nihilo*, in what Coleridge described as 'a repetition in the finite mind of the eternal act of creation in the infinite I AM' in contrast to fancy, which was the arrangement of already existing materials.[22] Frankenstein, however, needs an already created physical universe of 'dark materials' into which he can galvanise the spark of life. In the seventeenth century the essayist Michel de Montaigne had already described his literary pieces as 'grotesque and monstrous bodies, pieced together from sundry limbs, with no definite shape, and with no order, sequence or proportion except by chance', dramatising his distance from the divine creativity in which there is no grotesque element.[23] Shelley's *Frankenstein* too presents authorship as a modest assemblage rather than a bursting of creation out of nothing.

In her 1831 preface to the revised edition of *Frankenstein*, Shelley herself foregrounds the process of its composition, and her search for a plot, which she describes as having come to her in a dream – a dream *about* the process of literary inspiration that was so central to her anxieties at the time. She goes on to describe her tale as her 'hideous progeny', and thus a Montaigne-like grotesque assemblage, but without the transgressive over-reach of its protagonist (358). In this way Shelley reorients the grotesque away from Walpole's separation from the text, which aped the distance of a transcendent deity from his creation, towards a quite different, humbler understanding of the grotesque artwork as an assemblage of disparate ideas and influences. The fact that the story originates in a dream (which is itself the product, in associationist theory, of daytime concerns and images) only emphasises further its mixed and hybrid nature.[24] It was thought that in dreaming the relations between imagination, reason and memory became distorted. In *Frankenstein* the bad, fearful grotesque of Victor's monstrous creation is the result of his escape from the ties of memory (represented by Elizabeth and the Frankenstein family) and reason (represented by Clerval as his name suggests). Shelley offers, however, a more positive conception of the grotesque in the 'hideous progeny' of the novel itself, with its mixed influences and strong intertextual relations, which are the acknowledged child of its author, who disclaims creation '*ex nihilo*':

> Invention, it must be humbly admitted, does not consist in creating out of void, but out of chaos; the materials must, in the first place, be afforded: it can give form to dark, shapeless substances, but it cannot bring into being the substance itself [...] Invention consists in the capacity of seizing on the capabilities of a subject, and in the power of moulding and fashioning ideas suggested to it. (356)

This also is akin to Coleridgean conceptions – to the 'esemplastic power' that he describes in Chapter 13 of *Biographia Literaria* (1817) as the unifying force of the secondary imagination.[25] The difference between Victor's monster and Mary Shelley's is that the latter acknowledges a divine origin, and thus creates a *true monster* in the medieval sense, in which the power and strangeness of the dragon or gargoyle point to and reveal (from *monstrare* – the Latin verb meaning 'to show') the power and freedom of God.[26] Frankenstein's monster lacks this capacity to be a true wonder because his 'creator' claims quasi-divine status; the creature does not reveal Frankenstein's power and freedom so much as limit them. Shelley's use of the authorial grotesque therefore allows a specifically female model of authorship as childbirth, while also claiming all the artistic privileges and creative freedom of the masculine grotesque mode. And paradoxically, her 'hideous progeny' is *more* original in conception and narrative technique than any Gothic fiction hitherto.

The nineteenth-century turn to Hugoesque realism

So far I have sought to establish the grotesque as a marker of artistic creation and inspiration, as well as of a desire to burst physical and social barriers and aesthetic categories, and to enact transgression. It has, however, been used to describe supernatural forms – spectres, dreams and monsters – whereas in the later nineteenth century it comes to be more closely associated with realism, and less with artistic freedom than readerly *reception* and limitation of viewpoint. The poet Robert Browning, for example, was described as grotesque precisely because the rough, modern realism of his style made understanding difficult.[27] The central influence in this period is Victor Hugo, who celebrated the grotesque in his preface to the play *Cromwell* in 1827 as the specifically modern literary mode because of its democratic admixture of high and low elements, as well as its generic indecorum, which gives it the energy of the demotic. It is, moreover, true to the psychology of the human person.[28]

> From the day when Christianity said to man: 'You are double, you are composed of two beings, the one perishable, the other immortal, the one fleshly, the other ethereal, the one enchained by appetites, needs and passions, the other transported on the wings of enthusiasm and reverie, the former finally always turning towards the earth, its mother, the latter ceaselessly launching itself towards the heavens, its fatherland; from that day the drama was created. Is it anything else, indeed, than this contrast of all our days, than this contest of every instant between two opposed principles which are always present in life, and which dispute in man from the cradle to the grave?'[29]

The duality in man, which Hugo takes from Pascal, who described humanity as half-beast, half-angel, is what makes our life dramatic in character, and the grotesque therefore as appropriate a mode as the sublime in artistic composition. Comedy and the grotesque represent our bestial nature; tragedy the ethereal, but it is the struggle itself which manifests the spiritual dimension.

Shortly after the publication of this Romantic manifesto, Hugo published his great Gothic novel, *Notre Dame de Paris* (1831), which is dominated by the monstrously grotesque form of Quasimodo, the hunchback bell-ringer. Just as in the *Cromwell* preface, tragedy and comedy are interwoven, the spiritual and the bestial. Quasimodo's body may be as ugly as a gargoyle, but his spirit is sublime, and he devotes himself selflessly to the rescue and preservation of the gypsy girl, Esmeralda. But she too suffers the mental limitation and disjunction of the grotesque in her tragic mistakes and obsessive love for the worthless seducer, Phoebus. A gypsy, and thus quasi-oriental, and a dancer, the mobile Esmeralda is representative of the arabesque, which Hugo defines in his Shakespeare essay as akin to the fanciful operation of the imagination: 'the arabesque in art is the same phenomenon as vegetation in nature. The arabesque springs up, grows, entwines, exfoliates, reproduces, flourishes, flowers and grafts itself on all our dreams.'[30] Originally, in German aesthetics, interchangeable with the grotesque, from the late Schlegel onwards it was distinguished as the graceful labyrinth line without end, rather than the monstrous hybrid forms that might emerge from it.[31] The 'capricious movements' of Esmeralda's dance are made on the 'pattern of arabesques' of an eastern carpet. She shares the fanciful aimlessness of the arabesque, with her 'capricious' actions mirrored in those of her tame goat, who appears to have magical powers, but is just well trained, so that what seem intentional actions are mere tricks.

The tragic ending of the novel results from a complex mixture of social repression, the malevolence of Claude Rollo, and especially the *limited* nature of Quasimodo and Esmeralda's perspectives. Quasimodo mistakenly attacks those who storm Notre Dame to rescue Esmeralda, believing they wish her harm. The ending mixes tragedy and comedy in sending the rescued goat off with a writer of tragedies – the word 'tragedy' means a goat-song, from its origin in the worship of Dionysus – and the heartless Phoebus de Châteaupers to what the narrator describes as 'a tragic end: he got married'.[32] Quasimodo is also described as 'married' in the novel's final grotesque hybrid of two hideous carcasses. One skeleton is only recognisable as Esmeralda by the tatters of white and a little silken bag around the neck. The other is recognisable as that of Quasimodo by the curved spinal column, 'the head down between the shoulder blades, and one leg shorter than the other' (539). The final irony is that in death Quasimodo lacks the grotesque features of the other bodies in the pit, because his skeleton has no fracture of the vertebrae. He had come there of his own free will, to embrace the dead body of Esmeralda, and die in an embrace also of his monstrous body and equally monstrous fate. In so doing, embracing the hybridity of the grotesque and arabesque, he also becomes sublime, rather in the manner allowed to Shelley's creature, when he too accepts his monstrosity and ascends his funeral pyre.

In this way, Hugo's great novel turns the grotesque in a more positive direction, as a trope alike of the modernity of art, and the tragicomic in particular, and thereby rescuing the grotesque from the abject and disgusting. Unlike Walpole and Lewis, Hugo accepts the monstrous as Mary Shelley does her 'hideous progeny'. Hugo also brings the male and female versions of the grotesque body together in a more positive version of Frankenstein's hermaphroditic creature. As in Lewis and Shelley, the grotesque is a particularly appropriate mode for placing antonyms in tension, especially those of life and death. Hugo himself suggests that one of the key dialectical psychological tensions is that between the fleshly and perishable and the ethereal and immortal. In contrast to Lewis, however, and in accord with Mary Shelley, the tension between the dualities is what provides the energy of life.

In tracing a genealogy of the use of the grotesque in Gothic fiction, the association with the grotesque woman continues, especially in Hoffmann and in Poe's aptly titled *Tales of the Grotesque and the Arabesque* (1840). She is a more unsettling figure than her male counterpart because of her association from the Romantic period onwards with access to the spiritual and the ideal, summed up by the last words of Goethe's *Faust*: 'Eternal Womanhood/ Leads us above.'[33] One way of making sense of the infamous divide in this period between the spiritual and 'fallen' woman is as much to do with aesthetics and philosophy as it is with gender. As Terry Castle points out in *The Female Thermometer*, a post-Kantian world that accepts his claim that the only access we have to the world beyond the self is through our perceptions of objects, prevents any direct knowledge of the noumenal – of things-in-themselves – and renders phenomena, shorn of the transcendent dimension that gave them depth, spectral rather than real.[34] Women, as key heuristic tools among other phenomena, are therefore spectral (idealised) or abject (the real). Wilkie Collins is an interesting figure in this respect. Like Poe, he has a tendency to associate beauty in women with the monstrous, as in the celebrated description of Marian Halcombe in *The Woman in White* (1860), as seductively beautiful in body but ugly in visage, with a moustache on her upper lip. Her hybridity of gender and aesthetic value renders her wholly material and phenomenal and prevents her acting as any spiritual mediation. Her half-sister Laura, although given the accolade as 'the ideal' in contrast to Marian's 'real', has equally 'something wanting', and a pliancy that makes her closer to the arabesque than the classically beautiful.[35] Her incompleteness is partly the effect of Hartright having just met her unacknowledged sister, the ghostly 'Woman in White', and the uncanny effect bears out Freud's thesis that it is a marker for repression, since the likeness between the two women is the result of Laura's father's adultery and the consequent birth of an illicit half-sister. But she also represents the spectrality of the noumenal, shorn of its link to the phenomenal.

Laura does, however, become a bleeding nun figure who crosses the divide between death and life in the scene where she appears at her own graveside. Hartright returns to it to mourn the death of his lost love, only to be faced with the figure of a mysterious veiled woman. Like the bleeding nun of Lewis's tale, this figure 'had possession [of Hartright] body and soul' (419). And although she appears to be a spectre, she has a physical presence and her gown brushes the black letters of the tombstone inscription, which records her own death. In the original serialisation, readers had to wait a whole month for the resolution of this riddle: that Laura is alive but legally dead, and her identity lost. They were left with a precisely realised and visually clear picture of the dead woman by her own grave, but a conceptual impossibility. The figure, moreover, was the obverse of the spiritualised woman who mediates life and death, the spiritual and the physical worlds. Here, Laura's physicality was the problem rather than her spectral presence: it is a supernatural rather than transcendent effect, in which the material appears but cut off from its anchorage in spatial and temporal classification. Once the riddle is solved, however, Laura loses grotesque energy and is subsumed by the arabesque, while Marian too loses her monstrous duality and is subsumed to the domestic. The readerly response, moreover, requires duality for its hermeneutic key and without it the tale loses its edge.

Charlotte Brontë's embrace of the Hugoesque grotesque

Although Charlotte Brontë's fiction can seem more conservative than the sensation novel which postdates it, she is more ambitious than Wilkie Collins in her adherence to the contradictions of the grotesque, and she goes further in embracing fully the duality of the human – and particularly the female – person. Moreover, she may have had direct knowledge of Hugo through her education in French literature by M. Héger at the pensionnat in Brussels. Héger was, as Sue Lonoff has demonstrated, both a literary and educational innovator.[36] He welcomed the recent outpouring of Romanticism, including Hugo. One exercise mentioned by Elizabeth Gaskell's biography involved reading a range of different approaches to Oliver Cromwell, both French and English, which might mean that Charlotte read Hugo's play.[37] Certainly Brontë makes full use of the dynamics and possibilities of the grotesque as a heuristic and philosophical tool, and she uses it to expand the mode as a way of making sense of female subjectivity.

Her first novel, *Jane Eyre* (1847), contains in Bertha Mason, Rochester's violently lunatic first wife, a monster who has, since Gilbert and Gubar launched her career as avatar for the repressed energies of the female author and protagonist, been viewed as a transgressive and positive monster, whose murderous attempts against her husband enact Jane Eyre's justifiable rage upon him. Viewed in terms of Hugo's dualist conception of the self, Bertha, who 'grovelled seemingly on all fours; [...] growled like some wild animal' certainly represents the bestial aspects of the self, and Jane Eyre the ethereal.[38] In their bigamous union with Rochester, they undoubtedly provoke a grotesque image akin to that of Quasimodo and Esmeralda, which is central to *Jane Eyre's* concern with the relation of perishable body and imperishable spirit. Bertha is a literal blockage to the union of Rochester and Jane Eyre because she represents a non-signifying and non-transformed physicality: the phenomenal divorced from the noumenal. In risking his life to save Bertha from her own destructive capacities, however, Rochester makes her physicality 'speak', and accords it value. As she throws herself down from the roof, to be 'dead as the stones on which her brains and blood were scattered' (476), so Rochester too imitates her in having a hand amputated and in becoming 'stone-blind' (477). By admitting his sinfulness, his responsibility for Bertha, Rochester is able to experience a form of resurrection in a new life with Jane, which is a more positive version of a grotesque and arabesque union than Quasimodo's 'marriage'.

It is *Villette* (1853), the mature novel based partly on Brontë's experience in Brussels, which is also the more Hugoesque in its presentation of a female subjectivity constructed through dualities. The world of the novel is similarly dualistic: England versus Labassecour, Protestantism versus Catholicism, Reason versus Imagination are a few of the pairs of oppositions at play. Lucy Snowe may be a dull cipher to outward view but her inner life has a violent and colourful *psychomachia*:

> I seemed to hold two lives – the life of thought, and that of reality; and, provided the former was nourished with a sufficiency of the

strange necromantic joys of fancy, the privileges of the latter might remain limited to daily bread, hourly work, and a roof of shelter.[39]

The desire for imaginative expansion is dealt with by recourse to Jael's murder of Sisera in Judges 4:21.

> This longing, and all of a similar kind, it was necessary to knock on the head; which I did, figuratively, after the manner of Jael to Sisera, driving a nail through their temples. Unlike Sisera, they did not die: they were but transiently stunned, and at intervals would turn on the nail with a rebellious wrench; then did the temples bleed, and the brain thrill to its core. (176)

The narrator reverses the physical and spiritual here, so that the *latter* causes the visual clarity and grotesque image of a nail tunnelling into her forehead. Indeed, the vivid life of the mind repressed behind the impassive exterior makes Lucy Snowe's whole life one of a material-ised corpse, seeking continually, like Poe's Madeleine Usher, to escape the barriers of the tomb. Her own, an Arnoldian 'buried life', she views those around her either as spectres (in the case of Madame Beck) or grotesques, and the former never wholly bodiless but apt to turn into the latter, as in the beds in the empty dormitory which 'were turning into spectres – the coronal of each became a death's head, huge and sunbleached' (232).

And with the grotesque viewpoint on the material comes also the figure of the bleeding nun by whom Lucy is haunted. This veiled fig-ure, whom Lucy encounters so close to her places of resort, the school garret and the *allée défendue*, is too easily subsumed by critics as a figure of sexual repression or transgression, the removal of whom inaugurates a new adult, demystified Gothic, in which all terrors are now internal to the self.[40] For she is also a grotesque, being fully clothed, with the head bandaged, although presumed an immaterial spectre. There is a bizarre physicality to her image and like Frankenstein's monster, she has agency: 'she had eyes, and they viewed me' (381). A hybrid – lover/ nun, spectre/clothed – the nun, although terrifying, is a hopeful image, because, just as in *Jane Eyre*, an embrace of the grotesque is Lucy Snowe's liberation. Whereas, in *Jane Eyre*, it was Rochester who dressed as a female gypsy to gain access to Jane Eyre's secret desires, in *Villette* it is Lucy Snowe who holds on to a masculine cigar case won in a raffle, and refuses to exchange with John Bretton who has won a female headdress. Similarly, when asked to cross-dress for the school play, Lucy agrees, but only partially: she will appear as a man in the upper part of her dress, and woman below; she courts a grotesque effect of gender dissonance. M. Paul is her encourager here, but John Bretton reveals his unsuitability as rescuer of the buried Lucy when he derogates the performance of the actress, Vashti. The narrator registers a double response to her grotesque duality, 'It was a marvellous sight: a mighty revelation. It was a spectacle low, horrible, immoral' (339), but for Dr John there is only a single, negative response: 'he judged her as a woman, not an artist' (342). M. Paul also provokes in Lucy recourse to the grotesque at the art exhibition, where he moves her away from the grossly sensual Cleopatra, to view a series of conventionally pious depictions of female domesticity. To Lucy, Cleopatra is another Bertha, in being mere materiality without any spirit: she describes her as a slug. She gives a wonderful deconstruction of the painting in terms of its cost and comestibility. Cleopatra is weighed – 14 to 16 stone – her drapery's length estimated (7×20 yards), and her accessories revealed as such. A whole, a work of art, is reduced by Lucy's grotesquing eye to a series of disparate objects. But the pious paintings are no better, 'cold and vapid as ghosts' (275, 278). Indeed, there is a feminist critique at work here, but there is also an aesthetic and metaphysical one. How can one escape from the purely material without becoming merely spectral? How can matter reveal spirit? It is the quintessentially Victorian dilemma between the real and the ideal, the phenomenal and the noumenal.

At first it seems as if Lucy's trajectory will mirror that of Jane Eyre. Madame de Walravens, the jewelled hunchback, 'Malevola', the evil fairy, appears as at Sleeping Beauty's christening, to curse Lucy's growing relation with M. Paul by chaining him to the dead nun, Justine Marie. Greedy materialist and vapid spectre respectively, the women merely act to confirm M. Paul's kindness of heart and the threat posed by his attachment to Lucy for their plans for him. Where Rochester was enchained by the physicality of his wife and the spiritual bond of marriage by which they become 'one flesh', M. Paul is in spiritual thrall to his sense of duty towards his former fiancée, the dead Justine Marie.

The equivalent scene to that of Rochester's voice freeing Jane from St John Rivers' loveless marriage is that when M. Paul faces Madame Beck to take Lucy out of the school and Madame's control to offer her the little school of her own he has prepared for her. The date of her liberation is that of an important Catholic festival: 15 August is the feast of the Assumption, when Mary was taken, body and soul, into heaven, as the first fruits of the general resurrection of the dead at the end of time. Gaskell intimates that Charlotte and Emily Brontë were originally impressed and positive in their response to Catholicism during their time in Belgium, and here it appears that the holiday precipitated another of those proleptic reunions of soul and body, matter and spirit, that M. Paul speaks of earlier: 'in the future there will be a resurrection, as I believe to my soul's consolation; but all will be changed – form and feeling: the mortal will have put on immortality – it will rise, not for earth, but for heaven' (433). M. Paul is speaking of the transformation of his former affections, and his words are a message of hope to Lucy. But the words are coldly prescient of the actual ending of the novel which will not mirror the marriage of Jane Eyre and Rochester.

The nun, that embodiment of the grotesque, is finally demythologised as a bolster and some old clothes; she had been the disguise of the ridiculous Alfred de Hamal in his trysts with Ginevra Fanshawe. The nun is subsumed by the material, losing her agency and with it her grotesque character. Lucy treads her down like some latterday Miriam, in a manner commended by those who would see the novel as a rejection of Gothic grotesque in favour of modern realism. But her loss removes one of the engines of the grotesque that allow Lucy's desires expression. Like the whole Gothic plot of this novel, obstacles to Lucy's happiness such as Malevola and the phantom nun paradoxically *aid* her sense of self-worth: to become a fictional protagonist – to be haunted – is to acquire value and identity.

And the emancipatory moment of the assumption is also undone and spiritualised: M. Paul will sail to do his dependent's business in Guadeloupe, leaving Lucy as virginal as Mary, the Blessed Virgin, herself. Indeed, he sails on the Paul et Virginie, a ship named from the protagonists of the Romantic novel of Bernardin de St Pierre of 1787. Lovers from childhood, Paul and Virginie never consummate their union, and the latter dies at sea. As with *The Woman in White*, the grotesque appears to fail at this point. But *Villette* ends in uncertainty, as the narrator refuses to confirm that M. Paul returned or drowned, although the banshee wail brings back memories of the death of Miss Marchmont's bridegroom, and the fact that the three years of separation are described as the happiest of Lucy Snowe's life leaves all but 'sunny imaginations' little hope of a happy ending (596). But in the monstrously unfair fact that the evil junta of the novel all live long, prosperous lives, combined with the jaggedness of an unresolved ending, the narrator offers the novel itself as substitute for the spectral nun: neither living nor dead, nun nor bride, still bleeding. Where Quasimodo followed his Esmeralda to the gallows and the grave, Lucy Snowe also embraces death and the grotesque as a duality: the novel leaves her half in and half out of the grave, in a dubiety where Lucy and M. Paul, like Paul and Virginia, may be held together.

I have sought in this essay to give an aesthetic and philosophical account of the female grotesque in nineteenth-century Gothic writing. I do not necessarily mean to negate the interpretation of critics such as Mary Russo, who following Bakhtin looks to representations of monstrous femininity for inspiration for a socially transformative understanding of womanhood as free-ranging possibility and de-formation of the normal. There is no doubt, for example, that Lucy Snowe embraces grotesque performance as a sign of her unease at socially defined gender construction. Yet, by very virtue of its interest in acts of transgression and its concern with affect – especially in engendering horror and terror – the Gothic became a particularly appropriate medium for many different modes of philosophical and theological investigation, pushing all the time at the limits of its own generic construction. And what the articulation of the Gothic grotesque does in one gesture is to question our grasp of the meaning of what we see, challenge the idealist attempt to subsume the world as perception, and wonder at the uncanny dance of the grotesque. For what an embrace of the *distance* between self and world, and in Lucy Snowe's case, the duality of personality, enable is the possibility of reconfiguring that distance as plenitude, growth and possibility. G. K. Chesterton wrote of Charles Dickens's use of the grotesque: 'in beauty there is something allied to sadness, certainly there is something akin to joy in the grotesque.'[41] Frankenstein sought the decorum of beauty and was horrified by the active agency of the monster's eye. The Female Gothic seeks the vitality and joy of the Hugoesque grotesque and is energised by its contradictions.

Notes

1. Victor Hugo, *Cromwell*, trans. Annie Ubersfeld (Paris: Garnier-Flammarion, 1986); John Ruskin, *Complete Works of John Ruskin*, ed. E. T. Cook and Alexander Wedderburn, 37 vols (London: George Allen, 1905–12), V, 128–42, XII, 172–89; Walter Bagehot, *Wordsworth, Tennyson and Browning: or Pure, Ornate and Grotesque in Art in English Poetry*, in *Collected Works of Walter Bagehot*, ed. N. St John Stevas (London: 1965).
2. Edmund Burke, *A Philosophical Enquiry into the Origin of our Ideas of the Sublime and Beautiful*, ed. Adam Philips (Oxford: Oxford University Press [1757], 1990). The beautiful is allied to qualities of smoothness, smallness and delicacy (113), the sublime with fear, power, vastness and magnificence and terror (53–82). Kant, too, takes a gendered approach in *Observations on the Feeling of*

the Beautiful and Sublime, trans. John Goldthwait (Berkeley, CA: University of California Press, 1965).

3. Sarah Gleeson-White, 'Revisiting the Southern Grotesque: Mikhail Bakhtin and the Case of Carson McCullers,' *Southern Literary Journal* 33/2 (Spring 2001), 108–23.

4. Mary Russo, *The Female Grotesque: Risk, Excess and Modernity* (New York: Routledge, 1994), 11. The only full-length study of Bakhtin in relation to the Gothic novel, Jacqueline Howard's *Reading Gothic Fiction: A Bakhtinian Approach* (Oxford: Oxford University Press, 1994), focuses on dialogicity and makes no mention of his ideas about the grotesque.

5. Russo, *Female Grotesque*, 8–13; Margaret Miles, 'Carnal Abominations: The Female Body as Grotesque,' in *The Grotesque in Art and Literature: Theological Reflections*, eds James Luther Adams and Wilson Yates (Grand Rapids, Michigan: Eerdmans, 1997), 83–112, 83–4.

6. Mikhail Bakhtin, *Rabelais and His World*, trans. Hélène Iswolsky (Bloomington and Indianapolis: Indiana University Press, 1984), 352.

7. Bakhtin, *Rabelais and His World*: 'the grotesque imagery constructs what we might call a double body. In the endless chain of bodily life it retains the parts in which one link joins the other, in which the life of one body is born from the death of the preceding, older one' (318).

8. Wolfgang Kayser, *The Grotesque in Art and Literature*, trans. Ulrich Weinstein (New York: Columbia University Press, 1981).

9. Horace Walpole, *The Castle of Otranto: A Gothic Story*, ed. W. S. Lewis and E. J. Clery (Oxford: Oxford University Press [1764], 1996): 'he beheld his child dashed to pieces, and almost buried under an enormous helmet, an hundred times more large than any casque ever made for human being, and shaded with a proportionable quantity of black feathers' (19).

10. This tale is celebrated for Freud's use of it in his essay on the uncanny, which became so central to Gothic criticism that it was reproduced by Victor Sage in his casebook of critical material, *The Gothick Novel: A Selection of Critical Essays* (Basingstoke: Macmillan, 1990), 76–86. For Mary Russo, the grotesque and the uncanny are the same in being indices of repression (18). There is not space here to delineate in detail how I believe the two tropes are to be differentiated. Briefly, for Freud the uncanny is a seemingly *supernatural* or inexplicable doubling or repetition that is the result of an unacknowledged kinship, or repression. In the grotesque, one is faced by a *physical* reality (it is not the fact that dragons might be magical that causes the grotesque effect) that crosses *mental* categories. So excrement, for example, is grotesque not because one refuses to admit the lower functions of the body so much as because it is in the wrong place and challenges concepts of public and private. Excrement in a lavatory is not grotesque: dung on a human face is.

11. Geoffrey Harpham, *On the Grotesque: Strategies of Contradiction in Art and Literature* (Princeton, NJ: Princeton University Press, 1987), 5.

12. Quoted in Kayser, *The Grotesque in Art and Literature*, 30.

13. Kayser, 31. A similar emphasis on the fantastic and creative is found in Justus Möser's 'Harlequin, or the Defence of the Grotesque-Comic', published in 1761, in which the theatrical effects of the *commedia dell'arte* provide the examples. See Bakhtin, *Rabelais and His World*, 35.

14. William Taylor, 'Lenora: A Ballad,' *The Monthly Magazine* (1796), Vol 1, 135–7, 137.
15. Matthew Lewis, *The Monk*, ed. Christopher MacLachan (Harmondsworth: Penguin [1796], 1998), 136. All subsequent references are to this edition and are given in the text.
16. Quoted in the introduction to *The Monk*, xv.
17. Kayser, 53–5.
18. In his introduction to *Rabelais and His World*, Bakhtin seeks to critique Kayser's association of the grotesque with terror and alienation, but he is unable to deny that such a view is central to Romantic writers (36–42). He accuses them, therefore, of individualism in contrast to the solidarity of the medieval grotesque.
19. Mary Shelley, *Frankenstein: The Original 1818 Text*, ed. D. L. MacDonald and Kathleen Scherf, 2nd edition (Peterborough, Ontario: Broadview Press, 2001), 85. All subsequent references are to this edition and are given in the text.
20. John Milton, *Paradise Lost*, ed. Scott Elledge (New York: Norton, 1975), Book II, lines 650, 681 and 706, 46.
21. On Fuseli's importance for the Gothic novel, see *Gothic Nightmares: Fuseli, Blake and the Romantic Imagination*, ed. Martin Myrone (London: Tate, 2006). The *Paradise Lost* illustrations are reproduced and discussed in *Henry Fuseli 1741–1824*, ed. Gert Schiff (London: Tate, 1976), 87–93.
22. S. T. Coleridge, *Biographia Literaria*, in *Aesthetical Essays*, ed. J. Shawcross, 2 vols (London: Oxford University Press, 1907), I, 202.
23. Michel de Montaigne, *Essays*, trans. and ed. J. M. Cohen (London: Penguin, 1958), 'On Friendship', 91–105, 91.
24. Susan L. Manning discusses eighteenth-century theories of dreaming in 'Enlightenment's Dark Dreams: Two Fictions of Henry Mackenzie and Charles Brockden Brown,' *Eighteenth Century Life* 21/3 (1997), 39–56.
25. Coleridge, *Aesthetical Essays*, I, 195.
26. See Caroline Walker Bynum, 'Wonder,' Presidential Address to the American Historical Association, *The American Historical Review* 102/1 (February 1997), 1–26, 23. One of the limitations of Bakhtin's analysis of medieval gargoyles and monstrous carvings is his failure to acknowledge their religious function.
27. See G. K. Chesterton, *Robert Browning* (London: Macmillan, 1903), 149.
28. Jean-Bertrand Barrière, 'Character and Fancy in Victor Hugo,' trans. Beth Brambert, *Yale French Studies* 13 (1954), 98–113.
29. Victor Hugo, *Cromwell*, 78, my translation.
30. Victor Hugo, 'William Shakespeare' in *Oeuvres Complètes* (Paris: 1904), II, 1, 2, 110, my translation.
31. Kayser, 49–51.
32. Victor Hugo, *Notre Dame de Paris*, trans. Alban Krailsheimer (Oxford: Oxford University Press [1831], 1993), 537. All subsequent references are to this edition and are given in the text.
33. Johann Wolfgang Goethe, *Faust*, trans. and ed. Philip Wayne, 2 vols (Harmondsworth: Penguin, 1959), 2, 288.
34. Terry Castle, *The Female Thermometer: Eighteenth-Century Culture and the Invention of the Uncanny* (New York and Oxford: Oxford University Press, 1995), 125.

35. Wilkie Collins, *The Woman in White*, ed. John Sutherland (Oxford: Oxford University Press [1860], 1996), 33. All subsequent references are to this edition and are given in the text.
36. Sue Lonoff, 'The Education of Charlotte Brontë: A Pedagogical Case Study,' *Pedagogy* 1 (2001), 457–78.
37. Elizabeth Gaskell, *The Life of Charlotte Brontë*, ed. Elisabeth Jay (Harmondsworth: Penguin [1857], 1998), 230.
38. Charlotte Brontë, *Jane Eyre*, ed. Michael Mason (London: Penguin [1847], 1996), 327–8. All subsequent references are to this edition and are given in the text.
39. Charlotte Brontë, *Villette*, ed. Mark Lilly, introd. Tony Tanner (Harmondsworth: Penguin [1853], 1979), 140. All subsequent references are to this edition and are given in the text.
40. This theory is a venerable one, originating in R. B. Heilman's 'Charlotte Brontë's New Gothic,' in *From Jane Austen to Joseph Conrad*, eds R. C. Rathburn and M. Steinman Jr (Minneapolis, MN: University of Minnesota Press, 1958), 118–32.
41. G. K. Chesterton, *Criticisms and Appreciations of Charles Dickens* (London: House of Stratus, 2001), 62.

6
From Bluebeard's Bloody Chamber to Demonic Stigmatic

Marie Mulvey-Roberts

> One need not be a chamber to be haunted...
> Ourself, behind ourself concealed–
> Should startle most
>
> Emily Dickinson[1]

'Female Gothic' is a contested term which, when unveiled, is characterised by a number of recurring plots written by women writers. Ellen Moers, who coined the term, refers to the novels of one of its earliest exponents Ann Radcliffe, whose typical heroine is 'simultaneously persecuted victim and courageous heroine'.[2] Her predecessor may be found in the 'Bluebeard' fairy tale, which in turn is a reworking of the archetypal narrative of female disobedience prompted by curiosity which appears in classical mythology as in the tale of Pandora's Box, and in the Bible as the story of Eve. This chapter explores the relationships between desire, texts and death, including the connection between dangerous reading and sexual knowledge out of which spring archetypal narratives of female disobedience. Particular attention is given to the reworking of the motif of the forbidden room in the traditional Bluebeard fairy tale.

The bloody chamber is a haunted site to which both reader and writer endlessly return. This repetition is driven by desire through narrative circularity. In an essay entitled 'On the Pleasure Derived from Objects of Terror' (1773), Anna Laetitia Aikin (later Barbauld), writes of how the reader is propelled through the narrative by the 'pain of suspense'[3] and the imperative to satisfy curiosity. A metonym for the reader is Bluebeard's curious wife who cannot resist finding the secret behind the door[4] in a pursuit which allegorises epistemophilia, an excessive desire to know. Her initial impetus is to unmask the secret of otherness which is concomitant with defying the authority of her husband. In this respect her quest functions much as does literature, which according to Jacques Derrida in *Geneses, Genealogies, Genres and Genius: The Secrets of the Archive* (2004):

> delivers us over to the experience of the wholly other... literature... remains the absolute place of the secret of this heteronomy, of the secret as experience of the law that comes from the other, of the law whose giver is none other than the coming of the other.[5]

The heroine's knowledge of her husband's otherness is the shocking revelation that the chamber to which she is forbidden entry contains the corpses of his former wives. Other deaths ensue: her innocence, along with her marriage and the ideals of romantic love. In addition there is the ghostly arrival of her own murder which may be conceptualised through Derrida's theory of hauntology, 'Is it not already beginning to arrive and where is it going? What of the future? The future can only be for ghosts. And the past.'[6] So far the errant wife has followed in the haunted footsteps of her predecessors. 'I only did what he knew I would,'[7] admits the heroine of Angela Carter's 'The Bloody Chamber' (1979). Her action demonstrates Georges Bataille's assertion that taboo and transgression are inseparable.[8] On gazing at the macabre spectacle within his 'private slaughterhouse' (133), she uncannily recognises herself in the otherness of the marital victims and knows that a place has been reserved for her within her sadistic spouse's 'display of flesh' (141). What lies behind the door is self-knowledge including the ever-present realisation of her spectrality, which, according to Derrida, 'would harbour within itself, ... like circumscribed places or particular effects, eschatology and teleology themselves.'[9]

Originating at a time when women were deprived of legal rights within marriage the 'Bluebeard' fable is a test of wifely obedience and subjugation to the will of her husband. William Blackstone in his *Commentaries on the Laws of England* in 1765 declared that 'The husband and wife are one person in law; that is, the very being or legal existence of the woman is suspended during the marriage, or at least is incorporated and consolidated into that of the husband.'[10] Charles Perrault's tale, *La Barbe Bleue*, written in 1697,[11] is a cuckoo in the nest since it departs from the fairytale convention of ending with a happy marriage by beginning with a reluctant bride whose nuptials rapidly turn into nightmare.

Perrault noted that husbands were no longer as terrible as Bluebeard and that power relations between the sexes were now not as clear-cut.[12]

Yet this fairy tale has persisted as a cautionary warning about the abuse of male power and privilege in marriage. In common with most published versions of the tale, Perrault tends to excuse the husband's homicidal behaviour as a justifiable antidote to his wife's dangerous curiosity. As we shall see, Female Gothic writers resist this paradigm in their rewriting of the traditional 'Bluebeard' tale in which the female transgression of crossing the threshold between life and death is a replay of the Fall through which Eve helped bring death into the world. In Walter Crane's illustrations of 'Bluebeard' in 1874,[13] the wife holding the key en route to the forbidden chamber is set against a background of Eve picking the apple from the serpent-entwined Tree of Knowledge of good and evil. The Bluebeard husband is sometimes represented as God the father and the devil.

For centuries, marriage sanctioned husbands to be god-like and omnipotent in demanding obedience from their wives. In *The Bonds of Love* (1990), Jessica Benjamin explains how Sigmund Freud understands authority as

> what we may call the culture's 'erotic' means of binding individuals in spite of their resistance. Obedience to the laws of civilization is first inspired, not by fear or prudence, Freud tells us, but by love, love for those early powerful figures who first demand obedience. Obedience, of course, does not exorcise aggression; it merely directs it against the self.[14]

Domination, in a Freudian sense, is an extension of the bonds of love; it can be seen to be bound up with the death-drive (Thanatos) and life-instinct (Eros) and to coalesce with Freud's interpretation of the master–slave dichotomy. As Georges Bataille seems to suggest, 'we need the split unity of master and slave in order to maintain the boundaries that erotic union – the "little death" of the self – threatens to dissolve'.[15]

A woman's desire to acquire knowledge of the world, which might include sexual experience along with knowledge of the very power structures negating her existence, is surely life-affirming. Yet here the pursuit is ultimately death-driven. Bluebeard's wife seeks out the forbidden room in an affirmation of Eros while knowing that it will lead to punishment and, in some renditions of the tale, certain death. As Bataille declares of eroticism, it is 'assenting to life up to the point of death'.[16] In Carter's story the protagonist's fear is not directed towards her Marquis husband but towards herself, for such is the force of her awakened desire after her delayed wedding night that she unlocks in herself a secret room of corruption. Immediately after opening the door to the forbidden chamber Carter's heroine quotes her husband's favourite poet Charles Baudelaire: 'There is a striking resemblance between the act of love and the ministrations of a torturer' (130). She suspects that one of the wives has been tortured by being buried alive, which Freud asserts is for some people the 'most uncanny thing of all'.[17] This is a Romanian Countess who has been entombed within an Iron Maiden, whose spikes act as a grotesque parody of the sexual penetration of the female body. According to Freud in *Civilization and its Discontents* (1930):

> It is in sadism, where the death instinct twists the erotic aim in its own sense, and yet at the same time fully satisfies the erotic urge, that we succeed in obtaining the clearest insight into its nature, and its relation to Eros. But even where it emerges without any sexual purpose, in the blindest fury of destructiveness, we cannot fail to recognize that the satisfaction of the [death] instinct ... [presents] the ego with a fulfilment of the latter's old wishes of omnipotence.[18]

'Bluebeard' is a tale of sadism and sexual temptation. The threshold to the taboo space may be represented by the way in which Bataille views eroticism as a divide between subjectivity as tied to desire and non-individuation in being bound to its fulfilment. The door to the prohibited room has hymenal significance as does the lock, while the blood-stained key (or egg in some versions)[19] is a marker of sexual infidelity. In Carter's retelling the bloody chamber has walls which are compared to skin sweating in fright. It is also visceral in being a metonymy for bodily organs. In a stage adaptation by Bryony Lavery the Marquis pulls out the heart and womb of his opera singer wife to prepare her body for embalming.[20] Ironically, the name of this place of death is metonymic for the beating human heart. The two meanings of 'the bloody chamber' merge in the Brothers Grimm's version of 'Bluebeard' (1812) at the point at which the husband is about to plunge a knife into his wife's heart. Her Carteresque counterpart, at an earlier stage in the narrative, seeks to find some traces of her husband's heart in a file marked 'Personal' in his desk. Dissatisfied, she hopes that her trespass into the forbidden room will open the door to his soul only to find her quest for knowledge is gratified by the spectacle of his heartless cruelty. Here there is little comfort in Maurice Merleau-Ponty's apothegm: 'A man's sexual history provides a key to his life.'[21] On giving his wife the tempting key her husband had joked that it was 'Not the key to my heart' but 'Rather, the key to my enfer' (21), the French word for 'hell'. This is suggestive of the heroine's Dantean descent into the underworld from which she is reborn in a journey from tomb to womb. The prohibited space is also uterine as well as a sexualised sepulchre of pleasure and pain culminating in death. But the eroticism does not end there. The chamber is a timeless museum of morbid erotica where the wives are exhibits, resembling exquisite simulacra for the eye of the connoisseur surveying his pornography of death.

Carter's bloody chamber is a place of the imagination, paralleling the library in the 'Castle of Murder' (1812)[22] (135), where the heroine comes across her husband's private collection of decadent books with such telling titles as *The Secret of Pandora's Box*, *The Key of Mysteries*, *The Initiation* and *The Adventures of Eulalie at the Harem of the Grand Turk*. She gazes upon two engravings. The first is of an obscene sadomasochistic scene of a woman being punished with the 'Bluebeard' caption 'Reproof of curiosity' (120)[23] while the second is that of the immolation of a Sultan's wives. The Marquis's wry comment on her transgression is that 'My little nun has found the prayerbooks, has she?' (120). In the *Dictionnaire érotique moderne* (1864) written by Alfred Delvau, the erotic is encoded within a religious discourse so that the brothel was sometimes called 'convent', the madam was the 'abbess' and the prostitute the 'sister'. Delvau was a friend of artist Félicien Rops whose drawings include an orgy set in a monastic brothel depicting a nun and a prostitute, St Teresa masturbating to orgasm with a crucifix, and a crucified woman provocatively posing on a cross. The heroine sees in the mirror a reflection of herself in a pornographic etching by Rops as she waits for the consummation of her marriage. But at the stirring of her own desire her husband closes her legs like a book.

The connection between dangerous reading and sexual knowledge is evident in a Romanian version of the 'Bluebeard' fairy tale entitled 'The Enchanted Pig' (1874).[24] The story is about a king who, before leaving for war, forbids his three daughters to enter a forbidden room. Disobeying his command they find that it contains an open book which reveals the identity of their future husbands. Carnal knowledge which can be acquired through texts was usually off limits for the female reader who, until comparatively recently, had restricted access to books. Virginia Woolf complained of being turned away from an Oxbridge library on the grounds of her sex. She discusses the incident in the first chapter *A Room of One's Own* (1929), a history of women's writing which inspired the title of Elaine Showalter's *A Literature of Their Own* (1978) and, most probably, Suniti Namjoshi's feminist interpretation of the 'Bluebeard' story called 'A Room of His Own' (1981).[25] In Sabilla

Novello's 'The History of Bluebeard's Six Wives' (1875), the first victim is called Basbluella, or Bluestocking Ella.[26] Bluestocking is, of course, a disparaging name given to a learned woman. Since the transgression of wife number one could hardly have led her to open an archive of dead wives, it may have been her heroic quest for learning which brought about her death.

For Bluebeard's slaughtered spouses, whose bodies in some tales are pegged to the wall, there is no escape, even in death, from the control of such a husband. These rare artefacts displayed in the most perverse of private collections embody the perfectly submissive wife. In *The Sadeian Woman* (1979), Angela Carter declares that 'the moral of the fairy tale about the perfect woman' is: 'To exist in the passive case is to die in the passive case – that is, to be killed'.[27] In Carter's feminist rewriting, fairy tales are narrated from the woman's point of view and serve as a warning, in this case, of the possible dangers of violence in marriage. Thus the woman writer becomes a kind of ersatz Scheherazade who survives execution by telling and retelling tales in *The Thousand and One Nights*, which is a likely precursor for the 'Bluebeard' folktale. This is analogous to the cultural repetition of trauma through storytelling. Female Gothic writers from Ann Radcliffe through to Jane Austen, Charlotte Brontë and Daphne du Maurier have intercepted the traditional marriage plot by demystifying romance with a new type of heroine who is a sort of psychological detective in pursuit of her own fulfilment. In their reworkings the emphasis is no longer upon 'the just fate of her disobedience'[28] but upon the damaging effects of patriarchal control.

In *Northanger Abbey* (1818), Jane Austen's parodic retelling of Ann Radcliffe's version of the 'Bluebeard' tale in *The Mysteries of Udolpho* (1794), her heroine Catherine Morland believes that the mystery beneath the black curtain or veil is the body of Lady Laurentini who was the heir to the estate of Udolpho and who had mysteriously disappeared. Had she been fastened Bluebeard style to the wall by her suitor Montoni after it turned out that she had loved another? Radcliffe's heroine, the next heiress Emily St Aubert, fears that she will be Montoni's victim as she stands in the way of him inheriting the estate through marriage to her aunt. One way in which Radcliffe rewrote 'Bluebeard' was to recast the corpse within the forbidden space as male instead of female and as a representation rather than a reality. Emily discovers behind the black veil what appears to be a partially decayed body 'dressed in the habiliments of the grave'.[29] It is actually a wax effigy which was intended for penitential contemplation by a previous owner. Terry Castle points out that 'What is new in Radcliffe, however, is the fervour with which the finality of death is denied. Continuity is all.'[30] Yet in another part of the castle, when Emily peers behind an arras fearing that it conceals the bloody and mutilated body of her aunt, she finds instead that of one of Montoni's bandits. Once again a female corpse is transformed into a male corpse or its simulacrum and is connected with a patriarch. It turns out that instead of ending up dead and enclosed by the black veil, Laurentini had actually *taken* the veil in an enclosed order as punishment for her complicity in the poisoning of her lover's wife. It would appear that Radcliffe, by unveiling the male villainy behind Emily's fears, has moved away from representing the ultimate in female passivity: woman as cadaver.

The door, curtain or veil are threshold motifs for the mysteries of life, death and sexuality. In *The Coherence of Gothic Conventions* (1980) Eve Kosofsky Sedgwick points out that 'the attributes of veil and of flesh are transferable and interchangeable'.[31] What lies behind the bridal veil can be a fear of the unknown within marriage. In Charlotte Brontë's *Jane Eyre* (1847) Rochester's 'mad' wife Bertha tears the eponymous heroine's wedding veil the night before her husband is about to make his bigamous marriage. It foreshadows the destruction of the illusion of romantic love and dashes Jane's hopes into 'chill, livid corpses'[32] when Rochester, not Jane, opens the door to the forbidden chamber on a corridor as 'in some Bluebeard's castle' (122) to reveal how he had imprisoned his wife in a living death. There are hints that this is punishment for her sexual infidelity.[33] Indeed, Bluebeard is presented as the victim of faithless wives in Anatole France's version of the tale. In a poem on the same subject published in 1902 the last stanza warns: 'The Moral: Wives, we must allow,/ Who to their husbands will not bow,/ A stern and dreadful lesson learn/ When, as you've read, they're cut in turn.'[34] Bertha cuts back by biting flesh from bone (see 339), having already reminded Jane of the 'foul German spectre – Vampyre' (317). Her rage expressed through blood and fire is paralleled by Jane who, in an early episode, saw red and for which she was incarcerated in the haunted red-room at Gateshead by her Aunt Reed. This incident might also explain the heroine's lack of curiosity about Rochester's forbidden room, for unlike other 'Bluebeard' wives she already knew what lay inside: punishment for insubordination.

For Jane Eyre and for the heroine of the novel it influenced, Daphne du Maurier's *Rebecca* (1938), there is collusion with their husbands' crime against the first wife. Jane never really protests against Rochester locking up Bertha, while du Maurier's second Mrs de Winter is complicit in her husband's murder of her predecessor, Rebecca, whose shadow is 'sharp as a sword'.[35] In the latter novel the forbidden chamber is divided between the bedroom where the second Mrs de Winter contemplates suicide at the instigation of Mrs Danvers, the housekeeper who was infatuated with the first wife, and the boathouse where Rebecca was murdered. In her adaptation of Carter's text Lavery mentions the key to the boathouse which is 'empty now'.[36] Clearly within the 'Bluebeard' literary tradition there are chambers within chambers, just as text is interpolated within text. While Brontë and du Maurier's heroines do not escape their husbands they do achieve greater independence due to the actions of former wives. For example, the second Mrs de Winter acquires control over texts, in contrast to earlier in her marriage when her husband had monitored her reading. Indeed, it is Jane's unauthorised access to books which brings her into conflict with the burgeoning patriarch, John Reed, who declares: 'You have no business to take our books...I'll teach you to rummage my book-shelves: for they *are* mine' (17). Jane's eventual punishment is confinement in the red-room. Her doppelgänger Bertha Rochester escapes from her place of captivity by burning it down. When Jane eventually marries Rochester, he has been partially maimed and blinded by Bertha's fire. Indeed, blindness is a fate which Lavery's Carteresque heroine, who chooses a blind lover, wishes upon her husband before he sees the bloody evidence of her misdemeanour.

The Bluebeard wife's intrusion into a male domain is also an incursion into a feminised space where she has unwittingly carved out a place for herself. The ghosts of the murdered wives in Lavery's adaptation insist upon her staying: 'You are not allowed to go!!!!!' [*sic*] (72). In the Brothers Grimm's 'Fitcher's Bird' (1812),[37] the wife re-members the severed mutilated corpses of her blood sisters and helps them escape from Bluebeard's castle. In these dead wives clubs there is a female solidarity for, in Lavery's version, they gang up on the living and complain that Bluebeard's recent bride is unable to titillate their bodies with her pianist's fingers. Their entombment is portrayed as a cross between a mortuary and a harem for a visiting necrophile.

A formulaic ending for the fairytale version is for the wicked husband to be killed by the brothers of his wife. Thus 'Bluebeard' espouses an anti-marital myth, which breaks down the door of patriarchal oppression and frees the wife from her Gothic Bastille from which she emerges triumphant after having dispatched her lord and master. Even though in traditional versions she returns regressively to her childhood family, her value on the marriage market is likely to have diminished. In Female Gothic versions the last wife is exonerated rather then excoriated for her intrepid inquisitiveness. With the exception of Angela Carter these bloody chambers have been drained of blood and the stories of their horrors. For the heroine and her reader, psychological terror now prevails.

Yet in the hands of certain male writers, as I shall argue, the Bluebeard wife, both as victim and villain becomes a dark double of the demonic stigmatic.[38] This female monstrosity may even be seen as a horrific hybrid of Bluebeard's resurrected victims and the one who got away to demonstrate, however unconsciously, that female disobedience need not go unpunished. As a return of the repressed these characters rise from their interment to enter other texts including Matthew Lewis's *The Monk* (1796) and Bram Stoker's *Dracula* (1897). This category of horror marks the domain of a woman steeped in blood who is both victim and villain. The most obvious are Lewis's Beatrice de las Cisternas, the Bleeding Nun of Lindenberg and Stoker's female vampires. The demonic stigmatic is a projection of the castrating woman who is also a bringer of death. Her body is now the site of transference for the indelible blood-stain which had passed from homicidal husband to magical key. She is a blasphemous form of the femme fatale wandering the interstitial spaces between being and non-being. Bluebeard's heroine has been united with this sinister twin because of the way in which she crossed the boundary of life and death. Her punishment is to hover perpetually on that very threshold of desire as a creature of the abyss. Normally death is regarded as a release from infinite yearning and the loneliness of individuation, but it is also an object of desire, the *Todestraum* or dream of death to which the demonic stigmatic partially acquiesces. She is the bearer of a wound which is an interface between the exterior and interior that encroaches upon the distinction between the outer and the inner and as a site of abjection,[39] signifies the boundary between life and death which threatens the self.

Blood marks the milestones in the female rites of passage from menstruation and the loss of virginity to childbirth which is literally a body of knowledge experienced only by women. Prior to Freud, the first menstrual period used to be regarded as the awakening to sexual knowledge. In a variation of 'Bluebeard' by the Brothers Grimm there is a story called 'The Virgin Mary's Child' (1812) about a girl, who when she reaches the age of fourteen, the age of the menarch, is told by the Virgin Mary that she must not enter a certain room. The traditional 'Bluebeard' story dramatises the bloody terror of defloration whose irreversibility and impurity is symbolised by the stain on the key which cannot be washed away. For Carter's heroine and her husband the key, like the loss of her virginity, is 'a wounded presence between us' (122). This erotogenic wound is prescient of the penalty for her disobedience which is decapitation, associated by Freud with castration. The sword with which Carter's heroine is going to be beheaded is described as 'sharp as child-birth' (141) and serves also as a reminder of the dangers of a mother bleeding to death after giving birth. The setting for her tale is Brittany. An historical antecedent for Bluebeard is Cunmar or Conomor, a mid-sixteenth-century ruler of Brittany who killed his wives as soon as they became pregnant. Although this has Oedipal implications it may also be indicative of male anxieties about mother figures and female procreation. Carter uses a discourse of pregnancy when she describes how, after her heroine's initiation into sexual desire once her 'female wound had healed', she finds herself impregnated with a 'dark newborn curiosity' (125). The moral of Perrault's 'Bluebeard' is that curiosity is 'very very costly' and 'a fleeting pleasure',[40] which once satisfied ceases to exist. The demonic stigmatic does not have the luxury of that closure. She is a metaphor for the eternal return of desire and the unhappy-ever-after repost to the ideology of Romantic love. As an uncanny embodiment of the insatiability of longing she serves as a warning of the dangers of female sexual transgression.

In Lewis's novel, the bleeding nun, in common with the femme fatale, is a damned matrix of unbridled lusts who had broken her vows to become the mistress of the Baron of Lindenberg. She is doomed to be a revenant for having murdered her lover in pursuit of his younger brother who stabbed her to death. An atheist and murderess, she is a parody of the saintly stigmatic nun, particularly since her bleeding wound is not in imitation of Christ but is the effluence of violent sexual passion. Her spectrality proves to be no impediment to her sexual stalking of Don Raymond de las Cisternas, even though she is his grandfather's great aunt. As her face is veiled, not unlike a bride, she manages to dupe Raymond into exchanging marriage vows which specify the mingling of their blood: 'In thy veins while blood shall roll,/ I am thine!/ Thou art mine!'[41] When Raymond looks behind the veil expecting to find his lover Agnes who had disguised herself as the ghost of the bleeding nun in order to escape her monastic order, he finds instead a grisly apparition. Agnes is also the name of Laurentini who becomes a nun in *The Mysteries of Udolpho*, a novel which Lewis claimed had inspired him to write *The Monk*. In one sense, when Radcliffe's Emily and Lewis's Raymond look behind the veil they find the same thing: an icon of anti-Catholicism.[42] Emily sees the effigy of a dead monk while Raymond looks upon the 'animated corse'[43] [*sic*] of a dead

nun in a parody of holy relics, especially those of the miraculously pre-
served bodies of saints and stigmatics. These revelations were analogous
to fears for Protestant Britain that Romanish superstitions could come
back to life and, for the bleeding nun specifically, to suspicions of veiled
hypocrisy behind vows of chastity. Emily encounters the veil in a room
containing instruments of torture which might have inspired Lewis's
description of Ambrosio being tortured by the Inquisition. Radcliffe's
description of the iron chair which can entrap a human body pales
before Carter's Iron Maiden, which is a grotesque sarcophagus in which
a wife has been entombed. It is a metaphor for abusive marriage and
contrasts with the coffin of Emily's father, as an inviting home, being
heimlich (homely) and yet *unheimlich*.

For the undead the coffin is usually an abode of temporary rather than
of eternal rest but, as the heroine in Carter's story says of the quasi-vampire
Romanian Countess, 'I knew she must be dead to find a home there' (132).
She lies desanguinated in the deadly embrace of a rival femme fatale: the
Iron Maiden. Her name is Carmilla, which is a reference to the eponymous vampire heroine of Sheridan Le Fanu's novella of 1872, an antecedent
for Stoker's *Dracula*. Carmilla, in being identified by Carter as a Romanian
Countess, is an allusion-within-an-allusion to the sixteenth-century
vampiric Countess, Elizabeth Báthory, who was a kind of female Bluebeard
with her own torture chamber where she enticed women for sadistic sexual purposes.[44] Carter's heroine is drawn to the corpse of Carmilla, as if
being wound in on a spool by the lure of annihilation. As Julia Kristeva
writes in *Powers of Horror: An Essay on Abjection* (1982):

> I behold the breaking down of a world that has erased its borders:
> fainting away. The corpse...is the utmost of abjection. It is death
> infecting life. Abject. It is something rejected from which one does
> not part, from which one does not protect oneself as from an object.
> Imaginary uncanniness and real threat, it beckons to us and ends up
> engulfing us.[45]

This is perhaps the realisation of the ultimate 'knowledge' from which
no curious seeker ever returns.[46] According to popular belief Báthory
extracted the blood of young women in the hope of rejuvenating herself.
Stoker had read about the Blood Countess of Čachtice while researching his novel. She may have inspired him with the idea for his blood-
drinking Count who also contains sexualised women within his castle.
Carter's thanatophiliac husband on seeing multiple reflections of his
wife in a mirror ironically confesses: 'I have acquired a whole harem for

myself!' (118). Soon, Carter's heroine will see herself reflected in the tableau of a marital necropolis. The bodies of the Marquis's wives surrounded by rack, wheel and Iron Maiden are the collection of a debauchée along with the bottles of wine which 'inhabited in racks all those deep holes of pain in the rock on which the castle was built' (123).

These penetrations are metonymic with those of the body, the violation of which is a transgression of the boundary between the living and dead. In Stoker's novel it is Dracula's bite which turns Lucy Westenra into a vampire version of the demonic stigmatic. She becomes a sexual pariah preying on men and even children for their blood to quench her insatiable thirst. For Lucy's friend Mina Harker the sexual encoding of vampirism is indicated by the spearing of the skin being described as a 'thin open wound'.[47] The language is similar to that referring to the ruby choker wedding gift in Carter's story which when put around the bride's neck resembles an 'extraordinarily precious slit throat' (114). In the Arthur Quiller-Couch 1910 version of the 'Bluebeard' story, the throats of the wives have been cut. Carter's flashing jewels 'bright as arterial blood' (115) are a family heirloom from the Marquis's grandmother who wore them in imitation of the red ribbon worn around the necks of those aristocrats who survived the Terror of the French Revolution: 'Like the memory of a wound' (115). For the heroine, the wound haunts the guillotine of the past and the axe of the future[48] for, as Derrida reminds us, the spectre is always to come. The title of Carter's villain is a reference to the Marquis de Sade who lived during the Terror and whose life and fictions blended kisses with female blood.

His sadism has seeped into the pages of Lavery's adaptation through the rivalry of the dead towards the living in a conflation between vampirism and virginity, as when the ghostly Countess addresses the latest wife as a virgin and a vampire bride, and asks her 'Does he make you bleed a bit??? [*sic*]/ Does he like to drink *your* blood?/ Look how much he made *me* bleed!' (70). Besides being encased within an Iron Maiden in an erotic mausoleum, she also occupies a bloody chamber of Gothic literature. Bloody chambers, like Russian dolls, lie one inside another like layers of the narrative. In Bram Stoker's *Dracula*, the vampire coffin is yet another bloody chamber where Jonathan Harker finds the body of the Count whose 'mouth was redder than ever, for on the lips were gouts of fresh blood, which trickled from the corners of the mouth and ran over the chin and neck' (71).

'For the blood is the life' (301) is the Scriptural mantra of Dracula's disciple, the madman and zoophagist Renfield. In Stoker's novel, vampirism is a parody of the Roman Catholic doctrine of transubstantiation whereby bread and wine are turned literally into the body and blood of Christ. The metaphor also expressed anxieties about Catholic infiltration into the body politic. The stigmatic, for whom a synecdoche is 'the living crucifix', replicates on his or her body the marks of crucifixion. These are the portals of death transcended by the risen Christ as the redeemer of the fallen human race. The demonic stigmatic, a kind of resurrection of the profane rather than of the pious body, is representative not of redemption but of a Gothic reinforcement of the blood curses visited upon Eve and her daughters.

In *Dracula*, a 'curse' (486) is inflicted upon Mina Harker for her blood transactions and transgressions with the Count. When Van Helsing attempts to purify her by pressing the Eucharist to her forehead it sears her flesh leaving a vivid red mark, a ghost of the erotogenic wound. Similarly in Angela Carter's story the husband after discovering the blood-stained key presses it to his wife's forehead. From her reflection in the mirror she sees that 'the heart-shaped stain had transferred itself to my forehead, to the space between the eyebrows, like the caste mark of a Brahmin woman' (139). However hard she scrubs her forehead she knows that the stubborn stain will be inscribed on her flesh until the day she dies. Similarly, Mina Harker's forehead is scarred with a scarlet signifier which she believes will remain until the Resurrection of the Body on Judgement Day[49] for which the vampire is a prematurely parodic avatar. In both texts the woman plays a redemptive role in obliterating the homicidal marks of Cain imprinted upon female flesh.

Sedgwick writes about how 'the writing of blood and flesh never lies' and that

> The marks traced out in earth, flesh, paper...are often not part of any language but, rather, circles, blots, a cross...Whether stamps of authenticity or brands of shame, and however rich in symbolism, they act as pointers and labels to their material ground and not as elements in a syntactic chain that could mean something *else*.[50]

In *The Fabrication of the Late-Victorian Femme Fatale* (1996), Rebecca Stott explains how in *Dracula* men use circles to corral the vampire women in order to patrol their ungoverned sexual urges.[51] These are formed out of wreaths of garlic flowers, the circular holy wafer and circumferences made out of the scattered host. In Lewis's *The Monk*, the Wandering Jew draws a circle around the bleeding nun in a rite of exorcism with blood drawn on the end of a crucifix. The legendary sign of the cross that he bears upon his forehead, after having been blasted by the legendary curse of Christ, is not concealed by a veil but by a black velvet band to avoid instilling holy dread in the onlooker. Yet, unlike Mina and Carter's Bluebeard wife, he is allowed to keep the sign of his transgression hidden from view.

What immediately distinguished the femme fatale from other women was the boldness of her gaze. According to Bram Dijkstra in *Idols of Perversity* (1986), these are 'women with the light of hell in their eyes'.[52] They refuse to veil the eye in modesty, but to allow it to go where no woman has gone before in penetrating male sexual secrets with the castrating gaze of the Medusa. In Lewis's *The Monk*, Raymond is transfixed by the petrifying stare of the bleeding nun. Carter's heroine finds herself colluding in the desiring male gaze as she becomes an object of her own desire on seeing herself mirrored in the Marquis's frame of vision: 'When I had first seen [my] flesh in his eyes, I was aghast to feel myself stirring' (119). But she breaks his spell by entering the bloody chamber and witnessing the dialectical masculinity of the gaze and deadness of the feminine body. This is familiar 'Bluebeard' territory where the wives are passive objects hanging from the walls like unframed portraits in an art gallery. They are subject to the scopophilic gaze which frames the eroticisation of death that can become an endpoint of desire itself. Carter's Bluebeard is a connoisseur of desire, who knows that 'anticipation is the greater part of pleasure' (119). For Lewis's bleeding nun and Stoker's vampires whose voracious sexual appetites can never be satiated, Jonathan Dollimore's Wagnerian comments in *Death, Desire and Loss in Western Culture* (1998) have some relevance:

> The excess of desire is at once desire for death (released from desire), extinction of self in the ecstasy of desire, and a fantasy of desire's omnipotence which by extension becomes a fantasy of the omnipotence of the self in its very extinction.[53]

Even though the demonic stigmatic exists beyond death her existence must be finally extinguished by her author in a gesture of ultimate retribution. So the bleeding nun is exorcised and Lucy Westenra is violently laid to rest, spewing out crimson foam, when a stake is hammered through her breast.

Because much of how women have been perceived throughout the centuries has been bound up with fantasy, is it the case, as Elisabeth Bronfen asks, that 'only in death can Woman be real, autonomous, alterior'?[54] The demonic stigmatic in all her spectrality and undead manifestations refuses to be well and truly dead despite the best efforts of her creators to have her killed and re-killed. As a voyeuristic projection of the Bluebeard gaze she is a risen spectre of wayward female sexuality in all its bleeding horror to form part of a lineage stretching back to Eve and the resilient survivors and ghosts of the bloody chamber.

Notes

1. 'One need not be a Chamber', Emily Dickinson, *The Complete Poems* (London: Faber and Faber [1890], 1987), 333.
2. Ellen Moers, *Literary Women*, introd. Helen Taylor (London: The Women's Press [1976], 1986), 91.
3. J. and A. L. Aikin, *Miscellaneous Pieces, in Prose* (London: J. Johnson, 1773), 123.
4. In the Brothers Grimm German translation of the tale in 1812 the wife of Bluebeard discovers the strangled bodies of her husband's former wives. As a punishment for her curiosity her husband decides that she too must die but she is rescued in time by her brothers who kill Bluebeard.
5. Jacques Derrida, *Geneses, Genealogies, Genres and Genius: The Secrets of the Archive*, trans. Beverley Bie Brahic (Edinburgh: Edinburgh University Press, 2004), 48.
6. Hauntology is a play on ontology whereby the logic of spectrality makes it impossible to banish the haunting presence of otherness so that the present exists only in relation to the past: 'Repetition *and* first time, but also repetition *and* last time, since the singularity of any *first time*, makes of it also a *last time*. Each time it is the event itself, a first time is a last time.' Jacques Derrida, *Specters of Marx: The State of the Debt, the Work of Mourning & the New International*, trans. Peggy Kamuf, introd. Bernd Magnus and Stephen Cullenberg (New York and London: Routledge [1993], 1994), 45.
7. Angela Carter, 'The Bloody Chamber', *Burning Your Boats: Collected Short Stories*, introd. Salman Rushdie (London: Vintage, 1996), 140. All subsequent references are to this edition and are given in the text.
8. '*The transgression does not deny the taboo but transcends it and completes it*', Georges Bataille, *Eroticism: Death and Sensuality*, trans. Mary Dalwood and introd. Colin MacCabe (London: Penguin [1957], 2001), 63.
9. Derrida, *Specters of Marx*, 10.
10. Quoted by Diane Long Hoeveler, *Gothic Feminism: The Professionalization of Gender from Charlotte Smith to the Brontës* (Liverpool: Liverpool University Press, 1998), 6.
11. Folklorists claim that oral versions of the tale predated Perrault's written fairy tale. Angela Carter also published a translation in 1982.
12. See Charles Perrault, 'Bluebeard', *The Classic Fairy Tales*, ed. Maria Tatar (New York and London: W. W. Norton, 1999), 148.
13. This is reproduced by Maria Tatar, *Secrets Beyond the Door: The Story of Bluebeard and his Wives* (Princeton, NJ and Oxford: Princeton University Press, 2004), 34.
14. Jessica Benjamin, *The Bonds of Love: Psychoanalysis, Feminism, and the Problem of Domination* (London: Virago [1988], 1990), 5.
15. Quoted by Benjamin, 66.
16. Georges Bataille, *Eroticism*, 11.

17. Sigmund Freud ,'The Uncanny' (1919), trans. James Strachey, *Pelican Freud Library*, 14 (Harmondsworth: Penguin, 1985), 366.
18. Sigmund Freud, *Civilization and its Discontents*, trans. and ed. James Strachey (New York: W. W. Norton, 1961), 68. Originally published in German in 1930.
19. Margaret Atwood draws on this for her story 'Bluebeard's Egg' in *Bluebeard's Egg and Other Stories* (London: Virago Press, 1983).
20. There have been approximately 30 operas written around the Bluebeard theme.
21. Maurice Merleau-Ponty, *Phenomenology of Perception,* trans. Colin Smith (London: Routledge, 1995), 183.
22. This is the title of another Brothers Grimm fairy tale, first published in their collected tales in 1812 but which was dropped from the second edition of 1819, partly due to its similarity to 'Bluebeard'. See *The Complete Fairy Tales of the Brothers Grimm,* ed. Jack Zipes (New York and London: Bantam, 1992), 739.
23. The Bluebeard fairy tale was usually accompanied by a subtitle, 'The Effects of Female Curiosity' or 'the Fatal Effects of Curiosity'. See Marina Warner, *From the Beast to the Blonde: On Fairy Tales and their Tellers* (London: Vintage, 1995), 244.
24. This was first published by Petre Ispirescu in *Legends or Romanian Fairy-tales* (1874). See *Red Fairy Book*, ed. Andrew Lang (London: Longmans, Green and Co, 1890), 204–15.
25. This appears in her *Feminist Fables* and is reprinted in *Wayward Girls and Wicked Women: An Anthology of Stories*, ed. Angela Carter (London: Virago Press, 1986), 85–6.
26. See Marina Warner, *From the Beast to the Blonde*, 247.
27. Angela Carter, *The Sadeian Woman: An Exercise in Cultural History* (London: Virago [1979], 1984), 77.
28. Warner, *From the Beast to the Blonde*, 241.
29. Ann Radcliffe, *The Mysteries of Udolpho* (Oxford: Oxford University Press [1794], 1992), 662.
30. Terry Castle, *The Female Thermometer: Eighteenth-Century Culture and the Invention of the Uncanny* (New York and Oxford: Oxford University Press, 1995), 132.
31. Eve Kosofsky Sedgwick, *The Coherence of Gothic Conventions* (New York and London: Methuen [1980], 1986), 145.
32. Charlotte Brontë, *Jane Eyre*, ed. Michael Mason (London: Penguin [1847], 1996), 331. All subsequent references are to this edition and are given in the text.
33. Rochester refers to her 'infamous conduct' (348) and the humiliation of being bound to a wife who is 'at once intemperate and unchaste' (345).
34. Quoted by Maria Tatar, *Secrets Beyond the Door*, 205.
35. Daphne du Maurier, *Rebecca* (London: Arrow [1938], 1992), 12.
36. Angela Carter, *The Bloody Chamber*, adapted by Bryony Lavery (London: Oberon, 2008), 49. All subsequent references are to this edition and are given in the text.
37. See *The Classic Fairy Tales*, ed. Maria Tatar, 148–50. Tales of female triumph are common in the folklore tradition of the tale while published versions tend to favour the more anti-female cautionary tale.

38. This term was first used by Carol Margaret Davison during a question and answer session following my paper on the subject at the 'Female Gothic' conference held at the University of Glamorgan in July 2004.
39. See Julia Kristeva, *Powers of Horror: An Essay on Abjection*, trans. Leon S. Roudiez (New York: Columbia University Press, 1982), 3.
40. Perrault, 'Bluebeard', 148.
41. Matthew Lewis, *The Monk*, ed. Howard Anderson (Oxford and New York: Oxford University Press [1796], 1980), 160.
42. Victor Sage suggests that 'the veil is indeed a metaphor for the numinous mystery of experience... deliberately designed to titillate the conscience of the Protestant readership'. See *Horror Fiction in the Protestant Tradition* (Basingstoke: Macmillan, 1988), 30.
43. Lewis, *The Monk*, 160.
44. Female servants were lured to the castle and also the daughters of the upper classes. See Tony Thorne, *Countess Dracula: The Life and Times of the Blood Countess, Elisabeth Báthory* (London: Bloomsbury, 1997).
45. Kristeva, *Powers of Horror*, 4.
46. I am indebted to Avril Horner for this point.
47. Bram Stoker, *Dracula*, ed. Maurice Hindle (London: Penguin [1897], 1993), 366. All subsequent references refer to this edition and are given in the text.
48. This was the fate of St Cecilia, a name given to Carter's Bluebeard wife by her husband. After surviving premature burial in a hothouse room in Ancient Rome, she was beheaded.
49. The mark disappears once Dracula is slain.
50. Sedgwick, *The Coherence of Gothic Conventions*, 154.
51. Rebecca Stott, *The Fabrication of the Late-Victorian Femme Fatale* (London: Macmillan Press, 1996), 57.
52. Bram Dijkstra, *Idols of Perversity: Fantasies of Feminine Evil in Fin-De-Siècle Culture* (New York and Oxford: Oxford University Press, 1986), 252. In Stoker's *Dracula*, Lucy's eyes are described as 'unclean and full of hell-fire, instead of the pure, gentle orbs we knew' (225).
53. Jonathan Dollimore, *Death, Desire and Loss in Western Culture* (London: Allen Lane, The Penguin Press, 1998), 240.
54. Elisabeth Bronfen, *Over Her Dead Body: Death, Femininity and the Aesthetic* (Manchester: Manchester University Press, 1992), 63.

7
Keeping It in the Family: Incest and the Female Gothic Plot in du Maurier and Murdoch

Avril Horner and Sue Zlosnik

From Walpole's *The Castle of Otranto* (1764) to the present day, incest has repeatedly featured as a motif in Gothic fiction. This is hardly surprising because in Gothic novels the family is frequently represented as harbouring dangers, its structures at one and the same time regulating and focusing desire. Female sexuality is habitually the contested space in the family (both its control and exploitation) and in the Gothic plot young women frequently find themselves particularly at risk from the predatory attentions of tyrannical fathers, father surrogates or, indeed, rapacious siblings. James Twitchell suggests in his 1987 book *Forbidden Partners: The Incest Taboo in Modern Culture* that the prohibition of incest is the most defining trait of the human family and that 'if we want to understand the dynamics of the modern family we will have to study the unfolding of this trait in the nineteenth century as the modern nuclear family takes shape'. It does not escape Twitchell's attention that Gothic fiction in this period has a recurrent tale to tell: 'If the Gothic tells us anything it is what "too close for comfort" really means.'[1] Feminist scholarship has played a significant role both in establishing Gothic studies[2] and in providing detailed historical and discursive contextualisation for changing representations of incest in literature. Caroline Gonda's book *Reading Daughters' Fictions*, for example, examines the nature of representations of the father–daughter bond in the period between 1709 and 1834, beginning with the observation that expressions of excessive affection for a daughter were in the eighteenth century 'not merely expressible without disquiet but in some quarters *de rigueur*'.[3] Building on Gonda's work, Julie Shaffer argues that in the fiction of this period:

> familialization is made problematic in quite a different way at points, for it overlaps with the threat of incest, everywhere a possibility in Gothic novels, themselves closely related to the sentimental novel, the two linked through their reliance on suffering victims with whom the audience can sympathize as proof or practice of its own moral sensibility.[4]

This essay will consider representations of incest in the fiction of two very different but roughly contemporary twentieth-century women writers who, while not always identified as Gothic novelists, made inventive use of Gothic conventions and themes. Daphne du Maurier (1907–89) and Iris Murdoch (1919–99) seem an unlikely pairing: the best-selling middlebrow author set alongside the younger cerebral literary novelist noted for exploring philosophical problems in her novels. Both represent incest in their fiction but, as we shall argue, how they do this and what it signifies differ; in particular, it is the spectre of incest's female victims that haunts du Maurier's work whereas Murdoch appears to use the incest motif in a much more self-conscious manner, its relationship to female victimhood appearing more complex. For both, however, incest as a trope is a powerful presence. We shall be considering representations from each of the writers of both father–daughter incest and incestuous desire between siblings. Twitchell suggests that 'parental incest is an act so different in motivation and consequence that it may deserve a separate name and category'.[5] It is thus perhaps not surprising to find that, despite their differences, both du Maurier and Murdoch represent parental incest as particularly horrifying and that both use Gothic effects to suggest the threatening nature of such a relationship.

In the case of du Maurier, it was the clear delineation of family relationships and what they might mean for her own sense of self that presented a problem, as autobiographical writings not made public until later in her life indicate. In 1977 at the age of 70, she published a volume entitled *Myself When Young*, a memoir based on diaries kept from childhood until her late 20s. In this work, the figures of her actor father (Gerald du Maurier, referred to as D.) and her writer and artist grandfather (George du Maurier) are prominent, their artistic legacy contrasted with the dullness she associated with her mother's family. Du Maurier's relationship with her father appears to have been particularly complex. In *Gerald: A Portrait* (published in 1934 shortly after his death) she describes how 'he would watch in the passage for his own daughter to return, and question her hysterically, like one demented, if the hands of the stable clock stood at half past two'.[6]

In *Myself When Young*, du Maurier explores her complex feelings about her father's need for closeness and her reactions to the attentions paid to her by an older cousin, Geoffrey Miller. Reading a biography of the Borgias seems to have influenced her way of thinking about these familial relationships.[7] In *Myself When Young*, the word 'Borgia' is a coded way of referring to an increasingly uneasy intimacy both with Geoffrey and Gerald. She had become the focus of Geoffrey's sexual attention from her early teens; at the age of fourteen, she had noticed that he smiled at her in a particular way, although at this time he was 36 years old and married. Six years later he was kissing her passionately on the mouth. Describing what she calls her 'first experience' – presumably of an erotic kiss from a man – du Maurier writes:

It seems so natural to kiss him now, and he is very sweet and lovable. The strange thing is it's so like kissing D. There is hardly any difference between them. Perhaps this family is the same as the Borgias. D. is Pope Alexander, Geoffrey is Cesare, and I am Lucretia. A sort of incest. (*MWY*, 108)

Even as a young adult, du Maurier describes Geoffrey as 'still a brother. Brother and son. Such a muddle' (*MWY*, 127). The same sort of 'muddle' is evident in her portrayal of her relationship with Gerald, who is described as 'the Borgia father' (*MWY*, 110) and whose jealousy of her boyfriends du Maurier sees as unhealthily possessive. On one level, her marriage to Major 'Boy' Browning in 1932 resolved the 'muddle' for her: at the close of *Myself When Young* she writes: 'For henceforth I would come to know what it was to love a man who was my husband, not a son, not a brother' (*MWY*, 157).

The notion of incest, however, went on to haunt du Maurier's fiction for much of her long writing career. Most of the time it is treated allusively, coded and displaced into more socially acceptable relationships. In the more overtly Gothic works, the threatening father/father surrogate/husband figure sits within Gothic conventions. In *Jamaica Inn* (1936), for example, heroine Mary Yellan feels sexually threatened by and at the same time strangely attracted to her uncle by marriage; the novel resolves this ambivalence through her sexual commitment to his younger brother who is both like and unlike him.[8] The unnamed narrator and heroine of *Rebecca* (1938) marries the much older Maxim de Winter, who tells her, 'Listen my sweet...A husband is not so very different from a father after all. There is a certain type of knowledge I prefer you not to have. It's better kept under lock and key. So that's that.'[9] In du Maurier's first novel, *The Loving Spirit* (1931), the narrator describes four generations of the same family as being 'all bound together in some strange and thwarted love for one another',[10] thus suggesting complex familial bonds that transcend time and challenge the basis of individual identity. This question of individual identity is one to which du Maurier's fiction returns repeatedly; anxieties about the boundaries of self permeate her writing and endow it with a Gothic sensibility that is present even when more obvious Gothic trappings are not. In this sense she is a profoundly Gothic writer.[11]

Du Maurier's relatively neglected 1949 novel about a theatrical family, *The Parasites*, tells the story of three siblings, brought up by a famous singer father and dancer mother. Despite, or perhaps because of, the fact that Niall Delaney is not a full biological brother to the two sisters, family intimacies transmute into quasi-sexual desires that psychologically damage them all. The novel's title suggests obliquely the way in which, unable to break free of this 'strange and thwarted love', the siblings become parasitical upon each other and on others as they grow older. The novel's ominous epigraph is a passage on 'Parasites', taken from the *Encyclopaedia Britannica*, which concludes 'Parasites affect their hosts by feeding upon their living tissues or cells, and the intensity of the effect upon the hosts ranges from the slightest local injury to complete destruction'. The shifting narrative voice, a striking aspect of the novel, indicates an instability of identity: when referring to one of the siblings it is third person; when referring to them collectively it moves into the first person plural. Indeed, in the three Delaneys, Maria, Niall and Celia, the competing aspects of du Maurier's own life and personality are clearly visible in a dramatised version of the self as 'fractured', a classic Gothic trope.[12] The youngest, Celia, is the nurturer who cares for her demanding widowed father to the end, 'Mama' having met an untimely demise. She never breaks out of the paradigm of the dutiful daughter; repressing her own sexuality, she transfers her need to nurture to her sister's children. Strong female sexuality is embodied in the oldest, Maria, whose representation is clearly coloured by du Maurier's own experience of adolescence: the seduction of the pubescent Maria on the beach in Brittany by the much older Michel has clear echoes of the attentions paid to the 14-year-old Daphne by Geoffrey Miller. Perhaps the saddest of the three is Niall who, while having a successful career as a composer of light music, represents an undisciplined artistic impulse that makes him persistently unhappy. His quasi-incestuous desire for his 'sister' Maria adds to the muddle in his mind and represents unfulfilled desire: 'Our relationship to each other was such a muddled thing that it was small wonder that no one reached the truth of it correctly', says the first person plural narrative voice early in the novel.[13] Niall's troubled masculinity is a reminder of du Maurier's sense of her writing identity as masculine, what she called her 'boy in the box'.[14] Unable to conceive of desire outside the family, Niall eventually chooses his stepfather's first wife as a lover and, that relationship over, the novel ends with his impending death (which may or may not be suicide) as he drifts out to sea in a sinking boat. Du Maurier represents Niall as irreparably damaged, and finally destroyed, by a family that loves dysfunctionally; the failure to establish a firm border between self and 'sister' proves, in the end, tragic.

In 1933, du Maurier published a novel that represented the destructive effects of excessive paternal affection. Here, also, incest haunts the narrative but is represented metaphorically. One of her lesser-known novels, *The Progress of Julius*, was written by du Maurier when she was only 24. Many reviewers thought its subject matter unsuitable material for a young lady author.[15] Julius Lévy, by origin a Jewish French Algerian refugee and now a self-made businessman resident in London, makes a marriage of convenience with the daughter of a rich acquaintance and they have a daughter whom he scarcely notices while she is growing up. After Gabriel returns from a period at boarding school, he returns home one day to hear her playing his father's flute and memories of a childhood traumatised by war and the death of his musical father are stirred to life; this epiphanic moment stirs memories of his own lost familial relationships and is transformed into powerful erotic feelings that he experiences as desire for Gabriel:

> he looked at her, her face, her body, her hands on the flute, the colour of her hair; he looked at her figure outlined against the window, and a fierce sharp joy came to him stronger than any known sensation, something primitive like the lick of a flame and the first taste of blood, as though a message ran through his brain saying: 'I for this – and this for me'.[16]

Julius subsequently develops a 'voracious passion' (*J*, 213) for his daughter, ignoring his wife who then develops cancer and falls into despair, finally committing suicide by taking an overdose. He even thinks of his daughter as a replacement wife: deciding that Rachel's 'utility was over now' he is pleased that 'Gabriel would make as a good a hostess when she came out next year' (*J*, 232). Instead of sending her away to a finishing school, Julius involves Gabriel in three years of extravagant living. There is no description of actual sexual activity but his inappropriate sexual desire is rendered metaphorically in his response to Gabriel's playing 'the sight of her standing there so cool and undisturbed jarring upon him who felt dissatisfied and unrefreshed, an odd taste in his mouth, and a sensation in mind and body that was shameful and unclean' (*J*, 225–6). Their language and behaviour towards each other become that of lovers rather than parent and child: Julius showers his daughter with expensive gifts and calls her 'a bitch' when she upsets him (*J*, 232). Gabriel, too, is excited by her father's sophistication and worldly power that makes young men look 'callow and inexperienced' (*J*, 238); yet the emotional intensity of their relationship is clearly inappropriate and verges on the abusive. Indeed, Gabriel's perception of that relationship is expressed through metaphors of penetration and surfeit:

> She had no will of her own now, no consecutive thought, no power of concentration; she was being dashed and hurtled into a chaos that blinded her, some bottomless pit, some sweet, appalling nothingness... He was cruel, he was relentless, he was like some oppressive, suffocating power that stifled her and could not be warded off; he gave her all these bewildering sounds and sensations without pausing so that she was like a child stuffed with sweets cloying and rich; they were rammed down her throat and into her belly, filling her, exhausting her, making her a drum of excitement and anguish and emotion that was gripping in its savage intensity. It was too much for her, too strong. (*J*, 243–4)

This intimate relationship endures through the First World War but Julius becomes unbearably jealous of the young men who pay Gabriel attention. In the way of jealous lovers, he prefers to kill her rather than share her and so takes her on a Mediterranean holiday and strangles her in the sea with his own handkerchief. Gabriel thereby pays a terrible price for her complicity with her father. Julius is never suspected of a crime (it is assumed that his daughter drowned accidentally) but the novel ends with his lonely old age and death from a stroke. In this tragic tale, incest is never represented at the level of plot; perhaps in 1933, this was a step too far even for a novelist preoccupied with the 'Borgia'-like quality of her own family.

It was only as a much older writer that du Maurier was to represent incest overtly but even here she stops short of representing *knowing* incest. The short story, 'A Border-Line Case' published in 1971 (and in the same decade as *Myself When Young*), is constructed along the lines of a Greek tragedy in which the protagonists are unaware of each other's true identity until the catastrophe of accidental incest overtakes them. After the death of Shelagh Money's father (as she believes him to be), she sets out on a journey to find his old naval friend and best man, Nick Barry, described by her father as, 'Gallant as they come, but mad as a hatter. A border-line case.'[17] The search for Nick, who is believed to be living as a recluse, takes her into deepest rural Ireland, where she poses as a journalist and makes enquiries about 'Commander Barry'. This venture has the quality of a Gothic journey as she travels further into a strange and primitive countryside where the natives are taciturn and the very name of the 'eerie' Lamb's Island evokes for her barbarous images of prehistoric Ireland with 'sacrifices to ancient gods'...'a lamb with its throat cut lying amidst the ashes of a fire' ('BC', 127). She finds herself virtually kidnapped by the Commander's men who take her to a small community run with naval precision. While there, she sees her parents' wedding photograph and is disturbed by the fact it has been tampered with: 'Nick's head and shoulders had been transposed on to her father's figure, while her father's head...had been shifted to the lanky figure behind, standing between the bridesmaids' ('BC', 133). Shelagh fails to see the significance of this clue but experiences 'a feeling of revulsion, a strange apprehension' and reflects that 'the room that had seemed warm and familiar became kinky, queer. She wanted to get out of it' ('BC', 134). However, when she meets Nick she is reassured and is attracted to him. His business, it seems, is organising covert terrorist activities. She accompanies him on a bombing raid over the border and this furnishes them with the opportunity to have entirely consensual (and, as she readily admits, very good) sex.

It is only after her return home that she discovers the truth: that she is the product of an affair between her mother and Nick and has therefore slept with her own father. The revelation is traumatic and precipitates her into a self-loathing that urges her towards indiscriminate violence. She has been psychologically destroyed by her experience of incest; she becomes a victim. 'A Border-Line Case' is du Maurier's only work to represent incest directly and acknowledge its damaging consequences. As Gillian Harkins reminds us, 'according to earliest feminist interventions, incestuous trauma was the result of failed social recognition'; in other words, there has been not so much a taboo on incest as a taboo on talking about it.[18] As it became more possible to talk about incest, du Maurier's preoccupation realised its most explicit articulation.

No such taboo appears to have attached to incest in Iris Murdoch's writing; nor, apparently, was her interest in it precipitated by personal experience. The only child of happily married and cultured parents, Murdoch's early life was secure and 'idyllic'; she later described her family as 'a perfect trinity of love'.[19] As an intellectual influenced by existentialism, who was to become one of Europe's foremost moral philosophers, she developed an interest in incest, particularly in relation to current psychoanalytical discourse (about which she had many reservations) and, more importantly, to the moral conundrums it presented. Indeed, by the early 1960s an interviewer suggested to her that she had gained quite a reputation for writing about it.[20] The 1961 novel *A Severed Head*, ostensibly a comedy of manners, is a study of obsession that uses Gothic tropes to explore the troubled sexuality and familial relationships of its narrator, Martin Lynch-Gibbon. It is, in the words of Deborah Johnson, 'playfully Freudian',[21] a novel that self-consciously manipulates its central image both to echo and critique the Freudian trope of the Medusa's head as representing fear of the female genitals. Readings of the novel have tended to focus on its exposure of Martin's psyche;[22] such readings make it difficult to place *A Severed Head* in a category labelled Female Gothic in spite of the sex of its author. A more decentred reading, however, enables us to identify a different concern, Murdoch's representation of the two women academics, Honor Klein and her former student Georgie Hands.

Into the tightly knit clutch of smart and mannered London characters with their quasi-incestuous partner-changing comes the uncanny figure of Honor Klein, darkly powerful and enigmatic, who describes herself as 'a severed head',[23] representing the complex significations of the taboo (a term used repeatedly through the novel). The narrative represents sibling incest explicitly as a *mise en scène*. Looking for Honor at her Cambridge house, Martin goes into the bedroom to find her in bed with her half-brother (who is Martin's wife's analyst and lover, Palmer Anderson):

> Sitting up in this bed was Honor. She was sitting sideways with the sheet over her legs. Upwards she was tawny and naked as a ship's figurehead. I took in her pointed breasts, her black shaggy head of hair, her face stiff and expressionless as carved wood. She was not alone. Beside the bed a naked man was hastily engaged in pulling on

a dressing-gown. It was immediately and indubitably apparent that I
had interrupted a scene of lovers. (*SH*, 128)

This graphic representation must be seen in the context of the novel's
pattern. The Gothic figure of Honor constitutes an irruption into the
metropolitan comedy of manners narrated by the self-centred, emo-
tionally immature and amoral Martin. Honor remains enigmatic
throughout; in identifying herself as the 'severed head such as primitive tribes used to use, anointing it with oil and putting a morsel of gold
upon its tongue to make it utter prophecies' (*SH*, 182), she represents
both totem and taboo; what she is clearly not is a victim. Murdoch's
representation of Honor is disturbing on several levels. She is an abject
figure, the focus of both repugnance and desire for Martin. His first
meeting with her when he is expecting 'a poor old German spinster'
(*SH*, 52), takes place in the Gothic miasma of London fog and shocks
him. His description of her is couched in an Orientalist discourse that
evokes the anxieties of an earlier period of Gothic literature in which
sinister eastern entities manifest themselves in the capital itself,[24] 'Her
narrow dark eyes, which seemed in the strange light to be shot with red,
had the slightly Oriental appearance peculiar to certain Jewish women.
There was something animal-like and repellent in that glistening stare'
(*SH*, 55). He returns frequently to her Jewish features (her father was a
German Jew), suggesting that in spite of his urbanely modern outlook,
the bourgeois prejudices of an earlier period are still active in Martin.
Honor's profession as an anthropologist gives her arcane knowledge
about primitive cultures and her perspective presents a challenge to
the mores of the Lynch-Gibbons and to what Martin himself calls his
wife's 'metaphysic of the drawing room' (*SH*, 17). The game of sexual
musical chairs, in which everyone behaves with exquisite politeness, is
thrown into sharp relief by her insistence that Martin must react differently in response to his wife's defection to Palmer. Rather than falling
in with Antonia and Palmer's narrative of behaving as concerned parents towards him, he must reject such familial roles and assert his own
integrity and separate identity as an adult male. 'In such matters you
cannot have both truth and what you call civilization. You are a violent man, Mr Lynch-Gibbon. You cannot get away with this intimacy
towards your wife's seducer' (*SH*, 64). 'You cannot cheat the dark gods,'
she tells him (*SH*, 64). Martin's incipient violence comes to the surface
as an attack on Honor herself, after she has called him 'the knight of
infinite humiliation' (*SH*, 110), when he wrestles her to the ground and

strikes her three times across the face. In a strange reversal, it is Martin who appears the victim after this attack. Honor 'brushed down her coat and then without looking at me and still without haste she mounted the cellar steps' (*SH*, 112), whereas Martin is disoriented: 'With a choking sigh more profound than silence the fog enclosed me. I opened my mouth to call out to her but found that I had forgotten her name' (*SH*, 112).

Just before the attack, Martin had accused Honor of introducing his 'mistress', Georgie Hands, to his brother, Alexander, and this seems to account in large part for his rage. Martin fears that Alexander, who has a record of poaching his girlfriends, will steal Georgie away (although by the end of the novel it is revealed that he has in fact been having an affair with Antonia for many years and her eventual departure to Rome with him after the end of her affair with Palmer is for Martin the ultimate betrayal). At the opening of the novel, Martin is very satisfied with a life in which he has sustained his marriage to the older Antonia and 'kept a mistress' (in the terminology of the times) in the person of Georgie. Georgie leads a double life: she is hardly a 'kept woman', having already enjoyed career success through her appointment as a junior lecturer at the prestigious London School of Economics; however, she conducts a clandestine relationship with the selfish Martin and the relationship brings her anguish. She has had to abort Martin's child the previous year and he admits that 'Because of Georgie's character, her toughness and the stoical nature of her devotion to me, I had not had to pay. It had all been uncannily painless' (*SH*, 13). If there is a victim in *A Severed Head*, it is Georgie: an unlikely victim, yet nevertheless a victim. It is not incest that destroys her but the bad faith of her lover – and her collusion with his fantasies, which prevent him from paying full attention to her as a separate person. Honor Klein acts as a catalyst in bringing matters to a head; it is she who reveals the existence of Georgie to Antonia. When Martin is forced to arrange a meeting between them, Georgie is patronised by Antonia (as she often is by Martin), who insists on addressing this grown woman as 'my dear child' (*SH*, 89). Georgie is used and manipulated by all the main characters in the novel so that she eventually attempts suicide (having first, in a further inflection of the trope of the severed head, sent her hair in a box to Martin) and then gives up her academic post at the LSE to go off to America with Palmer Anderson. She is the collateral damage in Martin's struggle to escape the family demons that haunt him. The principle embodied by Honor and her propensity for incest in this symbolic drama is a primitive truth in the face of which 'civilised' arrangements such as that between Martin and Georgie cannot be sustained. In Honor and Georgie, Murdoch presents the reader with two contrasting images of apparently modern women. It is the atavism embodied in Honor and her willingness to transgress cultural norms as exemplified by the incest taboo that makes her such a strong figure. Ironically, it is the very act of finding Honor *in flagrante delicto* with her half-brother that jolts Martin out of his tendency to re-enact family relationships in his sexual liaisons (if Antonia has been a mother-wife, Georgie has been a daughter-lover). It is Honor Klein the anthropologist, not Palmer Anderson the psychoanalyst, who sets Martin free.[25] In contrast, the superficial bohemianism and intellectual sharpness of Georgie are no match for the intense egoism of a complacent bourgeois male and she passes from one to another in the rupture of her relationship with Martin and her new alignment with Palmer, the spokesman for an ineffective Freudianism. Sibling incest in this novel is therefore represented as a trope for empowerment, at least for some. In thinking about Honor, Martin reflects at one point that 'incest inspired *irrational* horror' (*SH*, 186). *A Severed Head* asks us to put aside our learnt responses to incest and to judge it in the context of a particular situation and its particular consequences. Arguably, Honor's relationship with her half-brother, which transgresses all social codes, is less damaging to others than Martin's immaturity and egoism. The novel therefore challenges conventional morality and asks us to look afresh at love, families and desire.[26]

However, not all incestuous or quasi-incestuous sibling relationships in Murdoch's fiction are thus exonerated by their author. In *The Bell* (1958), which features in true Gothic mode a legend concerning a nun who drowned herself, Nick Fawley's 'Byronic passion'[27] for his twin sister, Catherine, explains both her desire to enter a convent and her subsequent suicide attempt by drowning. She is saved but emerges from the ordeal completely distracted and is subsequently diagnosed as schizophrenic. The curiously intense, albeit not incestuous, relationship between David Levkin and his sister, Elsa, in *The Italian Girl* (1964) seems likewise to be a contributory factor to her instability. Roaming in the dark at night, she feels she is a ghost and later in the novel, having set fire to herself, finally dies from the burns. Hilary Burde's relationship with his half-sister in *A Word Child* (1975) is equally intense, as his confession to the reader reveals:

I should make it clear that there was nothing physical in my relation with Crystal ... I did not want to go to bed with her or kiss her or caress her or even touch her more than minimally. (Though if I had been told that I could never touch her I should have gone mad.) ... I simply was her ... She just had to be always available in a place fixed and controlled by me.[28]

Crystal's life is, not surprisingly, diminished and constrained by Hilary's bullying and possessive behaviour. For Murdoch, as for du Maurier, emotional incest can be as, or more, damaging than physical incest. Indeed, in *The Italian Girl*, Edmund traces the dysfunctional relationships in his family back to his mother's 'love' for her sons:

> My mother's affections had early turned away from her husband and focused with rapacious violence upon her sons, with whom she had had, as it were, a series of love-affairs, transferring the centre of her affection to and fro between us: so that our childhood passed in an alternate frenzy of jealousy and suffocation ... To say that I hated her for it was too flimsy a saying: only those will understand who have suffered this sort of possession by another.[29]

Murdoch saw such tendency to see the other as a mere extension of self – that is, to negate another in the pursuit of one's own desire – as particularly pernicious. And as in du Maurier's work, such intense 'love' is presented as all the more sinister and damaging when it is focused on a daughter.

Murdoch's 1966 novel *The Time of the Angels* places patriarchal tyranny and father–daughter incest at the centre of a tale that makes very self-conscious use of Gothic conventions. A London novel, it is set in a fog-bound and indecipherable East End, evocative of the murky world of Dickens's London novels and the even murkier world of Stevenson's Dr Jekyll, yet possessing its own sense of isolation as a product of the post-war world. The Rectory, stranded not only in the fog but also in a sea of bomb damage and demolition, stands alone as a Gothic edifice, its very foundations shaken by the rumbling of tube trains underneath it. The newly arrived Rector, Carel Fisher, is, for much of the novel, an enigmatic figure who has abandoned his belief in God, believing himself to be in 'The Time of the Angels'. These 'angels' are not benevolent figures but represent the licence to behave without restraint, or energies set free in a world without God. For Carel, this involves refinements of domestic evil,[30] from his coldness to his daughter Muriel, his callous sexual treatment of his black servant, Patti, and his sexual exploitation of the invalid Elizabeth, who for much of the novel is believed to be his niece but who is revealed later by Patti to be his daughter. As in many Gothic novels, the mother is absent; the mothers of both Muriel and Elizabeth are dead. Although Elizabeth is involved in an incestuous relationship with her father, Carel, the narrative does not elicit any sympathy for her as a victim. It is never focalised through her, concentrating instead on the feelings of the rejected daughter, Muriel. Like Carel, Elizabeth is also enigmatic, a sequestered figure, reminiscent of *The Unicorn*'s (1963) Hannah Crean-Smith.[31] She has androgynous qualities, with her black trousers and cigar smoking. She is also represented as an object of desire for Muriel, who recalls having kissed her on the lips once. The dramatic moment when Muriel sees her father and Elizabeth in bed together through a crack in a cupboard is thus a double betrayal. Murdoch's representation of incest here offers a *mise-en-scène* reflected in a 'big French mirror'. What she sees is graphic and unambiguous yet also has a spectral quality:

> She concentrated her vision at last into a small circle of perfect clarity. She saw the end of the chaise-longue close up against its mirror double. Beyond it in the mirror she saw the heaped and tousled bed. She began to see Elizabeth, who was on the bed. She saw, clear and yet unlocated like an apparition, Elizabeth's head, moving, half hidden in a stream of hair, and Elizabeth's bare shoulder. Then there were other movements, other forms, an entwining suddenly of too many arms. And she saw, slowly rising from the embrace, beyond the closed eyes and the streaming hair, white and dreadful, the head and naked torso of her father.[32]

This scene is both shocking and bathetic. Muriel has taken the ne'er do well son of the caretaker, Leo Peshky, to peep from the linen cupboard at Elizabeth, whose existence has hitherto been kept secret from him. This is one example of how Muriel, the aspiring poet, is shown to experience vicariously. However, she sees more than she bargains for; her idealised description of Elizabeth as 'a beautiful and solitary virgin' (*TA*, 105) is dramatically negated. Carel's behaviour not only transgresses social codes; it is also a sacrilegious act in which he betrays the pastoral duty of a priest in the most extreme way. At this point, Elizabeth is thought to be Carel's niece but the full horror of the act is thrown into relief when Patti reveals to Muriel that she is in fact his daughter, the result of his adulterous liaison with his sister-in-law. In comparison, his sexual abuse of the vulnerable Patti is more conventional and is apparent from the beginning of the novel. This suggests that Murdoch is staging the image of the incestuous bed to provide a significant moment in the novel, a turning point beyond which Carel articulates his loss of faith and ultimately commits suicide. This is a highly patterned novel in which Carel's transgression of the cultural taboo of incest signifies his abandonment of Christian belief and morality. Like Honor Klein, he is a powerful creation. In contrast with the self-absorbed characters of *A Severed Head*, however, those he is set against include several characters who attempt to find 'good' in this secular world. For his surviving brother, Marcus, this is an intellectual pursuit (he is writing a book of reflections on 'the good'); for the old family friend, Nora, it takes the form of philanthropy and a no-nonsense rationalism. Carel's suicide leaves the inhabitants of the Rectory to go their separate ways and the two sisters are seen departing for a life in the leafy suburbs. The image of the departure, described though the eyes of Marcus, and again framed, suggests a new dyad:

> Then framed in the doorway he saw the two girls, immobile as if they had been there for some time, their two pale heads close together, their bodies seemingly entwined. With a shock he realized that Muriel was carrying Elizabeth in her arms... Marcus saw her face turned towards him, long and without colour, half hidden in the drooping metallic hair which gleamed in the sunlight a faintly greenish silver. It was and was not the face of the nymph he had known. The large grey-blue eyes blinked painfully in the bright light and met his vacantly and without interest. (*TA*, 227)

This provides an enigmatic ending to the novel. Elizabeth appears to have been dehumanised by her life of confinement and the incestuous attentions of her father to the point that her entry into the outside world is painful and she is unable to make any social connection. Muriel has already been disconcerted by Elizabeth's refusal to acknowledge the witnessed scene of incest, coming to see her silence as a 'deliberate masquerade' (*TA*, 184) but by this stage of the novel, she has become effectively mute. Marcus's vision of the two girls also suggests possibilities of lesbian sibling incest but this is a narrative that remains at the level of suggestion. Whether the new life constitutes liberation for Elizabeth remains to be seen. Meanwhile, the already dispossessed members of Carel's household, the refugee caretaker and the abused mixed-race housekeeper, are freed to go their separate ways. For the latter this is liberation to pursue her dream of working in a refugee camp in Africa; for the former, it is one more displacement as he reflects, 'the world was just a transit camp' and carries his icon with its 'milky blue angels' with him (*TA*, 233).

In these novels by Murdoch, incest represents a self-conscious drawing on a tradition of cultural taboo. It is less the representation of deep-seated personal anxiety and more the manipulation of readers' responses in the service of each novel's wider agenda, which is to explore questions of morality. For Murdoch, whose thinking was much influenced by the work of Simone Weil, the Good consists of (among other things) paying extreme attention to the other and refusing the temptation to obliterate another in the pursuit of one's own desire. True love is an act of 'unselfing': 'Love is the perception of individuals. Love is the extremely difficult realisation that something other than oneself is real'.[33] Conversely, to wish to possess another totally is the opposite of good and constitutes evil – which is why we find Murdoch experimenting with Gothic effects in novels such as *A Severed Head*, *The Bell*, *The Unicorn* and *The Time of the Angels*. Well aware that her interest in moral philosophy informed her fiction, Murdoch nevertheless saw the novel as working on her readers in a way quite separate from that of philosophic discourse:

> The unconscious mind is not a philosopher. For better and worse art goes deeper than philosophy ... there is always something moral which goes down further than the ideas, the structures of good literary works are to do with erotic mysteries and deep dark struggles between good and evil.[34]

Very different in many ways, du Maurier and Murdoch are alike in others. Both produced novels in which one character's obsessive desire to possess another is exposed as destructive; both are keenly interested in what constitutes threats to the borders of identity; both represent a father's incestuous 'love' for his daughter as the most pernicious form of dysfunctional desire. However, whereas du Maurier dramatises such situations and perhaps unconsciously uses Gothic elements to represent the (invariably female) victim's fear and horror, Murdoch harnesses Gothic effects in a more self-conscious attempt to explore the moral questions precipitated by the desire of any individual – whether male or female – to possess and control another. They both, however, adapt the Gothic in order to convey to the reader what 'too close for comfort' really means and, in so far as their plots frequently involve the disempowerment and abuse of female characters, they can be seen as part of what we now broadly recognise as a Female Gothic tradition.

Notes

1. James B. Twitchell, *Forbidden Partners: The Incest Taboo in Modern Culture* (New York: Columbia University Press, 1987), xiii and 152.
2. See Lauren Fitzgerald, 'Female Gothic and the Institutionalization of Gothic Studies' in Andrew Smith and Diana Wallace, eds, *Gothic Studies* 6/1 (2004), 8–18. This essay provides an excellent overview of the area and is republished in this volume as Chapter 1.
3. Caroline Gonda, *Reading Daughters' Fictions 1709–1834: Novels and Society from Manley to Edgeworth* (Cambridge: Cambridge University Press, 1996), 1.
4. Julie Shaffer, 'Familial Love, Incest, and Female Desire in Late Eighteenth and Early Nineteenth-Century British Women's novels', *Criticism* 41/1 (Winter 1999), 67–99, 67.
5. James B. Twitchell, *Forbidden Partners*, xiii.
6. Daphne du Maurier, *Gerald: A Portrait* (London: Victor Gollancz, 1934), 215.
7. At about 18 years of age, she borrowed a life of Cesare Borgia from Hampstead Library. According to many biographies (including presumably this one) Cesare Borgia was reputed to have committed incest with his sister, Lucrezia, the illegitimate daughter of Pope Alexander VI. Alexander himself was also, by many sources, reputed to have slept with his daughter. (Daphne du Maurier, *Myself When Young: The Shaping of a Writer* [1977; London: Arrow, 1993], 82. All subsequent references are to this edition and are given in the texts, after *MWY*).
8. Daphne du Maurier, *Jamaica Inn* (1936; London: Arrow, 1992).
9. Daphne du Maurier, *Rebecca* (London: Arrow, 1992), 211. For a detailed discussion of Gothic desire in *Jamaica Inn* and *Rebecca* see our *Daphne du Maurier: Writing, Identity and the Gothic Imagination* (Basingstoke: Palgrave Macmillan, 1998), chapters 3 and 4.
10. Daphne du Maurier, *The Loving Spirit* (London: Arrow, 1994), 309.
11. Eugenia DeLamotte's feminist study of nineteenth-century Gothic recognises the significance of Gothic forms for female subjectivity:

    ...because the dividing line between the world and the individual soul has had, from the inception of the Gothic craze, a special relevance to the psychology and social condition of women, this interpretation of the 'deep structures' of Gothicism provides a new explanation of the appeal the genre has always had for women readers and writers (*Perils of the Night: A Feminist Study of Nineteenth-Century Gothic* (Oxford: Oxford University Press, 1990), 23).

12. Sheila Hodges, du Maurier's editor for many years, has reported that the author admitted to putting much of herself into the three characters and also notes the parallels between this novel and material in *Gerald* and *Myself When Young*. See 'Editing Daphne du Maurier' in Helen Taylor, ed., *The Daphne du Maurier Companion* (London: Virago, 2007), 25–43, 25.
13. Daphne du Maurier, *The Parasites* (Harmondsworth: Penguin [1949], 1965), 18.
14. This is discussed at length in our *Daphne du Maurier: Writing, Identity and the Gothic Imagination*.

15. Du Maurier's biographer, Margaret Forster, notes that although the *Observer* and *The Times* found some praise for it, 'the general reception was much more critical than expected'. Sir Arthur Quiller Couch, well-known literary critic and friend of du Maurier, considered it 'vulgar and cheap'. (Margaret Forster, *Daphne du Maurier* [London: Chatto and Windus, 1993], 103–4 and 97).

16. *The Progress of Julius* was reprinted by Arrow Books Ltd in 1994 as *Julius*. All subsequent references are to this edition and are given in the text, quote from 211. The Estate of Daphne du Maurier reduced much of what it saw as the anti-Semitic language of the novel (originally published by Heinemann in 1933) for the 1994 Arrow edition.

17. 'A Border-Line Case' in *Don't Look Now* (Harmondsworth: Penguin, 1971), 101–62, 117. All subsequent references are to this edition and are given in the text, referred to as 'BC'.

18. Gillian Harkins, 'Telling Fact from Fiction: Dorothy Allison's Disciplinary Stories' in Elizabeth Barnes ed., *Incest and the Literary Imagination* (Gainsville, FL: University of Florida Press, 2002), 283–315, 287.

19. Peter Conradi, *Iris Murdoch: A Life* (New York and London: W. W. Norton & Company, 2001), 33.

20. Cited in Tammy Grimshaw, *Sexuality, Gender and Power in Iris Murdoch's Fiction* (Madison, Teaneck: Farleigh Dickinson University Press, 2005), 144.

21. Deborah Johnson, *Iris Murdoch* (Brighton: Harvester, 1987), 17. Several other critics have noted how Freudian theory informs *A Severed Head*, among them Peter Conradi in *Iris Murdoch: The Saint and the Artist* (London: Macmillan, 1986) and Jack Turner in *Murdoch vs. Freud: A Freudian Look at an Anti-Freudian* (New York: Peter Lang, 1993).

22. A. S. Byatt, for example, sees the novel as a comic contest between Freudian and Sartrean truths in which 'the protagonist has to come to grips with his own sexual violence and fear, and with the "urge towards self-coincidence", or whether his acts are his own' (A. S. Byatt, *Degrees of Freedom: The Novels of Iris Murdoch* [London: Chatto and Windus, 1970], 105). Bran Nicol has offered a persuasive reading of the Freudian uncanny as repetition related to sexual desire in the novel (Bran Nicol, *Iris Murdoch: The Retrospective Fiction* [1999; 2nd edition Basingstoke: Palgrave Macmillan, 2004], 113–21).

23. Iris Murdoch, *A Severed Head* (1961; Harmondsworth: Penguin, 1963), 182. All subsequent references are to this edition and are given in the text, referred to as *SH*.

24. Richard Marsh's novella *The Beetle* (1897) (in which a monstrous and voracious beetle of Egyptian origin had dire effects on both men and women as it metamorphosed from human form) is an example of this. In the same year, Count Dracula appeared in London in Bram Stoker's novel, *Dracula*. (See Ken Gelder's discussion of Dracula's 'Jewish' characteristics in *Reading the Vampire* [London: Routledge, 1994], 13–14.)

25. Cf., however, Bran Nicol's view that Martin's choice of Honor at the novel's close reveals his compulsion to continue choosing mother figures, albeit this time a phallic mother. *Iris Murdoch: The Retrospective Fiction*, 116.

26. Ian McEwan, whose work seems to have been influenced by Murdoch's fiction, explores much the same territory in *The Cement Garden* (1978).

27. Iris Murdoch, *The Bell* (Harmondworth: Penguin [1958], 1969), 104.

28. Iris Murdoch, *A Word Child* (St Albans; Triad/Panther [1975], 1976), 60.
29. Iris Murdoch, *The Italian Girl* (London: Vintage [1964], 2000), 15, 16 and 17.
30. See Murdoch's *The Bell*: 'Could one recognize refinements of good if one did not recognize refinements of evil, Michael asked himself' (117).
31. 'The two most "Gothic" novels, *The Unicorn* and *The Time of the Angels*, with their persistent images of bowers, mirrors and tapestries, recall Tennyson's "The Lady of Shalott" but pose the question, as Tennyson does not, of why the lady was imprisoned in the first place.' Deborah Johnson, *Iris Murdoch* (Brighton: Harvester, 1987), 65.
32. Iris Murdoch, *The Time of the Angels* (1966; Harmondsworth: Penguin, 1968), 165. All subsequent references are to this edition and are given in the text, referred to as *TA*.
33. Iris Murdoch, from the essay 'The Sublime and the Good' in Peter Conradi, ed., *Existentialist and Mystics: Writings on Philosophy and Literature* (London: Chatto & Windus, 1997), 205–20, 215.
34. Iris Murdoch, from the essay 'Literature and Philosophy' in *Existentialists and Mystics*, 1–30, 21.

8
'I Don't Want to be a [White] Girl': Gender, Race and Resistance in the Southern Gothic

Meredith Miller

'By watching her I began to think there was some skill involved in being a girl.'[1] So says Scout, white tomboy narrator of Harper Lee's 1963 novel, *To Kill a Mockingbird*. Scout's one role model for femininity is Calpurnia, her family's African-American servant. In *Mockingbird*, Lee pastiches a generic formula established more than a decade earlier by Carson McCullers and Truman Capote. Crucial ingredients in this recipe include Gothic effects, gender dissident white focalising characters, black women servants and the violence of Southern racism. The film adaptation of Lee's novel makes the struggle between Scout and Calpurnia over femininity even more explicit. In a scene where Calpurnia urges Scout to be more ladylike, Scout responds angrily, 'I don't want to be a girl.'[2] This chapter explores the relationship between these three things – race, gender and the Gothic – especially as they work within mid-twentieth-century Southern American literature. What use are Gothic effects in this body of work, and how can we think through their entanglement with narrative constructions of both race and femininity? The term which is under erasure in Scout's protest is 'white' as her 'ladylike'-ness is clearly racialised as white, yet her only point of feminine identification is as a black woman. Throughout this genre, constructions of race and gender both uphold and undo each other, revealing their complex interrelation through Gothic effects. An examination of these relationships must necessarily involve sorting through a number of issues, both generic and methodological.

Generic contentions

'Southern Gothic' is a term widely used in popular discourse to describe a particular body of literature, but which critics are far more reluctant to employ. Both Carson McCullers and Truman Capote are more often referred to by critics as writers belonging to a 'Southern Renaissance' which began with Faulkner. Though the criticism must, and does, address the use of the uncanny and the grotesque in Southern writers of this period, the use of the term Gothic is always heavily qualified. The primary critical location of the Gothic in late eighteenth- and early nineteenth-century Europe, specifically for English studies, in Britain, is a structuring factor in terms of the genre. There is a recurring argument that the Gothic is a particular response to historical trauma and that American writers simply do not have the long view of history necessary for 'true' Gothic literature. As Teresa Goddu puts it: 'The gothic's connection to American history is difficult to identify precisely because of the national and critical myths that America and its literature *have no history.*'[3]

In *Gothic America* (1997), Goddu examines the critical positioning of Edgar Allan Poe as a Southern writer. She demonstrates convincingly that the South and the generic term Gothic function as abjections for an America whose racial violence belies the Enlightenment ideals on which it purported to found itself. Locating the problem of race in the South and in the work of Southern writers allows the creation of an American literature free from the haunting of slavery. The South, in its abjection, becomes an uncanny place, a location of Gothic effects. The darkness in writers like Hawthorne and Melville, Goddu points out, then becomes a universalised darkness of the soul. Goddu builds heavily on the work of Toni Morrison, who first elucidated the relation between this 'existential' darkness and the construction of race in America.[4]

The presence of the uncanny and the grotesque in the work of writers such as Truman Capote and Carson McCullers (and William Faulkner, Flannery O'Connor and Harper Lee) has, by the mid-twentieth century, become an articulation of Southern-ness, a way of speaking back to America from inside a dissident Southern identity. As a body, their work also makes it clear that racial categorisation, specifically the otherness of black Americans, is necessary to the Gothic structure of this identity. More recent criticism has focused on the dissident gender identities of writers of the post-war Southern Renaissance. Capote and McCullers articulate a dissent not only from the dominant ideal of the American individual, but also from gendered ideals of Southern whiteness: in the

Southern voice they find layers of otherness. What, then, is the relation between their use of the African-American other, their protest against Southern whiteness and their use of dissident gender identities? How is each of these mechanisms embedded in the others?[5]

Critical models

It is important to remember that late eighteenth- and nineteenth-century British Gothic drew heavily on the culture of slavery and the uncanny return of the colonial other to the centre of culture. The young woman at the centre of the classic Gothic novel provided the focus for images of imprisonment, entrapment, and the struggle for release and self-determination. As Cynthia Wolff has put it, 'her business was to experience difficulty, not to get out of it'.[6] The metaphorical equation of women with slaves informed both feminism and imaginative fiction of the period. The undefined threat which haunted the Gothic heroine often took the form of the cultural other, whether of Catholic Europe or the colonies. Her entrapment was the sign of her femininity, both as its positive expression in passivity and as the substance of her enlightened individual struggle against the constraints of culture. Gayatri Spivak has argued, in her reading of *Jane Eyre* (1847), that the presence of the colonial threat in the form of abject femininity is crucial to the articulation of the white feminist heroine of the nineteenth-century female Gothic novel.[7]

A move made by some more recent work on Southern Gothic shifts white central characters back into a position of otherness, as seekers of liberatory representation. Critics such as William White Tyson Pugh, Clare Whatling and Rachel Adams identify the description of white Southern Gothic characters as 'freakish' with their queerness, their refusal to conform to norms of sexuality and gender. 'I surmise', says Pugh, '[that earlier, more hostile critics'] indictment of the characters are based on the characters' location in a Gothic setting and the heterosexist labelling of both sexual-orientation difference and gender cross-over as grotesque.'[8] One interesting characteristic of this criticism is that it does not seem to take up the work of writers such as Jean Toomer or Richard Wright as Gothic. The argument might be usefully reformed into a question. Two questions, really. First, why do a particular group of white Southern writers at mid-century place sexually dissident characters together with Gothic elements? Second, what is the relationship between these sexually dissident white focalising characters and the stories they tell us about the racism which pervades Southern culture?

What is the relation between gender dissidence, racism and Gothic structures?

Such an analysis must raise questions of methodology. What is the most accurate or useful way to contextualise the operations of the uncanny and the grotesque and their relationship to the social and historical upheaval we associate with moments of Gothic resurgence in the history of the novel? Eve Kosofsky Sedgwick, in *The Coherence of Gothic Conventions* (1980), argues that a psychological model of the Gothic

> is one in which superficial layers of convention and prohibition, called 'the rational,' conceal and repress a deep central well of primal material, 'the irrational,' which is the locus of the individual self, which could or should pass to the outside.[9]

Within this model, as Sedgwick points out, the self is located in the 'true depths' and the Gothic thus becomes, through psychoanalytic discourse, explicable through an identitarian model of the self seeking emancipation (11). Sedgwick is not arguing for a dismissal of this model, but rather asserting that 'the major gothic conventions are coherent in terms that do not depend on that psychological model, though they can sometimes be deepened by it' (12). She reads the spatial metaphors of the Gothic in terms of isolation and entrapment (being 'massively blocked off') still very much focused on the self, though she does move on to complicate this. The psychological model, with its focus on the individual self, allows for a critique in terms of gender, and, following Fanon, of race through gender. Thus, the psychological critique can provide an extension to wider structures of social power, yet it sometimes limits or distracts from the wider structure by universalising the psychological self. Attempted cultural materialist critiques which place Gothic texts within these wider structures of power still fall back on something like a psychological model when explaining how these power relationships are displayed through uncanny and horrific effects in Gothic fiction.

Thus, from a range of critical perspectives, monstrously racialised and gendered characters represent 'others' in a psychological sense, projections of the inner self articulated through wider discursive structures of otherness. Hence, for example, the many discussions of Gothic doubles as split halves of the self.

I would like to follow Sedgwick in a way, and to extend her most basic premise to twentieth-century American Gothic. That is to say that these conventions are coherent in a way that may include, but does not depend on, a psychological model to explain them. I would argue that twentieth-century Southern American writers draw on the Gothic tradition because it is a facility for expressing the relationship *between* structures of masculine and feminine sexuality and structures of race and culture. This is specifically a relationship between the individual self (expressed through identity) and the social/culture machine expressed as structures of race, class, gender and sexuality. Gothic effects, in their dependence on both Enlightenment notions of the essential inner self and wider discourses of identity-based power (as race and gender, for example), are the perfect structures for this expression. The Gothic remains powerful not because we can theorise it as a relation between self and historical trauma, but because it is, *in itself*, the perfect method for the articulation of this relationship. The Gothic mode articulates what Raymond Williams might call the possible consciousness of these connections and in this sense the Gothic mode is already theoretical.[10]

The uncanny and the social machine

Rachel Adams gives a very suggestive reading of *The Member of the Wedding* (1946) and *Clock Without Hands* (1961) which begins to unpick the relations between racial and sexual categorisations in Carson McCullers' fiction. Adams' analysis is grounded in ideas of grotesque and transgressive bodies and bodily presentations. Following Clare Whatling, Rachel Adams and others, we can understand Frankie's freakish 'too tall' body, her inappropriate hair and unfeminine knees and elbows, her various transgendered experiences with clothing and her desire to be a 'boy' soldier as a kind of queering of puberty, a refusal of calm entry into feminine heterosexual signification. But we ought to read this grotesque, gender transgressive, Gothic body in its relation to the operations of the uncanny within the novel. Adams' discussion goes a long way in delineating the queer in terms of sexed and gendered bodies, but never fully articulates the operations of race in this formation.[11] The uncanny moments within the text, their structure, position and contents, reveal the complex embedding of race and sexuality within the semiotic material available to the white Southern writer at mid-century. One important exception to the critical trend is Thadious M. Davis' important essay examining the differences between the novel and the subsequent play. Davis sees the novel as an examination of the interconnectedness of racial and gendered identity and the play as an ideological recuperation that rests on more conventional and comfortable separations of identity.[12]

Throughout *The Member of the Wedding* the semiotic chain of blackness operates to create uncanny effects and structure Gothic operations.

Night, darkness, obscured visibility, radical absence and the realm of pre-verbal pleasure are all associated with African-American identity in the novel's descriptions and plotting. Berenice sings 'with a dark jazz voice' that beats 'like the heart that beats in your head when you have a fever' (44). A black horn player creates music that is 'low and dark and sad' and floats across the night-time town with 'sassy nigger trickiness' (54–5). In *Playing in the Dark*, Morrison examines the ways in which white American writers 'choose to talk about themselves through and within a sometimes allegorical, sometimes metaphorical, but always choked representation of an Africanist presence' (17). The method she articulates has particular resonance for the Southern Gothic, both in its textual effects and in their critical reception. At a central moment in the novel Berenice describes the state of blackness as Gothic entrapment, and likens it to the universal and existential alienation of selfness itself. In this conversation between Frankie and Berenice, the narrative allies Frankie's own pubescent alienation directly with the violent entrapment of black Americans and Berenice assures Frankie (and the reader) that 'the point is that we all caught. And we try in one way or another to widen ourself free' (141–2). Thus blackness becomes a metaphor for the self, a stand-in for subjectivity which precludes subjectivity itself. These are precisely the operations which Morrison describes in *Playing in the Dark*. Here also we can see that the traditional Gothic association of femininity and entrapment cannot be thought in America outside of the haunting association of entrapment with blackness. (Note, for example, the contemporary mid-century discourse of 'white slavery'.)

During Frankie's 'last dinner' in her father's house the novel's three central characters, Frankie, Berenice and John Henry spend a long afternoon philosophising. Here, Berenice remembers her dead husband as we are told that as she spoke 'the dead were walking in her heart' (109). There follows a series of images and descriptions in which death is associated with blackness, darkness, absence and African-American identity. F. Jasmine (Frankie) remembers, for example, seeing the dead Lon Baker, 'a coloured boy', with 'his throat cut open like a crazy shivering mouth that spoke ghost words into the April sun' (110). Finally F. Jasmine muses that 'the dead feel nothing, hear nothing, see nothing: only black' (112). Here Berenice, like her Big Mama, becomes a medium with uncanny powers of perception, ghostly black bodies uncannily speak and death itself becomes blackness.

So far McCullers' imagery and character constructions follow the pattern of an American Gothic tradition which associates African-American identity with blackness, death, absence and the revenant. But McCullers has also created Berenice as a character with a subjective position, struggling, as many white writers do, with the tension between their black characters both as markers of subjective positions and as objects marked by the white racial fetish. As Berenice speaks in the novel, her words and her gaze create whiteness as a marked category. She describes Frankie's brother and his bride as a 'nice white couple' (38). This description is not incidental; it marks a radical shift in the politics of the white American novel. In case we may miss it, Berenice reminds us of it by staring back at the reader with her one blue eye, the signifier of the white gaze, displaced and rendered uncanny, suddenly marked as artificial by its presence in her brown face. Introduced at the outset of the novel, Berenice's glass eye is the first entrance of the uncanny into the novel:

> There was only one thing wrong about Berenice – her left eye was bright blue glass. It stared out fixed and wild from her quiet, coloured face, and why she had wanted a blue eye nobody human would ever know. Her right eye was dark and sad. (9)

The Member of the Wedding is not, cannot be, free from the racial constructions which mark all of American literature – which in a very real sense *are* American literature. McCullers does not and cannot step outside of these, in the sense that, even in literature, one can only think oneself halfway out of any ideological structure. What she creates are tensions and paradoxes that make these constructions visible – again, a kind of possible consciousness. The novel's protest against the constraints of gender and the constraints of race make the interdependence of the two readable. The subjective positions it presents mark a dissent from within themselves, a fracturing of the identitarian self which is best expressed as Gothic.

As the title suggests, Frankie's obsession with her brother's wedding marks her own sense of herself as an outsider and 'a member of nothing in the world' (7). Her queer desire to be the third term in the signal heterosexual moment of coupling is her own answer to the sense of subjective loss that accompanies her entry into full social identity. In the scene where Frankie makes the decision to 'go with them' and become a part of their wedding, another fetish is laid, seemingly incidentally, alongside the heterosexual fetish of the wedding. 'It was the sad horn of some coloured boy' (54) which elicited in Frankie the first recognition of loss and desire. The horn is 'low and dark and sad' then 'a wild jazz spangle' (54) which transfixes her. When the music stops abruptly Frankie is stunned: 'The tune was left broken, unfinished. And the drawn tightness she could no longer stand. She felt she must do something wild and sudden that never had been done before' (54–5). It is this revelatory moment of loss that leads her to the decision that she is 'going off with the two of them to whatever place they will ever go' (55). This scene bears a remarkable resemblance to the one from Marie Cardinal's *The Words to Say It* (1975) which Toni Morrison describes in the opening of *Playing in the Dark*. The experience of jazz, sign of black sensibility, induces a moment of panic, loss and subjective revelation in the white protagonist. Frankie's profound moment of recognition and loss, of subjectivity itself, of her skewed relation to identity and sexuality, involves the interrelation of two fetish objects, one racial (the music) and the other heterosexual (the wedding). The impossibility of Frankie's desires, her inability to articulate them in readable ways, is never answered in the novel. At the climax she is excluded, turned out of the wedding, and the resolution finds her in blissful domestic enactment of her love for another girl and she remains as loquacious, yet as inarticulate, as always.[13]

The only character in the novel able to express desiring subjectivity is Berenice who is the only adult female fully present in the novel and thus the only model of femininity. (Janice, Jarvis' bride, is a ghostly white presence, occurring only twice in memory and never existing in the present tense of the narrative.) The stories Berenice tells about her lost husband Ludie and the men she has unsuccessfully replaced him with are clear and strong articulations of desire, and also tales of uncanny repetition. Having lost Ludie, Berenice pursues a series of men who signify him through either synecdoche or metonymy. One has Ludie's thumbs, the other has bought his overcoat in a second-hand shop; these pieces of her man, 'make a shiver run from [her] head to [her] heels' (124). Yet desire, for Berenice, is as tricky and misleading as prayer. The men who make her shiver are drunk and abusive and none matches the love or kindness of her first marriage. Ultimately, she marries the prosperous and unremarkable T. T., who does not make her shiver. These stories constitute the sum of Frankie's sexual education. Berenice is the role model for feminine sexual experience, but, despite her several marriages, is never the subject of bridal fantasies. Heterosexual feminine fantasy for Frankie is clearly white, associated with the novel's many images of snow and ice – of Northernness. 'For the wedding,' Frankie muses, 'I ought to have long bright yellow hair' (25). She as tomboy and Berenice as black are equally excluded from the ideal of heterosexual femininity: neither possesses its proper signifiers. The fantasy woman is both white and femme, with long yellow hair.

The structure of the novel follows, to some extent, the *bildungsroman* and Frankie's semi-orphan state foregrounds her identity formation and self-determination. Berenice is confined bodily to the maternal stereotype which characterises her position in the Southern novel, and her function as the mother substitute extends even to Frankie's continuing experiences of fractured subjectivity. During the long afternoon discussion of death, God and utopian fantasies which covers so much space in the novel, Frankie asks persistent questions about the nature of subjective experience, about this troubling separation called the self:

> Doesn't it strike you as strange that I am I, and you are you?... And we can look at each other, and touch each other, and stay together year in and year out in the same room. Yet always I am I, and you are you. And I can't ever be anything else but me, and you can't ever be anything else but you. Have you ever thought of that? And does it ever seem to you strange? (135–6)

Yes, Berenice has thought of that. She is black in America and the novel repeatedly invites us to read the question of subjective identity on two levels, as both a problem of existential loss and a problem of social segregation whereby each metaphorically figures the other. As the conversation stops, the three characters in the room dissolve together into inexplicable tears, joined in a place before words. At this moment Frankie, sitting on Berenice's lap, dissolves into her and the older woman's character function is revealed as the background material of Frankie's subjectivity. The place out of which her move toward *bildung* comes:

> F. Jasmine rolled her head and rested her face against Berenice's shoulder. She could feel Berenice's soft big ninnas against her back, and her soft wide stomach, her warm solid legs. She had been breathing very fast, but after a minute her breath slowed down so that she breathed in time with Berenice; the two of them were close together as one body... (140–1)

McCullers cannot, or does not, fully escape the racial-sexual paradigm which positions Berenice as the pre-symbolic ground of Frankie's white subjectivity. The Gothic map of the segregated town works in the same way, with its black preconscious half-concealed in alleyways speaking the ghostly words beyond death.

In McCullers' formation, the sexual experiences of Frankie and Berenice echo each other. Frankie, at 12 and five-sixths years old, is growing alarmingly tall and this height is a sign of excessiveness, of being outside the bounds of femininity: 'unless she could somehow stop herself, she would grow to be over nine feet tall. And what would be a lady who is over nine feet high? She would be a Freak' (25). Berenice later reflects that being married (sexually active) at 13 'stunted her growth' (35–6). Frankie's freakish, uncontrollable body makes puberty a queer place, a place where gender does not sit properly. Heterosexual experience, which makes women smaller, is a half-glimpsed horror just around the bend; Frankie cannot read its signs throughout most of the novel, and when she finally can she rejects them.

Her one sexual encounter, with a soldier in the Blue Moon, again associates heterosexuality with whiteness, and both with horror and terror. Frankie does not know what has happened physically when the soldier tries to kiss her, and she recoils in bodily horror from the abject experience of having another tongue in her mouth. Here, we are reminded of Berenice in the uncanny return of the blue-eyed gaze: 'His light blue eyes, set close together, were staring at her with a peculiar look – with a filmed softness, like eyes that have been washed with milk' (160). Whiteness, still tied to heterosexuality, is now rendered uncanny, thrown out of the centre and into the place of horror; yet these moments of subjective rupture, so easily read through psychoanalysis, are also profoundly historical.

In *The Member of the Wedding*, McCullers creates a set of characterisations and narrative structures that reveal the interdependence of race and sexuality as identity structures. Frankie's queer desire to become the third term in her brother's wedding is also a racial fantasy of whiteness. Likewise, Berenice's own sexual position is determined by her blackness, and vice versa. Neither is articulated without the other, for in the American South, the structure of race, and its violence, are enacted through the heterosexual economy.

Whiteness and the historical revenant

Truman Capote's *Other Voices, Other Rooms* (1948) also presents characters whose whiteness is the sign of horrific threat. The threatening Miss Amy, for example, is excessive in both her whiteness and her femininity. Like *Member of the Wedding*, *Other Voices, Other Rooms* is an interrogation of Southern white femininity which reveals the interdependence of heterosexuality and racial violence in the American South. The novel's central character, Joel Knox, is defined by his white femininity. We first see him through the gaze of a truck driver who is repulsed by his lack of masculinity:

> Radclif eyed the boy over the rim of his beer glass, not caring much
> for the looks of him. He had his notions of what a 'real' boy should
> look like, and this kid somehow offended them. He was too pretty,
> too delicate and fair-skinned; each of his features was shaped with
> sensitive accuracy, and a girlish tenderness softened his eyes...[14]

Here common signifiers of both race and gender (in skin colour and
features) define Joel as feminine, and femininity as whiteness and this
white femininity is his defining characteristic.

Later in the novel Joel expresses reticence about swimming naked in
front of his butch white friend Idabel. Idabel chides him thus:

> 'Son,' she said, and spit between her fingers, 'what you've got in your
> britches is no news to me, and no concern of mine: hell, I've fooled
> around with nobody but boys since first grade. I never think like I'm
> a girl; you've got to remember that or we can't never be friends.'...she
> knocked one fist against the other...and said 'I want so much to be a
> boy: I would be a sailor, I would ...' (108)

'I don't want to get married,' Idabel says later,

> 'Who the hell said I wanted to get married? Now you listen, boy: you
> behave decent, you behave like we're brothers, or don't you behave
> at all. Anyway, we don't want to do no sissy thing like pick grapes, I
> thought maybe we could join the navy...' (144)

Idabel's gender dissident desires suggest embarking on a process of *bildung*, leaving the rural setting in which the novel opens, confronting
the world and ultimately finding a place in social order and a sense of
self-identity. Indeed it seems that Idabel sets off to do just this, but her
quest takes her out of the Southern swamp and out of the novel, in both
of which Joel Knox remains firmly fixed. For Joel Knox is trapped in a
very Gothic way in a very Gothic setting. Action and passivity, mobility
and imprisonment, and their relation to positions of gender, remain one
of the abiding concerns of Gothic fiction. The novel uses established
Gothic conventions to place Joel in a narrative position which will fem-
inise him as effectively as possible: it is a position of passivity, entrapment and isolation. In contrast, Idabel is mobile and active, fighting,
running from one place to another, swashbuckling around the woods

and eventually leaving altogether. If this novel were a simple gender inversion of the Gothic formula, Idabel might be our hero but it is not, and she leaves. Joel, however, is most certainly a Gothic heroine, and his gender dissident positioning as such is one of many devices which Capote uses to queer the traditional structure of the Gothic novel.

At the outset of *Other Voices, Other Rooms* we learn that Joel has lost his mother and is going to find his absent father in a remote and decaying old mansion on a disused plantation ominously named Skully's Landing. Joel's father turns out to be trapped in a paralysed body, and Joel has been tricked into coming to Skully's Landing by means of a forged letter written by his predatory older uncle. If there is such a thing as a set of classic Gothic elements, they are here: labyrinthine and decaying architectural structures, rife with violent history; dead, missing and entrapped parents; false documents and misleading letters. In addition, the novel contains loquacious servants, dark forests full of secrets, apparently supernatural apparitions and a healthy dose of pathetic fallacy.

In his preface to the 1968 anniversary edition of the novel, Capote discusses his influences. He is careful to repudiate the critical placement of the novel in a twentieth-century Southern Gothic tradition, claiming that Carson McCullers, Eudora Welty and William Faulkner were not influences on the work. Instead he names a number of nineteenth-century writers, including Emily Brontë. Poe, he tells us, is the only writer who might be seen as 'a necessary antecedent'[15] to *Other Voices*. We cannot know how Capote means us to take this connection, particularly as he narrates the 'revelation' of the narrative as a sudden and 'unconscious' moment of creative vision. Capote's description of the novel's tropes and narrative structures as 'intuitive' tempts critics into a psychoanalytic/autobiographical reading of its personal and social fractures, and away from any historicist positioning of the novel.

In any case Capote was clearly aware of the nineteenth-century Gothic tradition on which he drew and he takes these Gothic conventions and deliberately makes them queer. Twice in the novel, Joel comes upon Skully's Landing to see a group of black birds winging ominously around its chimneys. These birds are identified as chicken hawks in a clear reference to the queer desires of Joel's uncle, Cousin Randolph. Zoo Fever, the talkative and eccentric granddaughter of Skully's Landing slaves, is the garrulous servant who seems at first to be Joel's only friend. She yearns to shoot these chicken hawks, but is forbidden by Cousin Randolph. This uncle is the queer version of the powerful and wealthy patriarch who imprisons and seeks to possess the Gothic heroine, in this case Joel. The apparition, of a woman in old-fashioned dress, which

Joel sees appearing and disappearing in the upper windows of Skully's Landing, is eventually given its customary rational explanation: it turns out to be Cousin Randolph in drag.

Both the novel itself and the 1968 preface show that Capote is well aware of the psychoanalytic potential of the Gothic. He deliberately presents and then undermines the models of interior and exterior, liberation and entrapment theorised by Sedgwick. He uses all of the familiar Gothic tropes and structures, exploiting them for their associations with the limits of the self, and the resonance of masculinity and femininity as they stand at those limits. But, by the end of the novel, the sinking and decaying house becomes a haven and the predatory older man becomes a desired partner. For Capote, these conventions neither uphold the oppositions which traditionally delineate them nor achieve the resolutions that would synthesise them. The conventions do their work, and then Capote takes them someplace where we might not have expected them to go in a Gothic novel. Our heroine is not saved, liberated or married, nor does he desire to be. Cousin Randolph is not revealed to be anything very different than what we see all along.

Within this narrative structure, Capote places Joel's trembling and resonating self, at moments of horror and terror, within wider structures of identity and social power. One such moment is a much-discussed passage in which Joel and Idabel confront a poisonous water moccasin snake which seems to Joel to possess his father's eyes. Once Joel sees the snake he begins to *come apart at the seams*. I use this phrase quite deliberately because as Joel stands confronted by the snake his consciousness, and its normal functions, break down. He cannot

> bring himself to make any sound, motion … and all over Joel began to sing, as though already bitten. Idabel, coming up behind him, looked over his shoulder. 'Jesus,' she breathed 'oh jesus,' and at the touch of her hand he broke up inside: the creek froze, was like a horizontal cage, and his feet seemed to sink, as though the beam on which they stood was made up of quicksand. How did Mr Sansom [his father]'s eyes come to be in a moccasin's head … (179–80)

Stranded here Joel tries to piece together a narrative of the day and of his life, but cannot:

> It was this way: they were bound for the Cloud Hotel, yes, the Could Hotel, where a man with a Ruby ring was swimming underwater, yes, and Randolph was looking through his almanac writing letters

to Hong-Kong, to Port-o'-Spain, yes and poor Jesus was dead, killed by Toby the cat (no, Toby was a baby), by a nest of chimney sweeps falling in a fire. And Zoo: was she in Washington yet? And was it snowing? And why was Mr Sansom staring at him so hard? It was really very, very rude (as Ellen would say) really very rude indeed of Mr Samson never to close his eyes. (180)

The narrative, focalised through Joel Knox, both telescopes and falls apart here. Many of the novel's major events are repeated in rapid succession, but confusedly and incorrectly because the consciousness of the narrative's focaliser has come unstuck in a classic experience of Gothic horror. The interior/exterior boundaries of the self are breached here and must be re-established. Once disrupted, the boundaries of Joel's self, reiterated through terror, are re-established through the action of gender.

Joel carries a confederate army sword given to him by Zoo's grandfather, Jesus, but it is Idabel, once Joel freezes with terror, who must seize the sword. 'Spinning [Joel] around and pushing him safely aside she pulled the sword out of his hand' (180) and killed the snake. The obvious psychoanalytic reading is often given to this passage. Idabel the butch seizes the phallic sword, which hangs ineffectually from femme Joel's waist and so slays the phallic father.

Again, activity and passivity are related to gender here, through the medium of the sword which Joel, paralysed, cannot use, and Idabel must come forth and forcefully wield. So Capote has inverted gender roles here, detached them from biological sex, and quite deliberately manipulated the by then widely popular psycho-sexual symbols in order to do so. Most queer readings of the novel, such as William White Tison Pugh's excellent generic reading of it, stop here.[16] In doing so, some critics have presented *Other Voices, Other Rooms* as a gay novel in terms which were not fully defined at the time of its creation and which reduce it to a kind of identitarian coming out story. What gets lost in this reading is what the novel does with race, or rather, the way in which what it does with race and what it does with sex/gender are part of one complete structure.

Gothic novels traditionally destabilise gender roles by presenting monstrous examples of masculinity and femininity. The likes of Lady Audley and the Marquis of Montalt demonstrate the dangers of excessive adherence to either masculine or feminine behaviours. Gothic heroines negotiate new relationships to femininity which allow them room for self-determination. At the same time, nineteenth-century Gothic novels represent and articulate anxieties around the relation of masculinity and femininity to race and culture. Ann Radcliffe promoted a specifically anti-Catholic masculinity; the Brontës, through characters such as Heathcliff and Bertha Mason, ask questions about the stability of categories of race, English whiteness specifically. Novels such as *Jane Eyre* explore the relationship between racialised and gendered categories of identity. Poe's work examines the philosophical problem of the subject within the context of colonial exploration, slavery and American racial hierarchies. And it is this that makes the established form so useful for Capote. For his characters are not just representations of masculinity and femininity, queer or otherwise. They are feminine and masculine within a context of race. Again, criticism on the novel seems to entirely ignore the way in which race structures the possibility of the queer self. Gary Richards, for example, gives a discussion of Joel's defining femininity, and its implications for models of gender and sexuality without ever mentioning the text's structuring racial formations.[17]

The relation between race, gender and the Gothic is evident on at least two levels within the structure of *Other Voices*. First, femininity and masculinity are a matter of whiteness and blackness at the level of characterisation. Idabel's properly feminine sister deplores her twin's butch aims:

> 'Sister's avowed...ambition is she wants to be a farmer.' Joel said, 'What's wrong with that?' 'Now Mr Knox, surely you're just teasing,' said Florabel. 'Whoever heard of a decent white girl who wanted to be a farmer? Mama and me are too disgraced ...' (84)

Zoo Fever, by contrast, hauls heavy loads, 'mannishly straddles a chair at the table' (45) and wields a gun without eliciting the slightest comment about her gender from the other characters. Femininity is not something that belongs to females; it is something that belongs to white people, since Joel and Randolph also possess it.

Second, at the level of plot structure, it is race which provides the secret horror of Gothic history within the architecture of *Other Voices*. The Gothic setting which imprisons Joel Knox, like most Gothic settings, contains a terrible history which threatens to erupt into the present. In this case that history is slavery. One day, as Joel plays in the yard, he runs between the pillars of a burned-down section of Skully's Landing.

> And then, midway, between the pillars and a clump of goldenrod, he discovered a bell. It was a bell like those used in slave-days to

summon fieldhands from work; the metal had turned a mildewed green, and the platform on which it rested was rotten. (66)

Later the narrative confirms that this was in fact a slave bell. The neurotic Miss Amy, owner of Skully's Landing, tries to dig it up and remove it. Or rather, ironically, she orders her black servant to do so. The bell will not budge, cannot be shifted and so it remains there, and its phantom tolling is heard at uncanny moments throughout the rest of the novel.

Certainly, the terrifying history and continuation of racial violence function recognisably as repression and its return for this, and other, Southern novels. What is unique here is the way in which Capote's narration consciously enables, or at least attempts, a subversion of the gendered structures which uphold racial violence. Myths of gender and sexuality keep racial power in place. American structures of racial violence are founded on the belief that white women are the repository of a femininity which must be protected from the excessive masculinity of black men. The belief in this excessive masculinity derives, as Frantz Fanon and Eldridge Cleaver have variously demonstrated, from a relegation to physical labour and the consequent association with the body. This in turn has the subversive effect of feminising white men in gendered racial contrast. Black women again are masculinised, as Zoo Fever is, as both working bodies and counterpoints to white femininity. Post-bellum lynchings and terror campaigns raised these race/gender constructions to the mythic proportions which Richard Wright exploited and exploded in his novels. The myth of the black rapist and his white female victim, and the reality of the rape of black women by white men delineated a system of race which rested upon mythical gender norms. It made necessary a collective reliance on visibility and invisibility, disavowal and repression.[18]

One can easily see the refusal of femininity by young white female characters, as those of McCullers' novels, as a refusal to participate in the gendered terms of racial violence. The material out of which this protest is formed involves a repressed historical violence and terror which cannot be fully contained in a psychoanalytic model. This model, dependent on the universalised self with its radically formed sense of interiority and exteriority, cannot usefully articulate the relations among this self and the social historical context within which it is formed. For this McCullers and Capote deploy the Gothic formula.

Other Voices exposes race/gender norms in the first instance through the use of Gothic conventions. Joel and Randolph expose the instability of white masculinity and Idabel, Florabel and Amy the absurdity and instability of white femininity. These characters resist the gendered positions on which the myths upholding American racial violence rest. At its final climax, the novel presents the story of Zoo's rape and torture at the hands of three white men. The rape of black women had been virtually invisible in the popular white American novel for nearly 80 years, since the end of the Civil War and, with it, the slave narrative. Here the repressed knowledge of American racial violence returns at the pivotal moment of the novel, the moment at which Joel's fundamental experience of the self within horror occurs.

The reader experiences the episode second-hand, as Zoo relates it to Joel, who remains the focaliser of our experience. Once two men have raped her, a third is forced to expose his impotence to Zoo, and he visits his shame and anger upon her body by burning her with the ubiquitous Southern cigar. Again, Capote manipulates the psychological model, depicting Joel's struggle to keep Zoo's story repressed, while voicing it transforms Zoo into the crucified saviour (her father's name is Jesus).

> Joel plugged his ears; what Zoo said was ugly, he was sick-sorry she'd ever come back, she ought to be punished. 'Stop that, Zoo,' he said, 'I won't listen, I won't …' but Zoo's lips quivered, her eyes twisted towards the inner vision; and in the roar of silence she was a pantomime: the joy of Jesus demented her face and glittered like sweat…she was a cross, she was crucified. He was without hearing and it was more terrible for that. (216–17)

Capote has made the connection between Zoo's rape and Joel's confrontation with the snake for us, through the climactic impotence of white masculinity within each scene. Zoo's narration of her rape, presented without any invitation to voyeurism, forms the second scene (after the snake episode) in which Joel's conscious perception fails in a moment of horror and terror. I have not seen a queer reading of *Other Voices* which discusses Zoo's rape as part of the book's overall presentation of sexuality. This is an omission which closes down the complexity of a very important period in queer American fiction. The period beginning with McCullers, perhaps, and ending in Harper Lee's easy pastiche in *To Kill a Mockingbird* of what had by then become a formula, allowed a fictional exploration of the multiplicity and complexity of race/gender systems which was later closed down by identity politics. Zoo's rape and Joel's (un)listening to it must be read as part of the whole structure of race and gender within the novel and must complicate it.

Race often remains under erasure as attempts are made to reclaim and canonise white Southern Gothic writers as radically queer or feminist. I would argue that this reflects a post-war world in which movements for liberation were/are based in an identity politics which forces subjects to choose between sets of monolithic positions. The queer narration of post-war Southern Gothic is specifically suited to exposing the structure of American racial power, because that power rests upon the construction of norms of identity both racial and sexual. These mythical norms, with an inordinate degree of power vested in them, and their dependence on the disavowal of historical violence and trauma, create monstrous anxieties. For mid-twentieth-century Southern writers seeking to express dissent from a violent history of raced and gendered power, Gothic conventions enabled the depiction of both the repression and the haunting of a violent past, and of the instability of gender. Joel's actions in the mediated rape scene are emblematic of the power and the limits of this utterance. Stopping his ears, he reveals his, and the novel's, ability to reach only halfway out of its ideological context. That moment of half-hearing and half-saying both employs and exposes the operations of the black fetish for white writers and readers. The Gothic mode, with its complex operations of repression and return, its function as interface between the psychological and the historical, was particularly suited to the task of expressing the crisis and resisting the power of American racial/sexual identities in the twentieth century.

Notes

1. Harper Lee, *To Kill a Mockingbird* (London: Vintage Classics, 2004), 125. All subsequent references are to this edition and are given in the text.
2. Robert Mulligan (Director), *To Kill a Mockingbird* (Universal Pictures, 1962).
3. Teresa Goddu, *Gothic America: Narrative, History and Nation* (New York: Columbia University Press, 1997), 9, italics in the original. All subsequent references are to this edition and are given in the text.
4. Toni Morrison, *Playing in the Dark: Whiteness and the Literary Imagination* (Cambridge, MA: Harvard University Press, 1992). All subsequent references are to this edition and are given in the text.
5. Cynthia Wu's discussion of McCullers' short fiction is significant here. Wu examines the use of ethnic white characters as 'substitutes' for African-American racial otherness in the short stories, and argues that this disrupts the fixed racial economy of the South in McCullers' fiction as it did historically. See Cynthia Wu, 'Expanding Southern Whiteness: Reconceptualising Ethnic Difference in the Short Fiction of Carson McCullers', *Southern Literary Journal* 34/1 (2001), 44–55.
6. Cynthia Griffin Wolff, 'The Radcliffean Gothic Model: A Form for Feminine Sexuality', *Modern Language Studies* 9/3 (Autumn, 1979), 100.

7. See Gayatri Chakravorty Spivak, 'Three Women's Texts and a Critique of Imperialism', *Critical Inquiry* 12/2 (Autumn, 1985), 243–61.
8. William White Tison Pugh, 'Boundless Hearts in a Nightmare World: Queer Sentimentalism and Southern Gothicism in Truman Capote's *Other Voices, Other Rooms*', *Mississippi Quarterly* 51/4 (1998), 663–82, 668.
9. Eve Kosofsky Sedgwick, *The Coherence of Gothic Conventions* (North Stratford, New Hampshire: Ayer, 1999), 11. All subsequent references are to this edition and are given in the text.
10. See for example Raymond Williams, 'Base and Superstructure in Marxist Cultural Theory' in John Higgins (ed.) *The Raymond Williams Reader* (Oxford: Blackwell, 2001), 158–78.
11. See Rachel Adams, '"A Mixture of Delicious and Freak:" The Queer Fiction of Carson McCullers', *American Literature* 71/3 (September, 1999), 551–83; Clare Whatling, 'Reading Miss Amelia: Critical Strategies in the Construction of Sex, Gender, Sexuality, the Gothic and Grotesque' in Hugh Stevens and Caroline Howlett (eds) *Modernist Sexualities* (Manchester: Manchester University Press, 2000), 239–50; and Brian Mitchell-Peters, 'Camping the Gothic: Que(e)ring Sexuality' in Truman Capote's *Other Voices, Other Rooms'*. *Journal of Homosexuality* 39/1 (2000), 107–38. In *Lovers and Beloveds: Sexual Otherness and Southern Fiction, 1936–1961* (Baton Rouge, LA: Louisiana State University Press, 2005), Gary Richards' discussion of *The Member of the Wedding* gives only a cursory discussion of race in a single paragraph.
12. See Thadious M. Davis, 'Erasing the We of Me and Rewriting the Racial Script: Carson McCullers Two *Member*(s) *of the Wedding*', in Beverly Lyon Clark and Melvin J. Friedman (eds) *Critical Essays on Carson McCullers* (New York: G. K. Hall, 1996), 206–19.
13. Interestingly, Louise Westling reads this scene against a later scene involving waltz music without ever remarking upon the racial construction of music in both. Westling is at pains to place McCullers in a high modernist tradition, following Kate Chopin and Virginia Woolf, and as such reads the novel as about psychic capitulation to femininity without remarking that this femininity is white. See Louise Westling, 'Tomboys and Revolting Femininity' in Beverly Lyon Clark and Melvin J. Friedman (eds) *Critical Essays on Carson McCullers* (New York: G. K. Hall, 1996), 155–65.
14. Truman Capote, *Other Voices, Other Rooms* (London: Heinemann, 1948), 4. All subsequent references are to this edition and are given in the text.
15. Truman Capote, 'Preface' to *Other Voices, Other Rooms* (London: Heinemann, 1968), x.
16. William White Tison Pugh, 'Boundless Hearts in a Nightmare World: Queer Sentimentalism and Southern Gothicism in Truman Capote's *Other Voices, Other Rooms*', *Mississippi Quarterly* 51/4 (1998), 663–82.
17. See, specifically, chapter 2, 'Truman Capote, William Goyen and the Gendering of Male Homosexuality' in Gary Richards (ed.), *Lovers and Beloveds: Sexual Otherness and Southern Fiction, 1936–1961* (Baton Rouge, LA: Louisiana State University Press, 2005), 29–61.
18. As early as 1919, the NAACP was working to upset this myth by publicising details of the lynching of Southern black women. See Barbara Foley, 'In the Land of Cotton: Economics and Violence in Jean Toomer's *Cane*', *African American Review* 32/2 (Summer, 1998), 181–98.

9
Children of the Night: Shirley Jackson's Domestic Female Gothic

Andrew Smith

Shirley Jackson was one of the most popular writers working in America from the 1940s to the 1960s. During her lifetime (she died in 1965 at the age of 48) she published six novels, a collection of short stories, two books of non-fiction focusing on her domestic life, and three books for children. Although it was not her first tale in print her literary career was effectively launched by the publication of her short story 'The Lottery' in *The New Yorker* in June 1948 which dealt with the inner tensions and murderously arbitrary rules of what otherwise appeared to be a 'civilised' community, and caused some considerable controversy at the time. Her work is often either explicitly Gothic or contains a strong interest in the sinister. It is, however, only since the 1990s that critical interest in her work has flourished.

The publication of *Shirley Jackson: Essays on the Literary Legacy*, edited by Bernice M. Murphy in 2005, brought together a range of important views·on her work by significant critics including Darryl Hattenhauer who in *Shirley Jackson's American Gothic* (2003), had argued that Jackson's writings should be seen within the context of an emerging postmodernism.[1] Indeed, how to critically situate and theoretically explicate Jackson's work became a key feature of the new critical approaches to it. Hattenhauer, for example, also claims that the complexities of her work can be helpfully understood via psychoanalytical perspectives. This is a view shared by Jodey Castricano who argues that Jackson's *The Haunting of Hill House* (1959) develops a discourse on telepathy which invites 'us to reconsider what we *mean* by subjectivity' in a way which enables a reconsideration of Freud's concept of the Uncanny (an approach that will be explored further in this chapter).[2] Steven Bruhm has also recently argued that teaching *Hill House* to undergraduates helps to introduce them to psychoanalytical theories and related models of sexuality because of the novel's covert representations of lesbian desire.[3] However, this chapter explores how Jackson's work contributes to our understanding of the Female Gothic, an aspect which has not received the same type of sustained critical attention, even though many of the psychoanalytical implications of her work have clear resonances with the form. One important article in this respect is by Roberta Rubenstein whose work on Jackson's relationship to the Female Gothic and Jackson's non-fictional domestic writings will be explored below.[4] This chapter will argue that in order to appreciate Jackson's reworking of the Female Gothic it is important to examine her critically neglected non-fiction writings about her role as a wife, and above all as a mother, and to place such writings at the centre of her *oeuvre*. Such a reading also enables a reconsideration of how the political contexts of the period relating to gender helped to shape her work.

Jackson's *Hill House* has attracted considerable psychoanalytical attention because it appears to be a disturbing book about mental disturbance, one which culminates in the suicide of 32-year-old Eleanor Vance, the novel's principal focaliser, and to that degree the novel manifestly lacks the kind of social, economic and moral optimism that characterises the Radcliffean Gothic. However, the novel is also concerned with absent mothers in ways which do suggest points of contact with the Female Gothic. Eleanor is invited to Hill House by Dr Montague, a psychic researcher, who wants to gather around him a team of people who in the past had documented psychic experiences in order to see if they would be especially receptive to the supposedly haunted Hill House. Eleanor, who had an apparent psychic episode as a child, is free to join him because of the recent death of her invalid mother whom she has looked after for 11 years. Her mother's death is a release for Eleanor because 'her years with her mother had been built up devotedly around small guilts and reproaches, constant weariness, and unending despair'.[5] However, this is tinged with feelings of guilt that become projected onto Hill House, the history of which reveals that it has been inhabited by a series of psychologically damaged and/or eccentric families. It has become somewhat of a critical commonplace to note that the house represents the projection of Eleanor's ambivalent feelings about her dead mother as her mother seemingly returns in the guise of a number of emotional pleas made to Eleanor that are written on the walls of the house including 'HELP ELEANOR COME HOME' (146). These make the others in the house suspicious that Eleanor, somehow, is making it all happen. Eleanor in effect finds herself trapped between feelings of grief about her mother and guilty feelings of liberation. The mother seemingly calls her back while Eleanor is enthralled by the prospect of fashioning an identity which is free from her mother's influence. She notes with pleasure 'what a complete and separate thing I am, she thought, going from my red toes to the top of my head, individually an I, possessed of attributes belonging only to me' (83). The promised freedoms of the house are ultimately challenged by her unconscious projection of her mother which suggests that she is unable to free herself from the past.

Hattenhauer notes, but does not develop, the view that Jackson's writing 'seems to be a text-book illustration of Nancy Chodorow's theory of the Pre-Oedipal'.[6] Chodorow in *The Reproduction of Mothering* (1978) examines how models of subjectivity become shaped by narratives concerning gender. Motherhood, she argues, replicates a patriarchal ideology which supports the close bonding between mother and female child. She claims that sons are raised to become independent whereas daughters are trained to become mothers and that this training takes place by the mother enforcing the female child's emotional and psychological dependency upon them so that they replicate such feelings of dependency, feelings which, considered in political terms, function to keep women within private, domestic spaces (which also makes it difficult for the daughter to psychologically separate from their mother). For Chodorow this ideological process only becomes visible when it is manifested in pathological terms, when 'the mother does not recognize or denies the existence of the daughter as a separate person, and the daughter herself then comes not to recognize herself as a separate person' but 'as a continuation or extension of her mother'.[7] Significantly Chodorow notes that 'In all cases the pathology reflects, in exaggerated form, differences in what are in fact normal tendencies' (109). Normality here represents an ideological model of conventionally understood scripts of female dependency. In the pathological state mother and daughter become blurred so that for Chodorow they appear to be doubled because they come to share the same identity (109). *Hill House* expresses this in Eleanor's projection of her absent mother. However, while for Radcliffe identity was assured through the discovery of a 'lost' mother (as in, for example, Ellena Rosalba's unconscious quest for her mother in *The Italian* [1797]) Jackson revisits the whole notion of motherhood and the binds that it places upon emancipation. Eleanor is trapped in the past (the pull of her mother) and unable to embrace a future characterised by independence. The novel, in other words, makes visible the ideological tensions of motherhood even while they appear as psychological conflicts.

These tensions are not just about motherhood. They are, to follow and perhaps develop Chodorow, about what it means to be a daughter. Jackson's works are characterised by the presence of troubling female children who question parental authority. Such children are often demonically represented, as in her children's book *The Witchcraft of Salem Village* (1956), which recounts supposedly demonically afflicted children in Salem who in 1692 were responsible for a number of adults being executed for witchcraft. Jackson's *We Have Always Lived in the Castle* (1962) also addresses a similar theme in its focus on the young Merricat Blackwood who has poisoned many of her family.[8] However, it is in her critically much maligned, and Gothically titled, non-fiction *Life Among the Savages* (1953) and *Raising Demons* (1957) that the roots of the aporia confronted by Eleanor in *Hill House* are to be found. Both books are compiled from articles that were originally published in magazines such as *Mademoiselle*, *Good Housekeeping*, *Harper's*, *Vogue*, *Woman's Home Companion* and *The New Yorker*. S. T. Joshi has argued that these texts articulate a horror of domesticity 'because Shirley Jackson so keenly detected horror in the everyday world'.[9] Joshi claims that 'The importance of this domestic fiction – as regards her other work, at any rate – rests in its manipulation of very basic familial or personal scenarios that would be utilized in her weird work in perverted and twisted ways' (188). However, the family scenarios are rather more complex than Joshi admits and analysis of them reveals how they underpin Jackson's representation of the mother and daughter relationship in *Hill House*. Also, although Joshi acknowledges that parallels can be drawn between images of houses in the fictional and non-fictional works, he nevertheless does not elaborate a theoretical or contextual account of motherhood and childhood which can bridge the two forms.[10]

Life Among the Savages begins with an account of buying a house, built in 1820, which is clearly the model for the house used in *Hill House*. Chodorow had noted how pathological mothering creates a language of doubling which implies (although it is overlooked by Chodorow due to her focus on pre-Oedipal experiences) Freud's concept of the Uncanny. For Freud, the domestic security of the home becomes supplanted by feelings of danger and uncanniness because the home is also the place where sexual identities become modelled through troubling Oedipal encounters, although this arguably relates to an alternative and covert narrative strain in Jackson which refers to her husband and his role as a father. However, the home as a site of trauma is clearly suggested in Hill House, and that this is related to the Female Gothic is implied in the idea that what is really dangerous is a circumscribed life of domestic duties.

Roberta Rubenstein has usefully developed the work of Claire Kahane who, in her 1985 article 'The Gothic Mirror', developed a theory of pre-Oedipal female subject formation that is indebted to Chodorow and applied to Jackson.[11] Rubenstein summarises Kahane's position on a Chodorow-inflected model of the Female Gothic in which:

> traditional elements of the gothic genre are elaborated in particular ways, notably through the central character's troubled identification with her good/bad/dead/mad mother, whom she ambivalently seeks to kill or merge with; and her imprisonment in a house that, mirroring her disturbed imaginings, expresses her ambivalent experience of entrapment and longing for protection. (130)

Rubenstein elaborates such a position in relation to Jackson's Gothic novels and a selection of her short stories and although she acknowledges that Jackson's non-fictional domestic writings also participate in a language of troubled mothering, she seeks to assign such texts to a different order of writing. For Rubenstein the novels and the tales are characterised by 'far darker relational anxieties' (129) than that found in 'the domestic comedies' (129) because the fiction addresses family issues 'from not only a maternal but a filial perspective' (129). However, this suggests that Rubenstein has been distracted by the supposedly 'wryly comic' antics of a 'doting if unorthodox mother' (129). As we shall see, *Life Among the Savages* and *Raising Demons* provide a complex re-evaluation of the notion of filial loyalties which are closely related to the issue of motherhood. The relationships between mother and child and child and mother are developed in these texts in ways which come to underpin the more orthodox Gothic writings of Jackson. However, Rubenstein, following Kahane, is correct in identifying the house as a source of Gothic entrapment in Jackson and this is an issue initially addressed in *Life Among the Savages*.

In *Life Among the Savages* Jackson tells the owner of the house that they are thinking of buying that ' "It looks so..." I hesitated. "Imposing." '[12] She discovers that the house, like Hill House, appears to have its own internal geometry, one that asserts the rights of its previous occupants, 'After a few vain attempts at imposing our own angular order on things with a consequent out-of-jointness and shrieking disharmony that set our teeth on edge, we gave in to the old furniture and let things settle where they would' (18–19). Jackson throughout the book focuses on the apparently comedic world of domestic duties that she carries out in relation to her four children and her husband (the academic

Stanley Hyman). Although the tone is one of humour and affection there are moments when a more Gothic language intrudes within the images of affectionate domestic chaos. Much of this Gothic language is initially associated with the house. Jackson notes that her daughter Jannie 'spoke for a long time about a faraway voice in the house which sang to her at night' (21). Later her son Laurie tells his parents about a house that is close to theirs that is supposedly haunted. This leads them to conceive of their own house as potentially haunted and prompts them to produce a fake handbill that would proclaim to the community the supernatural goings-on in the Jackson household, all written in a mocked-up seventeenth-century idiom which anticipates Jackson's book on the Salem witch trials. For Jackson, the house is haunted by its previous owners, by their histories and even by their furniture. However, this language is one that suggests an alienation from the domesticity that the book ostensibly celebrates. As in *Hill House*, it is a debate about mothering which relocates these issues of spectral influence as a coded reference to how a child's subject formation is ghosted by their mother's reproduction of the bonds which ensure the repetition of motherhood.

Jackson notes how the past plays a role in spectrally shaping both the children and how she perceives them. She writes:

Sometimes, in my capacity as mother, I find myself sitting open-mouthed and terrified before my own children, little individual creatures moving solidly along in their own paths and yet in some mysterious manner vividly reminiscent of a past which my husband and I know we have never communicated to them. (171)

Like Eleanor, they appear to be trapped between the past and a possible future. In *Life Among the Savages* the idea of the reproduction of mothering appears in her young daughters, Jannie and Sally. Jannie develops an imaginary family in which she is the surrogate mother to seven children. Intriguingly she does not imagine them as biologically hers because in her intricate fantasy she is their stepmother ('The second Mrs Ellenoy'). These fantasy children and how they behave and are treated clearly parallel, or double, how Jackson responds to her children. A trip to a restaurant, for example, descends into chaos as Jackson tries to get her children to behave in an orderly fashion only to find that Jannie's 'children' also behave in a disruptive way by making unreasonable demands for food which is not on the menu. For Jackson, such moments imply that children are fundamentally anarchic and

the recognition that their fantasies of motherhood are ones that simultaneously mock her and are, in Chodorow's terms, generated by her
appears in a particularly painful moment of self-reflection relating to a
fantasy of Sally's. Sally's fantasy is not about being a mother but rather
expresses an ambivalent self-sufficiency in which Jackson states that
Sally imagines that she:

> ... had a house of her own, located approximately and damply in the
> middle of the river near *our* house; we all heard a great deal about
> this retreat of Sally's, in which a number of small children Sally's age
> lived in utter happiness upon lollipops and corn on the cob. (174)

This adult-free world is disturbing for Jackson. Sally tells her, 'In my
river... we sleep in wet beds, and we hear our mothers calling us' (175).
This prompts in Jackson one of the many sombre moments which punc-
tuate the text when she states that it gave 'me a sudden terrifying picture
of my own face, leaning over the water, wavering, and my voice far away
and echoing' (175). It is a position occupied by the projected mother in
Hill House who is also distanced, frightened, but trying to exert some
influence over a daughter's attempt at asserting independence. Judie
Newman has also explored these patterns of motherhood and their
relationship to how children respond to the mother in a reading of *Hill
House*. Newman notes of childhood that, following Chodorow, within
'the brief period of immunity from individuality, the experience of
fusion with the mother, of mother as world, is both seductive and terrifying. Unity is bliss; yet it entails total dependence and loss of self'.[13]
Jackson's response to Sally's claim on an independent life with its vision
of her 'terrifying picture' of her own face as she attempts to reach out to
Sally represents the urge of the mother to control (and protect) and the
simultaneous (and more overtly politicisable) anxiety that motherhood
constitutes an aspect of a dangerous social control which has limited
the roles for women. As Newman notes this, becomes constructed as a
paradox in which 'Mothering [...] involves a double identification for
women in which they take both parts of the preoedipal relation, as
mother and as child' (171). However, this can also be construed in political terms when such impulses are regarded as the product of gender,
and so ideology, rather than biology.

The principal problem identified by Chodorow is that conventional
notions of motherhood simply replicate patterns of desire for intimacy
(which fathers cannot produce) in their female children. That Jackson
is wrestling with this is clear from repeated moments of self-doubt

about how to mother. These appear at points of apparent crisis, but the alternative option of simply adhering to accepted gender scripts for mothering is also stifling. Jackson, for example, recounts a dialogue between herself and her children where she reads from a pamphlet (some corporate literature from a company that made toys) about mothering:

> It says I should be relaxed ... It says naturally Mother is not going to handicap her children by teaching them insecure patterns of behaviour; what would we think, for instance, of a mother who believed herself fond of her children, who nevertheless allowed them to see her in a temper? Or who told them obviously untruthful stories, broke promises, or showed malice? (205)

To which Jannie replies, 'You better make those brownies' (205). Jannie's response thus knowingly links this model of good motherly behaviour to expectations of domestic competence.

The narrative structure of *Life Among the Savages*, family buys new house and has assorted misadventures therein or around, is also the structure of its sequel *Raising Demons*. The sense that moving into the house entails a loss of agency is suggested when Jackson drives out to view the house 'Feeling that I was in the grip of something stronger than I', later she notes of the house that it, as in the descriptions of Hill House, 'was waiting for us, eager, expectant, and empty'.[14] Sally throughout the book pretends to be a witch who can cast spells on anyone who annoys her, but as she matures this rebellious streak becomes tempered by an interest in domesticity, as referenced in a drawing she works on entitled 'Two Witches Drinking Tea in a Cave' (234). However, that the children intuit potentially malign presences in the house is captured in the image of Barry, the youngest child found shut out of his bedroom hammering on the door repeatedly shouting: '"Monsters," he was screaming, purple-faced, "monsters, monsters!"' (251).

The links made in *Hill House* between domesticity and the Gothic are therefore to be found in the earlier domestic narratives. These non-fiction writings represent ambivalence about the role of mothers, especially in raising female children. The dilemma that Jackson confronts is not one of the absent mother that so typifies the Female Gothic of the eighteenth century, but one of the all-too-present mother whose demands on the child pathologises motherhood but in doing so serves to make visible how motherhood becomes reproduced. Jackson reworks the Female Gothic's desire for emancipation but locates this within the necessity of casting off the mother's influence. In *Hill House* this is told from the daughter's point of view and in the non-fiction from the mother's (suggesting two Female Gothic plots one about daughters, which is familiar from Radcliffe, and the other about mothers – familiar from Mary Shelley's model of the reproduction of mothering in *Frankenstein* [1818]). The paradox is that the rebellious child effects their rebellion by resisting, through mockery, conventional gender expectations. The problem for Jackson is that she has no way of solving this tension between the demands of motherhood with the urge for emancipation. For this reason her texts hold conflicting states in an irresolvable dialectic. Jodey Castricano, for example, has noted that *Hill House*'s conclusion with Eleanor's suicide is both a liberation for Eleanor *and* a moment of anxious self-destruction which represents her abandonment (by her mother, family and the tentative friendships she has established among the characters in Hill House). She steers her car towards a tree: 'I am really doing it, I am doing this all by myself, now, at last; this is me, I am really really really doing it by myself.' However, 'In the unending, crashing second before the car hurled into the tree she thought clearly, *Why* am I doing this? Why am I doing this? Why don't they stop me?' (245–6).

Although these dialectical tensions are represented as constituting a kind of pathology, they also suggest the feelings of entrapment which run through the Female Gothic tradition. Indeed, it could be argued that Jackson's work, which spans the post-war period to the mid-1960s, also spans a period in which there was debate in America about feminism and class (in certain labour movements) and campaigns for equal rights. In other words her writing bridges the period of comparative disempowerment to the liberations provided by the passing of the Equal Pay Act in 1963 and the Civil Rights Act of 1964 and such an historical contextualisation is illuminating. Betty Friedan's *The Feminine Mystique* (1963) famously provided a synopsis of college-educated women of similar age to Jackson and 'the problem that has no name' that confronted them before the passing of these Acts. Friedan states that her researches began in 1957 when she sent a questionnaire to 200 graduates of the all-female Smith College who, like her, had graduated some 15 years before. She notes of her results that:

There was a strange discrepancy between the reality of our lives as women and the image to which we were trying to conform, the image that I came to call the feminine mystique. I wondered if other women faced this schizophrenic split, and what it meant.[15]

In part this disorientation was due to a sense that the present was constraining but that a positive future was quite literally inconceivable because 'an American woman no longer has a private image to tell her who she is, or can be, or wants to be' (63). Later Friedan notes of an interview she conducted with a group of high school girls that 'I found that these girls were so terrified of becoming like their mothers that they could not see themselves at all. They were afraid to grow up' (65). Ultimately for Friedan, 'It is the mystique of feminine fulfilment, and the immaturity it breeds, that prevents women from doing the work of which they are capable' (223). Such a view underpins the point made by Newman, following Chodorow, that there exists a dual identification in mothering in which the mother becomes both child and mother. The tensions between these states ensure that a state of immaturity is maintained because the child is unwilling to engage with the model of the adult woman that is available to them and the mother is worried that their child may emulate them and so come to participate in their limited world. To this degree Jackson's Female Gothic does not articulate the type of optimism about women's potential for upward social mobility that characterised the Radcliffean Gothic. It should be noted that Jackson gets a passing mention by Friedan who refers to her as part of a group of 'Housewife Writers' (51) who mock domestic duties (turning them into comedy) and thus attempt to exercise their superiority over such duties. Jackson's images of a restrained emancipation are therefore open to a historical reading which explains her conflicted images of motherhood, for which she can find 'no name' because they are irresolvable and so rework the tensions and conflicts that confronted women of Jackson's background during the period.

These conflicts can also be usefully understood by developing Jodey Castricano's reading of Eleanor's thoughts leading up to her suicide when she crashes her car. Castricano attempts an exploration of Eleanor's behaviour in light of the theme of telepathy which runs throughout the novel and is the principal reason why the characters have assembled at Hill House. Eleanor's sense of disbelief that she is 'really doing it' and that the others will not stop her indicates, argues Castricano, that Eleanor is not in control of her thoughts because thoughts are sent telepathically from elsewhere as in Eleanor's dead mother's attempt to communicate with her (90–1). Telepathy thus obliquely relocates the troubling issue of how the female subject is influenced by seemingly overwhelming outside forces. The issue of telepathy had been covertly addressed earlier by Jackson in *The Witchcraft of Salem Village* where Jackson informs her child readership that:

> If the specter, or ghost, or spirit, or apparition, or vision which resembled a person appeared to another person who was afflicted by witchcraft, it was regarded as absolute proof that the first person was a witch, whether she knew it or not. The judges reasoned that only a person in league with the devil could send a ghostly form to trouble innocent people.[16]

Messages cannot therefore be innocently sent or received even if they have not been solicited. In this way the sender and the recipient are always guilty even while they are being victimised. Such a position suggests that the female subject is trapped because they are unable to envision a world which is free of guilt, which is the dominant emotion in Jackson's repeated accounts of being a daughter *and* a mother. At the end of her book on witchcraft Jackson attempts to account for the behaviour of the female children who had incriminated women within the community of Salem in terms of guilt. She states:

> Psychologists have pointed out that there is such a thing as contagious hysteria. Groups of people can 'infect' one another and copy one another's symptoms. This kind of behavior is often caused by extreme fear or guilt such as the girls must have been suffering from dabbling in forbidden 'magic'. (144)

This 'guilt' is also associated with copying 'one another's symptoms' which glosses Chodorow's concept of the reproduction of patterns of mothering, but here played out as a disease in which people 'infect' each other. Read in these terms the suicide of the guilt-ridden Eleanor represents a moment of disempowerment which masquerades as a moment of apparent empowerment, one which can also be interpreted in Friedan's terms as part of the 'schizophrenic split' that she perceived as central to the experience of women of a certain class at the time. For Castricano the sense of unreality is manifested by the merger 'in which the house of fiction and the fiction of the house interpenetrate' (96) so that we cannot be sure of the reality of Eleanor's auditory and visual manifestations. The invisible and the unreal represent two sides of the ideology of gender in Jackson. A related issue concerns literature because the fictional, or the literary, plays an important role in this development of the 'unreal' and it is one which, although it concerns Jackson's role as a writer, also has links to a model of motherhood.

In *Hill House* repeated references are made to Dr Mortimer's leisure reading which consists of selected works by Samuel Richardson. Richardson's strictly male reading of women's plights can be read as an overt lampooning of Mortimer's apparent liberalism. It is noteworthy that Eleanor feels that she is excluded from reading. First, she is put off reading because it reminds her of her mother: 'I had to read aloud to her for two hours every afternoon. Love stories' (86).[17] She feels that she cannot enter the library because it has a smell of mould that reminds her of her mother. However, in a second episode she feels strangely drawn towards the library: 'she thought, But I can't go in there; I'm not allowed in there – and recoiled in the doorway before the odor of decay, which nauseated her. "Mother", she said' (228). It is in the library that Eleanor, climbing a staircase which has not been properly affixed to a wall, nearly causes a fatal accident and she is sent away from Hill House by Mortimer even though she has nowhere to go. Writing, for Mortimer, is potentially magical and he expects the ghost to materialise in the library because 'books are frequently very good carriers, you know. Materialisations are often best produced in rooms where there are books' (187). Whereas for Eleanor, what is materialised is a sense of the past (the mouldy books), from which she feels excluded because they manifest her mother as a negative presence. Writing, in other words, is not something that she owns and this can be related to Jackson's attempt to try and find a language which can resolve the conflicts that she is trying to write through. She touches on this in *Life Among the Savages* when she recounts her hospital admission prior to giving birth to her third child, Sally. The desk clerk takes some details:

> 'Age?' she asked. 'Sex? Occupation?'
> 'Writer,' I said.
> 'Housewife,' she said.
> 'Writer,' I said.
> 'I'll just put down housewife,' she said. (68–9)[18]

Here the role of the writer is supplanted by domestic duties. This connection to writing is, however, developed in much more sombre terms when Jackson articulates a sense of being trapped within a language which can represent conflicts but which cannot resolve them. This is suggested in Jackson's final entry in her diary shortly before she died and while she was being treated for a depressive illness: 'only way out is writing please god help me and do not show to anyone do not show to anyone someday please god help me do not show to anyone because locked'.[19] Writing is both the way out and the thing which paradoxically locks you in and for this reason Jackson provides us with an interesting, and poignant, insight into how her work foregrounds some of the specific ideological tensions which were associated with motherhood in America from the 1940s to the 1960s. It achieves this by examining motherhood through a Female Gothic idiom which reveals how an inherent Gothic narrative haunts domestic spaces during the period. Jackson's work also captures, as does Friedan's, a specific mood of pessimism which existed before the passing of various emancipatory acts that colour her model of the Female Gothic in which social, emotional, and intellectual advancement seems to be an impossibility. It was a mood given an ironically Gothic inflection in Friedan's quotation from a sympathetic article published in the *New York Times* on 28 June 1960, which noted of the college-educated middle-class housewife that 'Like a two-headed schizophrenic... once she wrote a paper on the Graveyard poets; now she writes notes to the milkman' (20). It is a historically specific mood which an examination of Jackson's representation of motherhood makes visible in texts which do not, and cannot, reach out to the era of comparative liberation that she tragically did not live to see.

Notes

1. Darryl Hattenhauer, *Shirley Jackson's American Gothic* (Albany, NY: State University of New York Press, 2003).
2. Jodey Castricano, 'Shirley Jackson's *The Haunting of Hill House* and the Strange Question of Trans-Subjectivity', *Gothic Studies*, 7/1 (May 2005), 87–101, 88. Italics in original. All subsequent references are to this edition and are given in the text.
3. Steven Bruhm, 'Gothic Sexualities' in *Teaching the Gothic*, eds Anna Powell and Andrew Smith (Basingstoke: Palgrave, 2006), 93–106, 99.
4. Roberta Rubenstein, 'House Mothers and Haunted Daughters: Shirley Jackson and the Female Gothic', in *Shirley Jackson: Essays on the Literary Legacy*, ed. Bernice M. Murphy (London: McFarland, 2005), 127–49. All subsequent references are to this edition and are given in the text.
5. Shirley Jackson, *The Haunting of Hill House* (London: Constable [1959], 1999), 6. All subsequent references are to this edition and are given in the text.
6. Hattenhauer, *Shirley Jackson's American Gothic*, 23.
7. Nancy J. Chodorow, *The Reproduction of Mothering: Psychoanalysis and the Sociology of Gender* (Berkeley, CA: University of California Press, 1978), 103. All subsequent references are to this edition and are given in the text.

8. Shirley Jackson, *We Have Always Lived in the Castle* (Harmondsworth: Penguin [1962], 1984).

9. S. T. Joshi, 'Shirley Jackson: Domestic Horror' in *Shirley Jackson: Essays on the Literary Legacy*, 183–98, 183–4. All subsequent references are to this edition and are given in the text. Joshi also makes reference to James Egan's relevant article 'Sanctuary: Shirley Jackson's Domestic and Fantastic Parables', *Studies in Weird Fiction*, 6 (Fall, 1989), 15–24.

10. See S. T. Joshi, 'Shirley Jackson: Domestic Horror', 195 for an argument about Jackson's representation of houses.

11. Claire Kahane, 'The Gothic Mirror' in *The (M)other Tongue: Essays in Feminist Psychoanalytic Interpretation*, eds Shirley Nelson Garner, Claire Kahane and Madelon Sprengnether (Ithaca, NY: Cornell University Press, 1985), 334–51.

12. Shirley Jackson, *Life Among the Savages* (Harmondsworth: Penguin [1953], 1997), 13. All subsequent references are to this edition and are given in the text.

13. Judie Newman, 'Shirley Jackson and the Reproduction of Mothering: *The Haunting of Hill House*' in *Shirley Jackson: Essays on the Literary Legacy*, 169–82, 170. All subsequent references are to this edition and are given in the text.

14. Shirley Jackson, *Raising Demons* (New York: Scholastic Book Services [1957], 1967), 12, 60. All subsequent references are to this edition and are given in the text.

15. Betty Friedan, *The Feminine Mystique* (Harmondsworth: Penguin [1963], 1992), 9. All subsequent references are to this edition and are given in the text.

16. Shirley Jackson, *The Witchcraft of Salem Village* (New York: Random House [1956], 2001), 37. All subsequent references are to this edition and are given in the text.

17. See also Judie Newman, 'Shirley Jackson and the Reproduction of Mothering', 175.

18. This is a scene also discussed in Joshi, 'Shirley Jackson: Domestic Horror', 188, and by Murphy in the Introduction to *Shirley Jackson: Essays on the Literary Legacy*, 17.

19. Cited in Hattenhauer, *Shirley Jackson's American Gothic*, 27.

10
Others, Monsters, Ghosts: Representations of the Female Gothic Body in Toni Morrison's *Beloved* and *Love*

Anya Heise-von der Lippe

Toni Morrison's novels *Beloved* (1986) and *Love* (2003), although published at an interval of 17 years, share a common narrative approach towards the Female Gothic body as a symbol of corporeal violence. The female body has been at the centre of definitions of the Female Gothic since Ellen Moers coined the term in 1976, describing it as 'the work that women writers have done in the literary mode that, since the eighteenth century, we have called the Gothic.'[1] Subsequent approaches, in accordance with theoretical reassessments of gender, have largely replaced the author's body with female bodies inside the text – spanning from the prototypical, or as Diane Long Hoeveler has suggested,[2] professional victim to the monstrous feminine. However, as Morrison's own critical approach shows, there is a crucial difference between narrative representations of black and white female protagonists in North American literary history: the white heroine's economic value in the marriage market depends on the preservation of her virtue/virginity. In comparison, the black (slave) woman's economic value is measured by her reproductiveness and 'an uncontested assumption of the sexual availability of black females',[3] which cast her in the role of the deviant, monstrous other. This narrative construction of African-American otherness forms the centre of Morrison's critical argument in *Playing in the Dark* (1993), while her novels explore gender and race as intertwined categories of power, discrimination and victimisation which have to be reassessed, undermined and deconstructed in various ways.

Beloved and *Love* focus on the black, female, Gothic body as a site of corporeal memory, marking both individual transgressions, like murder or sexual deviance, and the collective-historical past of slavery, exploitation and racial injustice. As Catherine Spooner points out, 'Gothic as a genre is profoundly concerned with the past conveyed through both historical settings and narrative interruptions of the past into the present.'[4] However, in Morrison's novels the past is not an abstract category of memory, it has a component of corporeality reminiscent of Kristevan theory, in its focus on female/maternal bodies and the return of the repressed, abject other.[5]

In addition to the thematic similarity suggested by the titles, *Beloved* and *Love* are linked by a striking parallel between their eponymous characters who are both dead, returning as ghostly embodiments of suppressed guilt and dark secrets. The repressed past returns as Gothic body and as Gothic text, reflected in the complex, disruptive narrative structure of the two novels. As George Haggerty has argued, 'Gothic fiction ... plays out a formal drama which is itself Gothic in its implications.'[6] With its ' "inclination" toward formal instability and fragmentation' (2), the structure of the Gothic text resembles a mutilated organism, a monstrous, dislocated Gothic body. Gothic text and Gothic body reinforce one another in their fragmented representation of past transgressions at what Cynthia Dobbs, referring to Morrison's *Beloved*, has called the 'crucial interface between body and story ... marked by the scar.'[7]

'Humming in the dark'

Morrison's critical text *Playing in the Dark* sets out to uncover a shadowy Africanist presence in American literature which is used as the defining counterpart of white, dominant, voiced characters. It also describes the narrative model of a spectral, black countertext – a function strongly reminiscent of the subversive possibilities of Gothic literature. Moreover, this concept refers to one of the central questions in postcolonial criticism: the difficulty of expressing otherness inside the given structures of established modes of representation. As Gayatri Spivak has argued, this raises a number of questions about the possibility of representing otherness in a Western cultural framework, with its inherent refusal to encounter the subaltern on an equitable basis.[8]

Toni Morrison's concern with voicing 'otherness' becomes clear in the context of open and equal representation which dominates both her critical and her fictional work. In a 1998 interview she replied to the question of whether she saw herself as a feminist:

> In order to be as free as I possibly can, in my own imagination, I can't take positions that are closed. Everything I've ever done, in the writing world, has been to expand articulation, rather than to close it, to open doors, sometimes, not even closing the book – leaving the endings open for reinterpretation, revisitation, a little ambiguity. ... I don't subscribe to patriarchy, and I don't think it should be substituted with matriarchy. I think it's a question of equitable access, and opening doors to all sorts of things.[9]

In order to undermine authoritative processes of 'othering', Morrison's novels frequently employ disruptive forms of representation, resisting simple forms of closure. Her texts focus on individual experiences to avoid generalisations and categorisations, evoking a sense of community by establishing multiple narrative perspectives – a sometimes consonant and sometimes dissonant cluster of different voices.

In an attempt to express traumatic experiences beyond words, both *Beloved* and *Love* resort to a non-verbal sort of vocal communication: a humming, described by Dobbs as 'a code of meaning that is simultaneously anterior, superior, and antagonistic to conventional language' (567). 'Humming in the dark',[10] as Morrison has termed it in her Nobel Lecture, can be read as a way to communicate something that is too painful to be put into words and, simultaneously, as a mode of resistance. For L, the spectral homodiegetic narrator of *Love*, humming is a form of quiet protest: 'My hum is mostly below range, private; suitable for an old woman embarrassed by the world; her way of objecting to how the century is turning out. Where all is known and nothing understood.'[11] In a similar way, humming amounts to a form of non-verbal public resistance in *Beloved*. The men on the chain gang, who are not allowed to speak, the women who gather in front of the haunted house to drive out a ghost that is an embodiment of their own pain, they all revert to an archaic form of communication: 'In the beginning there were no words. In the beginning was the sound, and they all knew what that sound sounded like.'[12] By using non-verbal sounds to communicate, the former slaves avoid the pitfalls of a language which they have repeatedly experienced as not being their own, but that of others – the white slave owners who have marked their bodies and abused them in writing. There is no alternative language they can use. Sethe's childhood memory of a different language, 'the same language her ma'am spoke and which would never come back' (63), is a weak reminiscence of one of many African mother tongues erased by the dominant English language. Short of a common language, the humming is a form of communicating pain, of voicing otherness, but it is also a way to reunite a community on the basis of a collective memory – the horror of the Middle Passage which cannot be put into words, or, as Beloved asks, 'how can I say things that are pictures?' (210).

'You can know me by this mark'

Beloved is set in the latter half of the nineteenth century – focusing on the inhumane consequences of slavery in the form of fragmented bits of personal memory. Haunted by the ghost of her baby daughter, the central character, Sethe, is represented as an outsider in a community of free African-Americans in Ohio. Her dramatic escape from slavery, pregnant, barefoot and feverish from a beating – and the birth of her daughter in a sinking boat – establish the novel's dominant themes of female corporeality and bodily harm. Sethe's urge to free her children originates from her particular idea of 're-memory' which Dobbs has termed 'a public place of haunting' (568). According to Sethe and Morrison's own concept of re-memory nothing ever dies; past events continue to haunt places even if the people have long gone. As Sethe tells her daughter Denver, 'even though it's all over – over and done with – it's going to always be there waiting for you. That's how come I had to get all of my children out' (37). As David Lawrence points out: '[o]perating independently of the conscious will, memory is shown to be an active, constitutive force that has the power to construct and circumscribe identity, both individual and collective, in the image of its own contents'.[13] Albeit existing independently from a particular remembering subject, memories have a tendency to return in the shape of bodies or embodied images to haunt the survivors.

The novel's subject matter is what Dobbs, with reference to Elaine Scarry's approach has termed 'black bodies-in-pain' (563). The text describes how, mutilated by inhuman forms of punishment, even those slaves who escaped alive are marked by the violence of slavery. For them '[t]he future [is] a matter of keeping the past at bay' (42). Around 'the desolated center where the self that was no self made its home' (140), they interpret their own bodies as changeable, split open or falling apart; their tortured, malfunctioning limbs and organs have moved beyond the possibility of literal representation into the realm of metaphorical narratives. Sethe's back has been marked by the slave-owner's whip, but, in a process of sublimation, she has learned to describe her scars as a 'chokecherry tree' (16). There are various interpretations for this image, ranging from a fruitful family tree, growing from her back to the poisonous fruit of her 'too thick' (164) motherly love, 'choking' her children, as Paul D, one of the central male characters of the novel suggests. What Dobbs calls Morrison's 'aesthetics of pain' (576) oscillates between the horror of pain and the strange beauty and fascination of the marked body.

Scars are bodily reminders of past traumata which can be neither told nor forgotten. Paradoxically for the slaves who have nothing else to pass on, they are also a form of family history, written on the body. A mark on her mother's skin, pointed out to Sethe so she would be able to tell her mother apart from all the other women on the plantation, is one of the few memories Sethe has of her mother:

> she opened up her dress front and lifted her breast and pointed under it. Right on her rib was a circle and a cross burnt right in the skin. She said, 'This is your ma'am. This,' and she pointed. 'I am the only one got this mark now. The rest dead. If something happens to me and you can't tell me by my face, you can know me by this mark.' (61)

However, the mark on the body is a treacherous form of corporeal history. Sethe is unable to identify the decaying body of her hanged mother, as the mark is lost along with its original meaning: '[b]y the time they cut her down nobody could tell whether she had a circle and a cross or not, least of all me and I did look' (61). Sethe is also blind to the peculiarities of Beloved's body. It is Denver, her younger daughter, who first recognises her sister by the fine-lined scar under her chin, 'the tip of the thing she always saw in its entirety when Beloved undressed to sleep' (74). For Sethe, the 'click' (176) of recognition comes in an epiphanic moment that draws on the memory of her mother's marked body: Sethe recognises Beloved by a tune that she made up and sang to her children. The soft 'humming' (175) establishes a wordless bond of love between them which is more powerful and more durable than the scar.

Apart from marks on the body, names are the only kind of family history available. Falsely named 'Jenny' in her papers, Sethe's mother-in-law renames herself 'Baby Suggs' in honour of her absent husband when she is bought out of slavery. This act of naming oneself is part of the liberation process along with an estimation of one's own body. As Sethe finds out in the 28 days between her arrival and the spilling of her daughter's blood, '[f]reeing yourself was one thing; claiming ownership of the freed self was another' (95). Baby Suggs' sermons encourage the community members to love themselves, to clearly name and love each part of their bodies, because nobody else will. In this process, as Lawrence states, 'the members of the community must put themselves back together – re-member themselves' (193). Learning to speak the 'body language' (194) of their own needs and desires, the former slaves have to let go of the traumatic experiences of the past by acknowledging their existence.

Under slavery, love and pain are intertwined so closely that to love somebody almost invariably means to lose them. Baby Suggs' eight children are taken away, one after the other, except for the unloved last one 'who gave her freedom when it didn't mean a thing' (23). Like Paul D, she knows that

[f]or a used-to-be-slave woman to love anything that much was dangerous, especially if it was her children she had settled on to love. The best thing, he knew, was to love just a little bit; everything, just a little bit, so when they broke its back, or shoved it in a croaker sack, well, maybe you'd have a little love left over for the next one. (45)

Sethe's love for her children and her pride at having liberated them all on her own are instances of hubris in the eyes of a community of former slaves who have seen most of their own family members sold down the river. Sethe's ultimate crime, however, consists of trying to kill her children so as to guard them from the white slave-hunters. Thus, when Sethe's dead daughter Beloved returns to haunt her house in the shape of a baby-poltergeist, most members of the community are quick to decide that it serves Sethe right. While the ghost can be read as an embodiment of Sethe's subconscious guilt, the novel's telling of the horrible deed itself is intricately constructed, avoided by and, at the same time, hinted at from different perspectives. Paul D's refusal to believe in Sethe's guilt, Denver's period of deafness, brought on by her inability to cope with her mother's deed, are all instances of avoiding the unspeakable, the horror of a mother killing her baby.

Like the novel, Sethe herself circles around the topic in both a direct and a metaphorical way, not quite telling what happened while moving in circles in her own kitchen: 'Sethe knew that the circle she was making around the room, him, the subject, would remain one. That she could never close in, pin it down ...' (163). The central tale of the murder and its causes emerges as a fragmentary text, as the novel's structure reflects the haunting of the house: three parts, each beginning with the same words respectively, describe the house as 'spiteful' (3), 'loud' (169) or 'quiet' (239). The characteristic structure of the text establishes a parallel between the house, Beloved's fragmented body and the spectral body of narrative. The ghostly girl's aura of uncanny familiarity is supported by her name which is not only the title of the novel, but also the inscription on the tombstone of Sethe's dead daughter – a construction evoking the memorial functions of the text. As Schapiro observes: 'Beloved's character is both the frame and center of the book.'[14] Her appearance as '[a] fully dressed woman [walking] out of the water' (50) is described as an uncanny event, accompanied by strange hollow breathing. The young woman's inability to stay awake for more than a few minutes hints at her emergence from a subconscious state. The embodiment of the ghost is, thus, staged as an actual 'return of the repressed'.

Apart from her strange, childlike behaviour, Beloved's monstrosity is established by her lineless, unmarked new skin. Contrasted with Sethe's body, Beloved's lack of visible scars gives her away as an outsider, a transient anachronism in corporeal history. Even in her own view her body lacks integrity – it seems to be held together solely by Sethe's attention: 'It is difficult keeping her head on her neck, her legs attached to her hips when she is by herself' (133). As Lawrence suggests, Beloved's narrative perspective reflects and reconstructs her fragmented body: 'her "word shapes" embody her tenuous physical and psychical shape' (196). Although provoked by fear, Beloved's insatiable hunger for Sethe's attention is an element of monstrosity as it hints at her wish to incorporate her mother, to become her, by devouring her. The monstrous swelling of Beloved's body, which is at one point described as a sign of pregnancy, could also be interpreted in terms of a post-human concept of flexible corporeality: the ability to assimilate external elements – to feed on information like a vampire. Beloved's hunger echoes the slave-masters' exploitation of the slaves' bodies. Evoking her past deprivation of her mother's milk, it refers back to the central transgressive act and the crucial point in her parents' past: the taking of Sethe's breast milk by the slave-master's nephews, while her husband was watching, unable to help, slowly going mad in the attic above.

On the structural level the growing symbiosis between Sethe and Beloved is achieved through a merging of their narrative voices: 'You are mine...You are my face; I am you' (216). In the ultimate state of integration the combined voices transgress interpersonal differences, overcoming the boundaries between life and death. The images of the Middle Passage of African slaves, which form part of Beloved's timeless, spectral consciousness, illustrate this transgressive process. They are based on an all-embracing model of racial, cultural memory, constructed from fragmented individual perspectives like the voices Stamp Paid hears when he approaches the haunted house: 'a conflagration of hasty voices – loud, urgent, all speaking at once' (172). Set in an oral narrative framework of broken, unpunctuated sentences, the horrors of the Middle Passage are nevertheless clearly placed in the context of the American Gothic tradition, thus creating a specific Postcolonial Gothic narrative style: 'I am always crouching the man on my face is dead [...] we are all trying to leave our bodies behind [...] the man on my face has done it [...] his teeth are pretty white points' (211). The abysmal conditions on the slave ship evoke the concepts of live burial and the enclosed space of the crypt – recurrent images of Edgar Allan Poe's grotesque aesthetics. Beloved's admiration of the dead man's white teeth, reminiscent of Poe's 'Berenice' (1835), is, accordingly, placed in the context of necrophilia – another, admittedly quite sombre, variation on Morrison's concern with the possibilities of love transgressing the boundaries between life and death which links *Beloved* to the later novel *Love*. In this context of aesthetic representation, it becomes clear how the novel's central concept of spectral embodiment is founded on the need for a retelling of American history from an African-American perspective. The 'conflagration of hasty voices' (172) has to be deciphered, the word order restored to read the tale of unspeakable horror and to incorporate the ambiguous narrative perspectives of Sethe's lurking re-memory into a broader cultural memory. It is in this sense that *Beloved*'s tale is 'not a story to pass on' (274) but an essentially Gothic body of narrative that has to be actively 're-membered'.

'A bad good man'

Love is an equally retrospective tale, concerned with representations of the (female) body in a complicated framework of sexual power politics. In a series of focalised flashbacks, the structurally complex narrative reconstructs the history of the Cosey family over much of the twentieth century. Each of the focalisers is haunted by their individual experiences, which are interlinked in a twisted narrative web. The plot hinges on the dominant figure of the wealthy African American hotel owner Bill Cosey who is curiously absent from the narrative itself. The gradual revelation of the puzzle of Bill Cosey's sudden death suggests a reading of *Love* as a murder mystery. The novel, however, offers several other textual levels, some of which are only revealed in re-reading it. The focalised chapters are framed and counterbalanced by five insertions of first-person commentary from Cosey's former cook, L. These are not only set apart typographically from the rest of the text by being printed in italics, but L also seems to take on the role of an external spectator watching the rest of the characters from a temporal rather than a spatial distance. Only in retrospect does it become clear, that she has been reconstructing herself in her own narrative, claiming to be working at a local restaurant, although she has been dead for over twenty years. When L's death is mentioned, almost casually, near the end of the novel, it calls for a re-reading of her comments – if not the whole text. Like *Beloved*'s tale, *Love* presents a body of narrative to be actively re-membered by the reader.

As Megan Sweeney notes, L's comments are the moral barometer of the text. Her criticism of 'the exhibitionism and false transparency'[15] of a world without secrets establishes her role as the keeper of secrets of both the novel and the Cosey's family history. L is represented as a mystery herself – she doesn't even mention her full name. It is only hinted at in her last, framing commentary: 'If your name is the subject of First Corinthians, chapter 13, ...' (199). Again, as in *Beloved* the ghostly presence turns out to be the eponymous character of the novel. Curiously enough, the absence of a body does not undermine L's narrative authority even in retrospect. L herself seems to be aware of her own death, although she interprets it as 'simply more of the same' (135) and describes it as shutting up altogether back in the 1970s – a period which she associates with the emergence of a new aesthetic of naked, fragmented, female bodies: 'when all the magazines started featuring behinds and inner thighs as though that's all there is to a woman' (3). The first-person narrator's claim to have shut up for good is one of the representational paradoxes of the novel. After all, she only continues to exist in and through her own narrative. This transfers the central dichotomy of presence and absence onto the structural level of the text, underlining the novel's central focus on the dominance of representation. Although, in accordance with the Female Gothic's tradition of powerful villainy, Bill Cosey is represented as the dominant figure in the text, it gradually turns out that his power has been undermined by the subtle humming of L's influence. As a compelling sub- or counter-text, L's humming subverts the previously established gender roles of powerful male patriarch and devoted female servant. Her true influence on the Cosey's family history is, nevertheless, only revealed in retrospect: L admits to having poisoned Bill Cosey to protect the Cosey-women from being disinherited. This rationally planned murder for charitable reasons turns the dominant patriarch into a victim.

Although, at the opening of the narrative, the patriarch has been dead for more than 20 years, Bill Cosey's prominent absence haunts his family as well as the pages of the novel. His commanding personality has influenced his family way beyond his death. He returns in narrative flashbacks from different perspectives. With Bill Cosey at its centre, the Gothic family plot harks back to Cosey's father, 'Dark', who accumulated some wealth by working as a police informer. Like the prototype of the Gothic villain, Manfred, Prince of Otranto, Bill Cosey tries to cover up this ancestral treason. He invents a more positive legend for his family and invests his father's blood money in a hotel and pleasure resort for black people. Although his business turns out a huge success and he manages to keep the white sheriff well paid and entertained, his patriarchal dream of founding a male lineage is doomed to fail. After the death of his only son – and again in line with the Gothic tradition – Cosey decides to marry a very young girl, his granddaughter's best friend. Cosey's motives are, however, not purely dynastic, as two flashbacks from the girls' perspectives reveal. His sexual deviance becomes obvious when he is aroused by 8-year-old Heed in a bathing suit and masturbates at the open window of his granddaughter's bedroom. What each girl sees as her fault and dares not talk about drives the first wedge of shame and secrecy between the two young friends. Christine, the granddaughter, sees 'an old man's solitary pleasure' lurking in the curtains of her bedroom at night and feels that 'his shadow ha[s] booked the room' (192). Cosey's paedophile marriage with 11-year-old Heed substantiates the central transgressive act of the novel. It turns the innocent, unconditional love between the two girls into lifelong hatred and ultimately destroys the family. To separate the girls, whose friendship is a constant reminder of the incestuous implications of Cosey's paedophile tendencies, Christine is sent away to school – a dismissal which she blames on her friend. 'You a slave! He bought you with a year's rent and a candy bar!' (129). Christine shouts after Heed in pig Latin, reminding her of the fact that Cosey practically bought the 11-year-old girl from her moneyless parents. Lacking metaphorical distance in an African American context, the accusation is an absolute one. Years later, after several exploitative relationships, Christine realises that she has been bought herself, and that most of the men resemble her grandfather in their attitude towards women. Even after her return home, there is no hope of reconciliation with Heed. On the contrary: the constant rivalry over Cosey's legacy keeps the two women tied to each other in mutual hatred, fiercely fighting each other. As Sweeney indicates, the novel is concerned with 'women's status as property vs. women's control over property' (228). *Love*, thus, echoes the Female Gothic tradition's crucial concern with questions of female economic ownership and agency.

Although *Love* has, so far, not been read as a Gothic text, the novel
draws on the Female Gothic tradition, introducing patriarchal structures and male dominance as its major threats. Bill Cosey's relationship
with his child-bride Heed, for example, evokes the Edward Rochester
or Maxim de Winter type of older, sexually experienced hero-villain a
nineteenth- or twentieth-century heroine might encounter in a Gothic
Romance. His jovial benevolence towards the young girl and his positive
image among the local black community are the only positive aspects
of his difficult character. 'You could call him a good bad man, or a bad
good man' (200), L suggests, or, in short, a classic Gothic hero-villain.

Bill Cosey's influence in the past is counterbalanced by his odd narrative silence: he is deprived of a voice, restricted to other people's
memories. On the surface, the text seems to reconstruct his spectral
body by assembling the different roles he performed in his life. In nine
chapters – each headed by a single, often ironically used noun, like
'Lover', 'Benefactor' or 'Friend' – the other protagonists remember their
difficult relationships with the patriarch. At the same time, his spectral presence is constructed as an absence. The chapter headings, which
seem to apply to Cosey at first sight, often turn out to refer to other protagonists. For example, the first chapter's title is 'Portrait' – ostensibly
referring to a painting of Bill Cosey which dominates his widow's bedroom. The major part of the chapter, however, does not describe this
artificial portrait, but the much more immediate physical appearance
of a young woman who calls herself Junior Viviane. Bold, sexy and
self-assured on the surface, Junior seems a typical post-feminist 1990s
woman. Her egotism and manipulative tendencies begin to show when
Heed engages her as a secretary. The young woman attempts to make
the most of her new job by trying to extract money from the older
women and by seducing young Romen, their after-school help. Junior's
history of violence reveals itself as sexual dominance in her relationship
with the teenager whom she considers as 'her gift' (63). Romen, in turn,
is fascinated by her 'sci-fi eyes' (179) and the rough sex. With her sadomasochistic tendencies Junior is cast in the role of a sexual predator.

Junior's body is represented in fragments. Assessed by different focalisers, her 'good legs' (23) are her most compelling feature in terms of a
Gothic aesthetic, because they turn out to be just the contrary. When
she finally takes off her boots in an intimate moment with her young
lover, her merged toes become visible, making her foot look like a hoof.
As a focalised flashback from Junior's perspective reveals, she was deliberately run over by her uncle's truck. This brutal heritage has had an
effect on the young woman's evolution as a psychopathic personality.

Her glorification of the deceased Bill Cosey as her 'Good Man' (116) opens up an interesting intertextual parallel: with her institution-ally induced recklessness and her complete lack of ethical categories, Junior evokes the sociopathic killer 'The Misfit' in Flannery O'Connor's story 'A Good Man is Hard to Find' (1955). Audacious and indifferent towards others, she is cast, both ethically and aesthetically, in the role of a psychopathic monster. As Rosi Braidotti argues, 'In the contempor-ary imaginary, the monstrous refers to the play of representations and discourses that surround the body of late postmodernity.'[16] Despite the recent aura of coolness surrounding the modified, post-human body,[17] monstrosity remains a way to describe physical as well as mental devi-ance. That is to say, the monster marks the point of excess.

Conclusion: *Agape*

The first sentence of L's framing commentary establishes the cen-tral picture of the novel: 'The women's legs are spread wide open, so I hum' (3). L's humming, which is a metaphor of her narrative voice, transfers the image onto a structural level, recasting the text itself in the role of both the rape victim and the rapist. Taking into account the similarity between the ambivalent Greek term for love, $\alpha\gamma\acute{\alpha}\pi\eta$ and the English adjective *agape*, *Love* oscillates between the two meanings of the word and the different concepts of emotional and corporeal relation-ships they denote. The selfless, unconditional form of love is, however, often overruled by the cruel image of legs spread wide open by force – of rape and bodily harm – which haunts the text. As Sweeney points out, *Love* shows how women's resistance against their status as 'sexual com-modities' (455) is punished by a system which reads these acts of resist-ance as criminal. L's ominous 'old folks' tale' (10) of 'Police-heads' (5) drifting in from the sea at times of upheaval and particularly 'to scare wicked females and correct unruly children' (10) suggests a similar read-ing. However, L's narrative also shows that resistance to the system sym-bolised by the Police-heads is possible: Celestial, long-term prostitute to Bill Cosey and glorified by Heed and Christine as bold and smart in their private code word 'Hey Celestial' (188), confronts the sea and the Police-heads with a sound that keeps L spellbound: 'I don't know to this day whether it was a word, a tune, or a scream. All I know is that it was a sound I wanted to answer' (105). Again, as in L's humming narrative and the humming of male and female communities in *Beloved*, resist-ance is expressed in what Sweeney terms 'the eloquence of not-yet-born language' (459). Like *Beloved*'s tale, which has to be re-membered from scars and the fragments of corporeal narrative, this tale is represented as a black, female countertext that has to be assembled from different narrative perspectives. By concentrating on the humming/countertext both novels manage what Helene Myers describes as 'negotiating the minefield of contemporary discourses about female victimisation'.[18] L's theory-conscious meta-commentary includes an appropriate description of Female Gothic varieties – from what Diane Long Hoeveler has termed 'victim feminism' (7), L's observation that '[e]ach story has a monster in it who made them tough instead of brave, so they open their legs rather than their hearts where that folded child is tucked' (4) – to a tale of female empowerment that L describes as '[s]omething better. Like a story that shows how brazen women can take a good man down' (10). Focusing on the individual, fragmented perspectives of their ghostly/scarred protagonists *Beloved* and *Love* recast the Gothic body simultaneously in and as a narrative text establishing a particular narrative aesthetic which is set somewhere between these two bodies of the Female Gothic – the victim and the monster.

The two novels I have discussed here in terms of their Female Gothic elements form part of Morrison's substantial project, both as a literary critic and a writer, to (re)incorporate African-American perspectives into the canon of North American literature. In *Playing in the Dark* she argues that '[t]he contemplation of this black presence is central to any understanding of our national literature and should not be permitted to hover at the margins of the literary imagination' (5). Moreover, Morrison suggests, major characteristics of North American literature have developed in response to this Africanist presence. These include 'the thematics of innocence coupled with an obsession with figurations of death and hell' (5) – core concepts of the (Female) Gothic which are also central to Morrison's narrative texts. A reading of Morrison's novels as Female Gothic texts, thus, not only establishes a dialogue between Morrison's literary criticism and her work as a writer – it also considers these texts as part of the Female Gothic narrative tradition they are rooted in.

Notes

1. Ellen Moers, *Literary Women* (London: The Women's Press [1976], 1978), 90.
2. Diane Long Hoeveler, *Gothic Feminism* (University Park, PA: Pennsylvania State University Press, 1998), 7. All subsequent references are to this edition and are given in the text.
3. Toni Morrison, *Playing in the Dark* (London: Vintage, 1993), 23. All subsequent references are to this edition and are given in the text.

4. Catherine Spooner, *Contemporary Gothic* (London: Reaktion, 2006), 9.
5. Julia Kristeva, *Powers of Horror* (New York: Columbia University Press, 1982), 5.
6. George Haggerty, *Gothic Fiction/Gothic Form* (University Park, IL: Pennsylvania State University Press, 1989), 3. All subsequent references are to this edition and are given in the text.
7. Cynthia Dobbs, 'Toni Morrison's Beloved: Bodies Returned, Modernism Revisited', *African American Review*, 32/4 (Winter, 1998), 563–78, 575. All subsequent references are to this edition and are given in the text.
8. Gayatri Spivak, 'Can the Subaltern Speak?' in *Marxism and the Interpretation of Culture*, eds Cary Nelson and Lawrence Grossberg (Urbana, IL: University of Illinois Press, 1988), 271–313.
9. Zia Jaffrey, 'Toni Morrison – The Salon Interview', *SALON* (2 February 1998), <http://www.salon.com/books/int/1998/02/cov_si_02int.html> Accessed 15 August 2007, 1.
10. Toni Morrison, 'Nobel Lecture', in *Nobel Lectures, Literature 1991–1995*, ed. Sture Allén(Singapore: World Scientific, 1997), <http://nobelprize.org/nobel_prizes/literature/laureates/1993/morrison-lecture.html> Accessed 22 March 2009 (no pagination).
11. Toni Morrison, *Love* (New York: Knopf, 2003), 4. All subsequent references are to this edition and are given in the text.
12. Toni Morrison, *Beloved* (London: Vintage [1986], 1997), 259. All subsequent references are to this edition and are given in the text.
13. David Lawrence, 'Fleshly Ghosts and Ghostly Flesh: The Word and the Body in *Beloved*', *Studies in American Fiction*, 19/2 (Autumn, 1991), 189–201, 189. All subsequent references are to this edition and are given in the text.
14. Barbara Schapiro, 'The Bonds of Love and the Boundaries of Self in Toni Morrison's *Beloved*', *Contemporary Literature*, 32/2 (Summer, 1991), 194–210, 209.
15. Megan Sweeney, ' "Something Rogue": Commensurability, Commodification, Crime, and Justice in Toni Morrison's Later Fiction', *Modern Fiction Studies*, 52/2 (Summer, 2006), 440–69, 447. All subsequent references are to this edition and are given in the text.
16. Rosi Braidotti, 'Teratologies', in *Deleuze and Feminist Theory*, eds Ian Buchanan and Claire Colebrook (Edinburgh: Edinburgh University Press, 2000), 156–72, 162.
17. See Erich Kasten, *Body-Modification* (München: Reinhardt, 2006), 185.
18. Helene Meyers, *Femicidal Fears* (Albany, NY: State University of New York Press, 2001), 2.

11
'Unhomely Moments': Reading and Writing Nation in Welsh Female Gothic

Kirsti Bohata

[I]ssues of suppression in a stateless national culture can find a mode of expression which has much to do with the Gothic, and [the study of this writing] can help us to illuminate some key points about Gothic as a mode of telling, and remembering, of history.

(David Punter)[1]

By making visible the forgetting of the 'unhomely' moment in civil society, feminism specifies the patriarchal, gendered nature of civil society and disturbs the symmetry of private and public which is now shadowed, or uncannily doubled, by the difference of genders which does not neatly map on to the private and the public, but becomes disturbingly supplementary to them. This results in redrawing the domestic space...the personal-*is*-the political; the world-*in*-the-home.

(Homi Bhabha)[2]

Castles, houses and ruins are paradigmatic tropes of Gothic writing, ubiquitous and multivalent signifiers from its inception to the present. Family, 'race' and nation are evoked by the sense of the word house meaning 'lineage', making houses emblematic of nation. Houses are also used figuratively in Female Gothic writing to encode and deconstruct the female body and psyche. If houses have traditionally symbolised imprisoning structures of patriarchy by which women are confined and from which they must escape, the house is a potentially troubling and problematic Gothic trope of nation for those reading or writing female nationhood. One of the aims of this essay will be to consider how ideas of nation(hood) and gender intersect and complicate each other in twentieth-century Anglophone Welsh Female Gothic. A second aim is to indicate some common organising features, in addition to houses, that might be associated with 'the Welsh Female Gothic'; this essay will suggest ruined buildings, fire, disease and mental illness as prominent images which express gender and cultural crisis.

If the construction of a 'tradition' of Welsh Female Gothic represents a contribution to the idea of a national literature, the idea of nation and nationhood (as constructed through the Gothic houses) in the Female Gothic texts read here is a problematic and embattled one. In the twentieth century, a trajectory can be traced from romantic, feminised, yet spiritually enriching and attractive decay, through violent conflict (between sexes and nationalities), to an apocalyptic picture of disease and devastation, dereliction and ruin, homelessness and dislocation. Women's relationship with nation is haunted by the spectre of desertion as an implicit or explicit option, even an imperative to escape. Ruined, deserted, cursed, haunted, burning or demolished buildings rather than inhabited houses are at the centre of the national picture constructed by twentieth-century Welsh Female Gothic. This is not necessarily the metanarrative which might emerge in a wider critical engagement with ideas of gender, nation, illness and the house in Welsh writing in English, but what is striking about an important strand of the *Female Gothic* in Wales is its foregrounding of anxieties about national culture and the politics of gender in a manner which becomes increasingly apocalyptic as the century progresses.[3]

A chapter of this length cannot attempt to be a comprehensive survey of the various forms, tropes or themes which can be gathered under the heading Welsh Female Gothic; rather it attempts to foreground some of the issues raised by considering Welsh Female Gothic as a variety of national literature and, more importantly, a literature concerned with nation. I adopt Punter's suggestion, quoted above, that the Gothic may be a mode particularly suited for illuminating 'issues of suppression in a stateless national culture', but want to consider how Female Gothic writing is complicated by its attempts to engage with suppression of gender as well as stateless national culture. This chapter also builds on postcolonial approaches to Gothic. In *The Location of Culture*, Homi Bhabha suggests that, 'Although the "unhomely" is a paradigmatic colonial and post-colonial condition, it has a resonance that can be heard distinctly, if erratically, in fictions that negotiate the powers of cultural difference in a range of transhistorical sites' (9). Moreover,

Andrew Smith and William Hughes have suggested that the Gothic may be particularly suited to expressing the fractured experience of colonisation and the postcolonial moment where the past is a haunting, disruptive presence.[4]

The manifestation of the past in the present and a sense of the inescapability of the past, which is a feature of Gothic writing, is an apt representation of the postcolonial experience of history and a pervasive feature of Welsh writing. Wales is characterised by internal fractures and uncanny doublings which emanate not least from the uneasy history of the two languages of Wales. Tony Brown has drawn attention to the way that the uncanny, particularly in the sense of feeling estranged in a familiar space, has a special resonance for English-language Welsh writers. With reference in particular to writers growing up in the first half of the twentieth century, he notes

> the individual writer's situation between, on the one side, the Welsh-language cultural tradition in which generations of his/her family had been at home but from which the writer, no longer able to speak or write in it, is uprooted and, on the other, the English literary tradition in which s/he has been educated but which expresses a cultural and social experience very different from the Welsh experience of the writer.[5]

Brown describes a kind of schizophrenic[6] fracture in the experience of these writers resulting from belonging to a culture from which one is simultaneously distanced by exclusion from the Welsh language. He suggests the 'psycho-cultural situation' of writers who are 'Welsh in experience, but express...themselves in English can be manifested...in a sense of the world as an insecure, uncanny place' (111) and, indeed, the Welsh language is a ghostly presence in much twentieth-century Anglophone Welsh writing and the rendering of Wales as an uncanny space through linguistic fracture is certainly present in Welsh Female Gothic.

The presence of houses in Welsh Female Gothic writing overtly concerned with ideas of nation is notable throughout the twentieth century. While the house in such texts clearly functions in ways consonant and continuous with wider Anglo-American Female Gothic in its representation of female, feminine and feminist concerns, it has another dominant dimension (particularly when these texts are read as part of a body of national literature) in signifying nation. In Welsh Female Gothic, houses tend to represent patriarchal repression at the same time as they stand for the nation, as in Hilda Vaughan's *The Soldier and the Gentlewoman* (1932), rendering the house a problematic, troubling metaphor in a feminist nationalist reading. Vaughan's novel (discussed in more detail below) reprises several of her earlier engagements with the house as symbol of contested inheritances and national and cultural conflict, this time in the form of a psychological thriller which depicts a battle over an ancestral home. Ostensibly a battle between the sexes, this is also about the viability of Wales as a modern nation capable of self-regeneration. The national and cultural crisis of Wales is elsewhere inscribed in metaphors of disease on the bodies and minds of women as well as the Gothic buildings which they haunt, as in Mary Jones's extraordinary novel *Resistance* (1985) (discussed in more detail below) or Glenda Beagan's emblematic story 'Scream, Scream' (1992). The latter is about the mentally disturbed Mrs Jenkins, the 'last of the Jenkinses of Sgubor Fawr',[7] who is taken to a mental ward for what we learn is a recurring (three-yearly) scream. The scream is an unnerving, uncanny yet eloquent expression of her intolerable position as a woman and also the cry of a nation. Her scream is explicitly described as expressing the various agonies and frustrations of the staff and patients on the ward: 'the scream slowly *inhabits* them all, slowly *expresses* them all' (31, my emphasis). The metaphor of habitation is important here; it links women's bodies and minds with domestic space (in a familiar trope) and reinforces the meaning of the scream as expressing something not only female but specifically Welsh.

> Mrs Jenkins comes from a farm, a farm in the middle of nowhere. A farm so old it's like a fungus, an excrescence of the land, breeding barns...full of...ancient harrows and flails. Enough to fill a museum with fascinating glimpses of our agricultural past. But this isn't the past. It's the present. Little has changed at Sgubor Fawr since Owain Glyndwr rode by...But this is the end of the line. The very end. This is the scream of the last of the Jenkinses of Sgubor Fawr, this is. (32)

The fungus-like farm is a part of the land from which it emerges and by which it is imminently likely to be reclaimed. Mrs Jenkins's scream is both a lament for the farm/nation's demise and a cry of horror for the suffocating horizons it represents, the individual sacrifices it has demanded of her. Even the farm implements listed, the harrow and the flail, suggest pain while there is a suggestion of failed military resistance in the mention of Owain Glyndwr who once passed that way and whose campaign left all but one son of the farm dead.

A monument to the dead and departed, deserted or ruined houses recur in Welsh writing in English, particularly that concerned with mid-twentieth century rural depopulation. In a sequence of Gothic poems, 'Valley-before-Night' (1992), Ruth Bidgood memorialises a lost people and culture through her elegiac depiction of empty houses, ruins in a mid-Wales upland landscape. 'Valley-before-night' uses Welsh superstitions (such as the sighting of corpse candles and its 'auditory equivalent', *cyheuraeth*, 'a [howling] death omen'[8]) to memorialise the cultural specificity of this community (and community as nation) and to reinforce the loss of this way of life. Matthew Jarvis and other critics have emphasised 'Bidgood's recurrent attention to decaying buildings...[which] offer a potent sense of a landscape in which something is dying (and has been dying for a long time)'.[9] The empty houses in 'The Given Time' (1972) and 'All Souls' (1978) retain an echo, a memory of the lives lived there, but even these memorials are threatened by encroaching alien conifer plantations, which will render

> ... all meaning gone
> From the broken shape of the house,
> Blurred like a thicker shadow
> Than tree-shadows in the silent forest; ('The Given Time')[10]

By the end of the century, Female Gothic writing is most remarkable for its fractured, ruinous places, cityscapes characterised by absence, as in Trezza Azzopardi's *The Hiding Place* (2000) and her later work.

The remainder of this chapter will discuss Hilda Vaughan's *The Soldier and the Gentlewoman* and Mary Jones's *Resistance* as outstanding examples of twentieth-century Welsh Female Gothic, but it is necessary briefly to sketch in the earlier literary history of Welsh Female Gothic in order to provide some context. The course of the Female Gothic in Wales has been traced by Jane Aaron in her wider study of nineteenth-century women's writing. In the early 1800s, women writing Gothic fiction set in Wales tended to be outsiders to Wales and the country provides a sublime or terrible backdrop for Gothic romance, replete with wind-bitten towers, remote castles and aristocratic villains. As the century progressed, a sense of Welsh nationhood evolved into self-conscious nationalism and both political separatism and cultural nationalism were important concerns for women writers by the end of the nineteenth century.

At the beginning of the twentieth century, Gothic writing from Wales still had some affinities with the earlier romantic texts which portray Wales as a wild location geographically and culturally distant from the

metropolitan centre and metropolitan readers addressed. This location is also temporally remote, a country holding on to its superstitious
and exotic traditions and old fashioned ways so that to visit is to step
back in time. Jeanette Marks (1875–1964), for example, an American
author with an affinity for Wales, wrote short stories that play with
Gothic themes and highlight the links between Welsh superstitions
and Gothic.[11] Bertha Thomas (1845–1918) had closer ties to Wales and
although her *Picture Tales from Welsh Hills* (1912) is still indebted to the
idea of Wales as a romantic, mysterious and wild backdrop for Gothic
tales, she repeatedly undermines this outsiders' view while yet mobi-
lising its powerful tropes.[12] Indebted to romantic stereotypes though
they are, Thomas's stories are interesting because of their valorisation
of Welsh hybrid identities and stress on the importance of women to
nation and economy. In later texts, the resolution of tensions through
idealisations of British–Welsh hybridity is replaced by much more conflicted imaginings of nationhood and gender roles which appear to
result in a greater ambivalence towards nation, or at least the prospect
of a sustainable national identity.

The conflicting and complex loyalties engendered (the pun is
intended) when the residual, emergent or imagined nation is conceived as a correlative of patriarchy, as 'the Land of Our Fathers' (as
the national anthem figures Wales), is an important theme in Welsh
Female Gothic writing and these texts draw attention to the way gender inflects or cuts across experiences of national identity.[13] Indeed,
the ambivalence towards nation which I suggest is a characteristic of
twentieth-century Welsh Female Gothic may perhaps be accentuated as
a consequence of the employment of tropes of nation and nationhood
(namely the house) which have traditionally been used to encode (and
critique) patriarchal power. While these tropes are easily mobilised to
critique the *patriarchal nation*, they perhaps do not so easily facilitate the
reclamation of this national space for feminists. It is also worth remembering that the Welsh nation signified by the house is simultaneously
a profoundly phallocentric structure and yet also weak, even impotent,
in its statelessness. Thus the tired old attack against feminism in emergent nations makes an insidious entrance: if gender becomes a second
(internal) front, a fault-line on which battle commences, there may be a
perceived danger that the 'integrity' of the house already facing threat
from without may be weakened, undermined, or even come crashing
down. Certainly, in Welsh writing in English, the autonomy and safety
of the house (nation) is never taken for granted.

Kate Ferguson Ellis 'locat[es] in the feminine Gothic a "deep subversive impulse" to undermine the constitution of home as a "place of

peace" ',[14] but what are the implications of this subversive project if the home is also the embattled nation? Escape from an oppressive, imprisoning house has implications beyond feminist resistance or female survival in Welsh Female Gothic: if the heroine flees, she may be escaping domestic or patriarchal oppression but is this an escape into the 'no country' of post-national feminism ultimately at the cost of deracination and the desertion of nation? What, on the other hand, are the implications of staying to fight this internal battle, for an equitable or even dominant place in 'her father's house'?

A great deal of the tension, conflict and the unsettling resistance to closure or univocal readings which is characteristic of twentieth-century Welsh Female Gothic writing arises from the complexity of the house as both a gendered and a potent national signifier and nowhere more so, perhaps, than in Vaughan's novel. On the surface, *The Soldier and the Gentlewoman* describes a battle between the eponymous protagonists over control of the estate, but more important perhaps is the battle between Gwenllian (the Welsh gentlewoman) and her father's chauvinism. Gwenllian's challenge is to forge a way of life which allows her full emotional expression *and* possession of her beloved estate (thus empowering and valorising a female nationhood). Yet, although apparently triumphant, her victory is a grotesque replication of patriarchal models. As a child and young woman Gwenllian loves and idolises her father, the squire of Plâs Einon, yet 'she cursed him and his sex in the name of the meek dead [her mother] and of all women living'.[15] The injustices suffered by herself and her sex, 'the penalty of womanhood' (42), are the cause of her 'hatred and passion' (38). Like her father, Gwenllian's first love is for the house and estate, yet she is disinherited: disqualified from ownership by her father's will which demands a male heir. In common with much of Vaughan's writing and, indeed, other texts which use a marriage plot to explore themes of nationhood, *The Soldier and the Gentlewoman* problematises notions of inheritance and regeneration, evoking Wales as a feminised nation excluded from the discourse of law and privileges of ownership.[16] Early in the novel, in a chapter which explains her childhood's disappointments as she learned the 'penalty of womanhood', we are told:

> If she had been bred a nun, she might have ignored men; but in her world there was no power but through them; they were in possession, hour by hour and generation by generation, of all that she desired to possess; they invaded her integrity, usurped the inheritance of her soul. (38)

After the death of Gwenllian's two brothers in the 1914–18 war, the required male heir is a 'stranger' (45), an inadequate 'common little suburban with a pale moustache' (46), the anglicised, war-damaged, nervous, emasculated young Dick. Plâs Einon becomes a battleground (the imagery of war pervades this text) as Gwenllian seduces, marries and finally murders Dick. Her action is a defiant strike for her sex. Her act apparently frees her from both her husband's and her late father's domination. Her father's haunting presence has been symbolised by the oppressive, distorted portrait which hangs in the room Gwenllian uses as an estate office. Coming directly from the chamber of death, Gwenllian holds a match up to the portrait of her father (to illuminate it, but the suggestion of burning is implicit too): 'She feared him no longer; she had transcended him. Would you, a man, have dared as much? she asked silently. Then with an abrupt twist of her shoulders, final and contemptuous, she turned her back on him' (268). A battle of the sexes, then, in which the woman apparently triumphs twice in the conquest of husband and father.[17] Yet it is her unwavering, obsessive adherence to tradition, the desire to preserve her father's estate unaltered, which causes her ultimately to murder the 'illegitimate' heir, Dick, so as to enable her *sons* to inherit, suggesting she has not ultimately challenged or rewritten the terms of her father's legacy.

This battle is not just between the sexes but also a battle for land, ownership and nation, as the inscription on the plaque Gwenllian erects in the church to memorialise her dead husband makes clear: 'Dulce et decorum est pro patria mori' (281). The intended meaning is that Dick's final illness and demise was a direct consequence of his war service, yet the 'odd claim' (which is suddenly illuminated in blood red by a ray of light thus revealing Gwenllian's guilt to her sister who flees in horror) has another meaning. He has died for *her* country, for her house. Gwenllian, as well as the estate, is constantly associated with the Welsh; she is dark-haired, innately aristocratic, she speaks in Welsh to an adoring retinue of servants and tenants whom she treats with a semi-feudal sense of responsibility for their welfare and exacts appropriate homage. Conservative Wales, allegorised in Gwenllian and the Plâs Einon estate, is in the grip of an irredeemably conservative patriarchy. In her mimicry, Gwenllian appears set to replicate its pernicious structures. Mimicry, however, is a destabilising act and Gwenllian's mimicry of traditional values 'act[s] out and hyperbolize[s]'[18] and thus exposes the profound problems of this phallocentric society and, by extension, a national identity which demands conformity to a narrow, limiting patriarchal model.

The defence of tradition and estate in *The Soldier and the Gentlewoman* is loaded with an awareness of cultural crisis, yet the grotesque gender roles imposed by tradition problematise Gwenllian's defence of this house. The choices made in the novel by the two sisters, Gwenllian and Frances, reflect two (unsatisfactory) options for Welsh women and ultimately the nation: Frances chooses to go and embrace a bohemian, intellectual and apparently internationalist left-wing life in London, while Gwenllian stays to fight for her inheritance. One sacrifices home and nation, the other embraces a living death. Plâs Einon is a troubling representation of nation, a place, ultimately, of death and stagnation. The first and last chapters depict a character viewing Plâs Einon from above, atop 'an old burial mound'. In the opening chapter, 'He Looks on His Inheritance', this character is Dick and thus his death at the hands of Gwenllian (acting to save the estate from his expenses) is prefigured. The final chapter, 'Frances looks on her former home', witnesses Frances's flight having realised Gwenllian's guilt. Determining never to return, she climbs the tumulus and, ostensibly talking about the cairn but looking pointedly towards the house, describes Plâs Einon as 'a place of burial' (287). An escape for this life-loving feminist, but an ambivalent future at best for her 'former home'.

One of the most accomplished examples of twentieth-century Welsh Female Gothic writing is Mary Jones's novel, *Resistance*. Published after the failed referendum of 1979, it is profoundly concerned with representations of Welsh cultural crisis, suppressed histories and linguistic fracture. The house, familiar from other Gothic narratives, is transformed into a hotel, an unhomely home for Ann, the first-person narrator, who has fled to rural mid-Wales to await surgery for a devastating tumour which 'exploded' into her mouth during a dental examination. The bizarre and disorienting architecture of the hotel, its labyrinthine corridors full of cul-de-sacs and unexpected turns and an extraordinary wooden fire-escape which dominates the courtyard, represents Ann's disturbed physical and psychological condition. But the hotel and, indeed, Ann's own diseased body also represent aspects of the national condition, particularly the sense of imminent cultural catastrophe which is driving the covert activities of the (all-male) nationalists who haunt (and eventually accidentally blow up) the old farmhouse around which the rest of the hotel has been built.

David Ronneburg has noted that in Anglo-American Gothic 'houses are frequently used as...junctions in the traffic between this and other world(s)'. He suggests '[a]t least three configurations', all of which seem relevant to the hotel in *Resistance*: 'the house is the *gatehouse* guarding the entrance to the other world, the house *is* the *other world*...or the house equals a *crossroads* and incorporates both worlds which interact'.[19] The hotel is certainly a gateway for Ann; she struggles through the mirror-like revolving doors of the front entrance of the hotel into a world full of signs she fails to comprehend. In the bizarre world she repeatedly fails to interpret accurately, she appears to have entered a foreign country (emphasised by the demand for her passport on arrival and her inability to speak the local language). When she finally leaves the burned hotel, she struggles out again through the revolving doors: 'I half tumbled out onto the dazzlingly bright pavement, much as Alice must have emerged from behind the looking glass.'[20] Furthermore, the hotel becomes, in the meeting of Ann and Aled (the leader of the nationalist activists), a liminal cultural space, a meeting point for different world views. Ann is an English-speaking Welsh woman from the city (although her claim to a Welsh identity is contested by some in the novel who claim that speaking Welsh is a requirement of Welshness); Aled is a charismatic Welsh speaker and a committed nationalist whose ambition is to open a Welsh bookshop but who will accidentally blow up himself and the old farmhouse in which he is preparing a bomb, setting fire to the rest of the hotel.

Resistance has been read by M. Wynn Thomas as a novel that 'traces out' the complex 'nexus of feelings and attitudes' which characterise the 'dominant ideology of modern Wales, the ideology of Britishness'.[21] This ideology of Britishness is seen as 'influencing and maybe deciding the vote against devolution in 1979' (159) and Thomas suggests the ideology of Britishness reflects mixed feelings of attraction and fearful repugnance towards Welsh-speaking Wales, with the latter in the ascendant. Dominic Head argues that Ann's ' "resistance" is Janus-faced [...] denoting an intermediary position between cultural capitulation and regressive nationalism.'[22] While both assessments are valid, I want to argue here that in addition to ambivalence and the ideology of British Wales which are conveyed through Ann's character and beliefs, the novel offers a trenchant and uncompromising reading of the national condition through its metaphorical use of cancer.[23]

If the hotel is a potent and highly Gothic signifier, the specific nature of Ann's cancer is perhaps even more revealing of the cultural crisis signalled in this text. The Welsh-language poet Gwenallt once wrote of Wales in terms of illness and physical pain, where 'The cancer desiccates your face and form,/.../ You are merely a nightmare in your own land.'[24] Ann's cancer of the jaw and mouth is repeatedly linked metaphorically with the English language in Wales. The cancer begins as an invasive growth which goes unnoticed in her jawbone. Specifically we are told it is an ameloblastoma – a 'locally malignant tumour' (97) according to the library encyclopaedia Ann consults. Her confusion – what does *locally* malignant mean? – leads her to think sarcastically, 'Chop my head off, I suppose, and I'd be alright' (97). But the confusing medical definition clearly has resonance as a metaphor for the impact of English in Wales, it is *locally* malignant but equally a fundamental part of the nation (Ann can't chop off her head and survive).

If the cancer begins as an invasive yet imperceptible tumour, it becomes a void in her jaw after it explodes into her mouth, leaving her face vulnerable to collapse at the slightest impact. This damaging emptiness can be read as a description of the cultural impact of the decline of the Welsh language.

> He [Aled] must watch the state of the language like I watched the state of my jaw, noticing here a little improvement, there an alarming setback, and pledging himself to make more effort. For an unhealthy language, like an unhealthy body, needed to be watched and cosseted and self-consciously cared for. (88)

And a little further on, 'I expect that's the way you think of me' says Ann to Aled, 'As a tumour – a painful presence, threatening you. The enemy in your midst. The native who has betrayed the culture and the language. There's nothing more subversive' (89). From the opening of the novel, Ann feels both unwelcome and culturally dislocated as an English speaker, albeit one who describes herself as Welsh. Her inability to speak Welsh is connected with her complete failure to grasp the significance of events and utterances, such as the manager's loaded greeting on her arrival at the hotel, '*Mae'n boeth iawn, ond yw hi?*' (1). The phrase (meaning 'It's very hot, isn't it?') is not translated in the text, but it refers to the unrelenting and oppressive heat of late summer (and foreshadows the pervasive images of fire in the text) which in turn gestures to the fraught cultural tension Ann senses but cannot fathom. It is one of her many failures to grasp the meaning of signs which would reveal the incendiary situation in which she finds herself and when she does begin to suspect double meanings she ironically searches for a clue as to what a delivery of 'fertiliser' really is, failing to understand that fertiliser is just that – it is the main ingredient of the explosives being manufactured.

The cancer itself is, in fact, associated with fire. The bomb-making and fire-setting of the activists is euphemistically passed off as making

'Welsh whiskey', while to mask the nauseating smell of putrefaction in Ann's jaw she drinks whiskey. When a row of holiday cottages are burned to the ground after Plaid Cymru squatters have been forcibly removed, their gutted remains are described: 'The charred facades stood stubbornly as black teeth' (98). The gutted remains prefigure the hotel fire when the nationalist bomb blows a hole in the roof of the ancient farmhouse and both echo the way in which Ann's cancer was discovered by accident when the probing of an unsuspecting (negligent?) dentist causes the tumour to explode into her mouth from under a tooth.

The fault lines of this novel are linguistic rather than overtly gendered, yet it is interesting to observe that the traditional gendering of the authentic, indigenous culture and invasive colonising culture is reversed in *Resistance*. It is Aled, the Christ-like (or at least priest-like) believer who represents an ancient Wales, not an allegorised female figure as in earlier romantic texts, while Ann, the apparently infertile, middle-aged spinster, represents if not England then the anglicised majority of Wales. The suggested infertility of her body is nevertheless disturbingly linked with Wales's future. Aled says that 'We come out of your past, us lot – but you sit there at the fender in the Hungry Cheese [the hotel pub] like our future' (89–90) and Ann muses that Aled must see in her

> the descendants who would no longer talk in the same tongue or read his books or sing his songs or share his ideas or beliefs, but whose connection with him was betrayed, perhaps, by an unusual word or expression here and there, the origins of which had been lost sight of. (90)

Like so much in this novel the meaning of the word betrayed is unstable, its double meanings are richly ambivalent. As a kind of intimacy develops between the two, Aled appears to offer Ann absolution as he gently touches her cancerous jaw; it is an act of tenderness and has mildly sexual undertones. But the potential for greater understanding and contact and the suggestion of cultural compassion which is implicit in this scene is undermined and rendered uncanny, indeed horrifying, for Ann. At this first human contact Ann realises she cannot *feel* Aled's touch – the cancer has made her face numb – a realisation which sends her into a terrified panic which ultimately, after the fire at the hotel, sends her back home, to the life and energy and light of the city (which 'miracle of organisation' [149] is suddenly transformed into a vibrant human body about to be cured of its small malignant corner). This flight seems to deny the validity of the place she leaves behind – the stagnant, burned-out body of the hotel with the empty exploded farmhouse at its heart – thus complicating any nationalist reading of *Resistance*. The closing lines of the novel are a guilty but defiant answer to the final look of 'disgust with which [the hotel manager] was watching my desertion ...'(148) and constitute a grim prognosis for the Welsh-speaking Wales from which she flees '...dear God, oh let me be alright, let me be alright, let me be alright. / It is a basic instinct, the will to survive' (149).

Illness and disease, imprisonment and (implicitly deracinating) escape, decay and displacement, appear to be central to the depictions of the Welsh nation in the Welsh Female Gothic texts I have discussed here, albeit in various measures at different times during the twentieth century. It is significant too that the endings of these texts, which show characters departing the stagnant, imploded or otherwise untenable houses they have depicted in the main narrative, suggest that life must continue outside Wales (or beyond the particular version of Welsh culture being portrayed). In *The Soldier and the Gentlewoman* Vaughan's life-embracing Frances turns to London; at the end of *Resistance* Ann returns to the anglicised (English?) city rejecting rural, Welsh-speaking Wales. In Azzopardi's *The Hiding Place* (mentioned above as an example of late twentieth-century apocalyptic Wales), all the characters depart a ruined, derelict Butetown. Mrs Jenkins, in Beagan's story, leaves the hospital ward to return to her farm, but it is only a matter of time before the land reclaims their farm (and their lives) like the houses swamped by forest in Bidgood's poems whose inhabitants have all left the valley. In this list, only Bidgood in the persona of the memorialising poet remains within her chosen community, life-affirming, recording, leaving the lights on in her own home, the curtains undrawn to keep the dark depopulated valley company.

Thus the houses representing the nation and national culture which are abandoned by women seeking survival appear at best beleaguered (as in Gwenllian's estate), at worst a burned-out (as in *Resistance*) or crumpled ruin, a pile of debris (as imagined by Bidgood, Beagan and Azzopardi), evoking the fall of the house of Usher. Welsh Female Gothic writing, in the examples I have discussed here at least, represents the intolerable pressures on women in a phallocentric society and as a correlative of this account produces an *accentuated* sense of cultural crisis. That is, the sense of a *national* cultural crisis is heightened in these texts by the representation of Welsh women as doubly 'socially and culturally dispossessed',[25] subordinated by gender and nationality. Indeed, their richness, complexity, paradox and resistant ambivalences arise directly from multiple concerns with cultural dispossession, nation and gender and a profound sense of the conflicted nature of these categories.

Notes

This chapter confines itself to *English-language* Welsh writing.

1. David Punter, 'Heart Lands: Contemporary Scottish Gothic', *Gothic Studies* 1/1 (August 1999), 101–18, 101.
2. Homi Bhabha, *The Location of Culture* (London: Routledge, 1994), 10–11. All subsequent references are to this edition and are given in the text.
3. Other paths through Anglophone Welsh women's use of the Gothic might have been followed, taking in, for instance, Margiad Evans's Gothic short stories such as 'The Black House' which foregrounds the creative, artistic impulse, or the same author's novel *Creed*. Another course is illustrated by Jane Aaron's current unpublished research on Welsh Gothic which has foregrounded the Welsh figure of the sin eater, highlighting the work of Edith Nepean and Alice Ellis Thomas among others, as outlined in her paper 'Shifting Gothic Locations: The Case of the Welsh Sin Eater' at the 'Gothic Locations' conference at Cardiff University, September 2008. Of course, inclusion of Welsh-language texts might alter this narrative considerably.
4. Andrew Smith and William Hughes have discussed the Postcolonial Gothic in 'Introduction: Defining the Relationships between Gothic and the Postcolonial', *Gothic Studies* 5/2 (November 2003), 1–6 <http://journals.mup.man.ac.uk/cgi-bin/pdfdisp//MUPpdf/GOTH/V5I2/050001.pdf>, Accessed 23 March 2009, and Andrew Smith and William Hughes, 'Introduction: Enlightenment Gothic and Postcolonialism' in Smith and Hughes, eds, *Empire and the Gothic: The Politics of Genre* (Basingstoke: Palgrave Macmillan, 2003), 1–13. Recent postcolonial approaches to Welsh literature and culture include Stephen Knight, *One Hundred Years of Fiction: Writing Wales in English* (Cardiff: University of Wales Press, 2004), Jane Aaron and Chris Williams, eds, *Postcolonial Wales* (Cardiff: University of Wales Press, 2005), and Kirsti Bohata, *Postcolonialism Revisited: Writing Wales in English* (Cardiff: University of Wales Press, 2004).
5. Tony Brown, 'Glyn Jones and the Uncanny', *Almanac: Yearbook of Welsh Writing in English* 12 (2007–08), 89–114, 90–1. All subsequent references are to this edition and are given in the text.
6. Welsh culture is often characterised as schizophrenic, but Juliann E. Fleenor, among others, has noted that 'The Gothic has long been characterised by a kind of schizophrenia...' 'Introduction', Juliann E. Fleenor, ed., *The Female Gothic* (Montreal and London: Eden Press, 1983), 3–28, 4.
7. Glenda Beagan, 'Scream, Scream' in *The Medlar Tree* (Bridgend: Seren, 1992), 26–33, 32. All subsequent references are to this edition and are given in the text.
8. Ruth Bidgood, 'Valley-before-Night', *Selected Poems* (Bridgend: Seren, 1992), 149–58, 149 (the quotation is from an explanatory note at the beginning of the poem).

9. Matthew Jarvis, *Welsh Environments in Contemporary Poetry* (Cardiff: University of Wales Press, 2008), 62.
10. Ruth Bidgood, 'The Given Time', *New and Selected Poems* (Bridgend: Seren, 2004), 13, lines 2–5.
11. See, for instance, Jeanette Marks, 'An All-Hallow's Honeymoon' in Jane Aaron, ed., *A View Across the Valley: Short Stories by Women from Wales c. 1850–1950* (Dinas Powys: Honno, 1999), 59–69.
12. See 'The Madness of Winifred Owen' and 'A House that Was' in particular, for their use of decaying houses to achieve Gothic affects and dramatise the characters who dwell within. A third story, 'The Only Girl', might also be read as a Gothic allegory of nation. I have discussed these stories elsewhere, see Bohata, *Postcolonialism Revisited* and my 'Introduction' to a collection of Bertha Thomas's short stories, *Stranger Within the Gates* (Dinas Powys: Honno, 2008), i–xxii. The latter volume reprints *Picture Tales from Welsh Hills* in its entirety along with other prose.
13. Of course, I am not suggesting that this concern is unique to Female Gothic writing or, indeed, writing by women alone. Rhys Davies's *Dark Daughters* can be read as 'feminine' Gothic text in its concerns with gender identities and Welsh identities. See Jane Aaron, 'Daughters of Darkness: Rhys Davies's Revenge Tragedies' in Meic Stephens, ed., *Rhys Davies: Decoding the Hare* (Cardiff: University of Wales Press, 2001), 216–30.
14. Kate Ellis Ferguson, *The Contested Castle: Gothic Novels and the Subversion of Domestic Ideology* (Urbana and Chicago: University of Illinois Press, 1989), 219.
15. Hilda Vaughan, *The Soldier and the Gentlewoman* (London: Victor Gollancz, 1932), 41. All subsequent references are to this edition and are given in the text.
16. See Jeni Williams, 'The Intertexts of Literary History: "Gender" and Welsh Writing', in Patsy Stoneman and Ana María Sánchez-Arce with Angela Leighton, eds, *European Intertexts: Women's Writing in English in a European Context* (Oxford: Peter Lang, 2005), 156–76.
17. An interesting comparison could be drawn between Vaughan's novel and Rhys Davies's *Dark Daughters* (1947) which could arguably be described as a female (or feminine) Gothic novel. *Dark Daughters* is also about intergenerational battles of the sexes with father and daughters all trapped in a Gothic house which has been linked to a vision of Wales and the hypocrisies of Welsh Calvinistic Methodism in particular. See note 14 above.
18. Diane Long Hoeveler, *Gothic Feminism: The Professionalisation of Gender from Charlotte Smith to the Brontës* (Liverpool: Liverpool University Press, 1997), 12. Hoeveler is drawing on Irigaray to suggest how Gothic mimicry exposes phallocentric discourse.
19. David Ronneburg, *The House as Gothic Element in Anglo-American Fiction (18th–20th Century)* (Munich: GRIN Verlag, 2002), 24.
20. Mary Jones, *Resistance* (Belfast: Blackstaff Press, 1985), 148. All subsequent references are to this edition and are given in the text.
21. M. Wynn Thomas, *Internal Difference: Twentieth-Century Writing in Wales* (Cardiff: University of Wales Press, 1992), 159. All subsequent references are to this edition and are given in the text.

22. Dominic Head, *The Cambridge Introduction to British Fiction, 1950–2000* (Cambridge: Cambridge University Press, 2002), 146.

23. Here I am indebted to Susan Sontag's *Illness as Metaphor and Aids and Its Metaphors* (London: Penguin, 1991), although, interestingly, she does not describe *cultural* or linguistic decline or protest as an area which appropriates cancer as a metaphor. She does, however, draw attention to the language of military conquest, invasion, colonisation, attack and resistance (see pages 65–6) all of which appear in *Resistance*. She also notes that 'to describe a phenomenon as cancer is an incitement to violence. The use of cancer in political discourse encourages fatalism and justifies severe measures – as well as strongly reinforcing the widespread notion that the disease is necessarily fatal' (84).

24. Gwenallt, 'Wales', in Menna Elfyn and John Rowlands, eds, *The Bloodaxe Book of Modern Welsh Poetry: Twentieth Century Welsh-language Poetry in Translation* (Tarset: Bloodaxe, 2003), 94.

25. Smith and Hughes, 'Introduction: Enlightenment Gothic and Postcolonialism', 1.

12

Monstrous Regiments of Women and Brides of Frankenstein: Gendered Body Politics in Scottish Female Gothic Fiction

Carol Margaret Davison

> A thinking woman sleeps with monsters.
> The beak that grips her, she becomes. And Nature,
> That sprung-lidded, still commodious
> Steamer trunk of *tempora* and *mores*
> Gets stuffed with it all: the mildewed orange-flowers,
> The female pills, the terrible breasts
> Of Boadicea beneath flat foxes' heads and orchids.[1]

Feeling himself and his family increasingly persecuted by his creature three years after its creation, Victor Frankenstein agrees, after a lengthy and impassioned conversation during which the creature relates his tragic tale, to provide him with a female companion. Only in this manner, Victor rationalises, may he appease his resentful, homicidal monster and regain peace and normalcy. This incident notably coincides with Victor's agreement, at his ageing father's urging, to marry Elizabeth after completing a two-year European tour with his beloved friend, Henri Clerval.[2] In order to 'compose...[the] female monster' (124) over the course of his tour, Frankenstein determines to retire to 'one of the remotest of the Orkney [islands]' in Scotland (136). Thus are the two 'brides' of Frankenstein inextricably connected in Mary Shelley's compelling novel, a significant association in keeping with the Gothic's longstanding engagement with anxieties relating to sexual desire and such key rites of passage as marriage and death. Thus, too, is Scotland represented as the domain of female monsters in this iconic Gothic work.

Victor's reconsideration of his promise to his creature in the following chapter seems decidedly uncharacteristic given his past history. While it may be inspired, in part, by lessons learned from his previous careless experiment, the fact that this new, contemplated creation is female seems to be pivotal to his reassessment. Indeed, the scenario he envisions is rife with biblical echoes explicitly derived from the book of Genesis. A true daughter of Eve, the female creature may become, Victor contemplates, 'ten thousand times more malignant than her mate, and delight, for its own sake, in murder and wretchedness' (138). Perhaps more worrisome to him is the fact that she may possess a mind of her own and, because she did not consent to the compact with Victor, may decide to reject the creature and refuse to quit the neighbourhood of man with the hopes of mating with this 'superior beauty' (138). (Clearly, Victor wants to retain a monopoly on procreation, especially of the monster variety.) It would seem that her reproductive powers raise the most fearsome spectre, however, as Victor considers that she may, with the creature as mate, propagate 'a race of devils' upon the earth, for which disaster Victor may be despised by future generations (138). With these ideas in mind and cognisant of the creature's presence at the casement window of his Orcadian laboratory, Victor passionately tears the female creature to pieces (138–9), a sadistic act that is subsequently reciprocated by the creature's brutal and heartless strangulation of Elizabeth on her wedding night (166). Thus does Scotland become the site of both the creation and violent destruction of female monsters.

Mary Shelley's choice of Scotland for this crucial textual event seems curious given her own positive, even liberating experience in that country just two years prior to writing *Frankenstein*. As she claims in her 'Author's Introduction to the Standard Novels Edition [to *Frankenstein*] from 1831', Scotland was to her, as it was to many Romantic writers and others since the mid-eighteenth century,[3] 'the eyry of freedom, and the pleasant region where unheeded ... [she] could commune with the creatures of ... [her] fancy' (193). It should be noted, however, that, despite her own positive, personal experience, Shelley's choice of Scotland was not without significant precedent. In fact, various noteworthy works – both literary and otherwise – made Scotland the natural choice for the location of female monsters. John Knox's venomous diatribe, *The First Blast of the Trumpet Against the Monstrous Regiment of Women* (1558),[4] which was aimed primarily at undermining the authority of Mary Queen of Scots, did much to establish the association between female monsters and Scotland. In Knox's words, such powerful, authoritarian women were nothing short of an abomination – 'repugnant to nature' and subversive 'of good order' (9) – a philosophy that also served to justify the brutal persecution of so-called Scottish 'witches' a century later.[5] Likewise, William Shakespeare's domineering and ambitious femme fatale, Lady Macbeth, was also inextricably linked to that nation.

Perhaps most important for Mary Shelley's novel, however, is the fact that several contemporary British Gothic works published in the decade prior to *Frankenstein* employed Scotland as the site of female monsters. In so doing, these novels helped to forge the image of a Gothic Scotland. Indeed, 'North Britain' is frequently represented therein as a divided, jingoistic nation unnaturally misguided by superstition and a monstrous regiment of passionate, treacherous and domineering women. In scenarios where rational benevolence is often opposed by vengeful malice, these phallic femme fatales embrace the latter standpoint and seem to take such figures as the fictitious, stereotypical Scottish witch, Lady Macbeth, and Mary Queen of Scots as their models. Francis Lathom's *The Romance of the Hebrides* (1809), for example, is set against the backdrop of a Scotland rife with a belief in mantology where the greatest threat is sorcery.[6] The most terrifying and bizarre role is played by the 'dreaded Abdeerah' (I. 179), 'the famed witch of Iona' (I. 153) who is essentially half-woman, half-beast. At least 100 years old, Abdeerah is a cave-dweller garbed in a wolf's hide and ragged tartan who possesses unearthly red eyes filled with rheum, pointed, beastlike fangs, and talon-like fingers (I. 179–80). She is also a prominent player in an argument about the capabilities of female rulers, which is notably one of the novel's principal debates. When Ulina, the daughter of the Laird of Cornic from Lewis, seeks Abdeerah's assistance in getting pregnant because her husband Starno threatens to annul the marriage otherwise, Abdeerah readily assists, enabling Ulina to give birth to a daughter. When Starno contests the claim that women can properly rule a country on the grounds that 'the capacities of a female mind are ill-adapted to the weighty task of governing a state' and 'a scepter swayed by the hand of a woman can never reflect honour on herself, or prove a blessing to her subjects' (I. 201), Ulina vigorously disagrees, citing numerous examples of countries flourishing under queens. She suggests that her daughter may be an intelligent woman of sound judgement. Starno's response that such a daughter would be nothing short of a prodigy echoes Knox's position (I. 202), a stance ultimately undermined by the nature and actions of Ulina's daughter, the Lady Alexandra, who, after consistently exhibiting sound judgement and faithful devotion while facing tremendous persecution, is gloriously installed as a ruler by novel's end and her greatness proclaimed (III. 252).

Catherine Smith's *The Caledonian Bandit* (1811) presents yet another case in point in the form of the crafty and ambitious Lady Margaret of Monteith.[7] Although her husband, the usurper Duncaethal, is unarguably the novel's greatest villain, he is entirely overshadowed, simply by virtue of his gender, by his extremely passionate, proud and villainous wife whose future doom is sealed when she falls in love with another man, Donald, and has the audacity to discard propriety and express her desire. The narrative reaches its Gothic pitch in several sequences where Margaret attempts to exact revenge on her womanising husband who drugs and, presumably, murders her. Perhaps most compelling is the episode where the protean Margaret enacts a bleeding nun scene in front of Duncaethal, the imprisoned Donald, and his beloved Matilda, assuming the role of a 'tall spectral figure... [with] a deep wound... in her breast, from which the sanguinary stream still seemed to flow'. Her injunction to 'give peace to the suffering spirit of the murdered Margaret' (I. 201) raises a mystery that is so unsettling even the hard-hearted Duncaethal is 'conscience-stricken' (I. 202). Margaret remains unremittingly venomous to the end as she daringly cross-dresses (replete with beard) as a bandit named Darthalgo and kidnaps and terrorises both Matilda and Donald. Although this plot is ultimately foiled, she successfully attacks and kills her husband, thereafter committing suicide in a final fit of 'ungoverned temper and unrestrained passion' (II. 230).

The popular image of Scotland as a nation inhabited by female monsters and a site of gender subversion in much early nineteenth-century British Gothic fiction was bolstered by established propaganda emasculating Scottish men that dated from, at least, the mid-eighteenth century and John Wilkes's virulently anti-Scots newspaper, *The North Briton*. In such propaganda, the skirted, filthy, famine-plagued Scot is regularly ridiculed, an image directly countered by the twentieth-century 'cult of masculinity' that came to characterise models of Scottishness.[8] While Scottish Gothic literature of the nineteenth century frequently exposed the dark underbelly of British paternalism and, as Cairns Craig has noted, civilised capitalism,[9] it was only in the late twentieth century, against the backdrop of a growing Scottish independence movement, that Scottish Female Gothic narratives began to engage with and critique the loaded and problematic conception of a feminised, 'castrated' Scotland. Among them, Iain Banks's *The Wasp Factory* (1984) and Alasdair Gray's *Poor Things* (1992)[10] – two works notably written by men – wield post-structural poetics to construct dark comic allegories about the state of Scotland and the contentious Act of Union (1707). In a canny semiotic turning of the tables, these Female Gothic works strategically adopt and manipulate the idea of the female monster – what I will call the Bride of Frankenstein motif – in order to engage with such loaded questions as the source and nature of 'monstrosity,' Scottish and otherwise, and to reflect on various complexities relating to Scottish national history and identity. These novels also craftily employ this motif with the aid of such suitable structural strategies as narrative patchworks and/or generically 'doubled' narratives that may be classified, for example, as both Gothic and Female Gothic.

The Wasp Factory: Narrative Doubling/Generic Doubling

Iain Banks's 1984 *succès de scandale*, *The Wasp Factory* is, as most critics have recognised and as Victor Sage has articulated, 'the story of Frankenstein's monster written ironically from the monster's deceived point of view set in the world of the 1980s'.[11] An unsettling first-person confession of homicide and mental instability, this highly Oedipal 'horror Gothic' narrative graphically chronicles the ritualistically violent life and worldview of 16-year-old Frank Cauldhame and his perverse relationship with his father, a scientist-anarchist hippie who retreated in the 1960s to a castle-like house[12] on an island off the north-east coast of Scotland. Unknown to Frank until the novel's end, this distant, enigmatic and combative father has conducted some rather peculiar experiments on his children, Frank, Eric and Paul. In order to retain a sense of authority and power, he has consciously woven a web of mystification perhaps best symbolised by his locked study, a prototypically Gothic space that obsesses Frank. He has also deliberately miseducated his son, who fashions, in the face of such mystery, a Calvinistically inflected, sign-filled cosmology and fetishistic world of ritual that is, at its core, militaristic, misogynist and patriarchal. In no uncertain terms, Frank's very warped education ranks under the heading 'Lies My Father Told Me', the most treacherous of which concerns Frank's gender and what he refers to as his 'unfortunate disability' that requires him to sit down at the toilet like, as he describes it, 'a bloody woman' (17). According to one of his father's many lies, this position is necessary because Frank was dentally castrated at the age of three by his father's 'bandy-legged and ancient white bulldog' named Old Saul (105). The ultimate, startling truth, however, is that *Francis Leslie* Cauldhame is actually *Frances Lesley*

Cauldhame, a gender alteration accomplished by a perverse, criminal socialisation process and fictionalised history coupled with the sustained use of male hormones that Frank is surreptitiously fed in order to suppress any tell-tale signs of 'female' development.

By way of this final revelation that Frank is, in fact, Frances, Banks enacts a brilliant sleight-of-hand whereby he cleverly 'doubles' his narrative generically and prompts its reassessment as a work of *Female* Gothic. Frances's systematic isolation and imprisonment, combined with her detective-style process of self-expression and discovery, are notably in keeping with that genre. A fuller consideration of this aspect of this 'doubled' narrative, however, must follow an examination of both its role as a Gothic novel and the tremendous significance of its systematic use of the doppelgänger motif. In the first instance, *The Wasp Factory* is a highly intertextual Gothic work whose primary agenda is national allegory. To date, the limited critical interpretations of this novel have tended to overlook *The Wasp Factory*'s position as a work of *Scottish* Gothic. While, for example, Andrew M. Butler entirely bypasses any assessment of the national aspects of this novel,[13] Berthold Schoene-Harwood draws a parallel between the relationship Frank has with his brother Eric – who may or may not exist[14] – and the longstanding idea of Scotland's split psyche. In support of this postulated parallel, he explains that '[w]ithin the imperial framework of English–Scottish relations, the Scottish male is already feminised as a disempowered native (br)other'.[15] Although, as this essay hopes to illustrate, ample and compelling textual evidence exists to illustrate *The Wasp Factory*'s role as a carefully, conscientiously constructed work of Gothic national allegory that consciously works within the Scottish Gothic tradition, Schoene-Harwood's claims are surprisingly bereft of supportive textual evidence.

Banks may situate the Victor Frankenstein-monster dialectic at his novel's core, but it is the Scottish Gothic tradition that drives it, especially James Hogg's chillingly modern psychological portrait, *The Private Memoirs and Confessions of a Justified Sinner* (1824). *The Wasp Factory* is a highly intertextual work that identifies some of its influences but consciously veils some of its more major ones. Banks is highly indebted, for example, to two adolescent classics – J. D. Salinger's *Catcher in the Rye* (1951), which features the similarly aged and named 16-year old protagonist Holden Caulfield, who is likewise an immature, unreliable narrator and outcast highly judgemental of social hypocrisy, and William Golding's *The Lord of the Flies* (1954), an allegory likewise set on an island that chronicles the descent of stranded schoolboys from a state of civilisation to one of savagery during wartime. Their ritualistic, violent and increasingly militaristic male behaviour parallels Frank's.

Much has been made of Banks's masterful use of the doppelgänger motif, perhaps the novel's crowning structural strategy, and of Banks's own self-fashioning as a writer with dual creative drives and personas,[16] but an analysis of how *The Wasp Factory* functions as an updated 'double' of Hogg's masterpiece is strikingly absent from the critical literature. In terms of narrative structure, *The Private Memoirs and Confessions of a Justified Sinner* (1824) is also a doubled narrative in that Robert Wringhim's story is twice-told – once by the realistic Editor and again by the religious fanatic Robert Wringhim himself.[17] The effect, as in Banks's ironic novel, is to cast doubt on both the protagonist's reliability and mental stability. In the broadest possible sense, both works function as typical Gothic cautionary tales that warn against excesses, in this case extreme ideologies that produce distorted psychologies. While Robert Wringhim is a fanatic Antinomian Calvinist who believes that God's elect can sin with impunity, Frank is a fanatic for patriarchy. Both worldviews are problematically fed by 'the sins of the fathers' – lies circulated as truths by father figures that have severely damaging results: Robert Wringhim senior's proclamation that Robert Wringhim junior has been elected 'to the society of *the just made perfect*' (115) is matched in its tragic consequences by Frank's father's litany of lies about the world and Frank's history. Notably, such distorted worldviews provoke similar results, namely severe mental instability and various coldblooded acts of fratricide and homicide. The resulting psychological division in Frank as suggested by the telephone calls from his insane, pyromaniacal half-brother and 'double', Eric,[18] is a clever modern adaptation of Hogg's brilliant creation of Gil-Martin, Robert Wringhim's 'brother' in ideology and evil (117), who provokes, applauds and justifies Wringhim's varied criminal activities.

Like Hogg's novel, *The Wasp Factory* assumes a much richer resonance on a variety of levels when one considers its role as a Gothic national allegory, a form overtly signalled by its author in several key episodes. In one of many incidents involving Frank's father's twisted, dark sense of humour, he purchases his 'son' a copy of Günter Grass's *The Tin Drum* (51), a national allegory about Germany's stunted growth while under the demonic sway of the National Socialist Party. (Ironically, Frank reads neither that book nor his father's other gift – a copy of Gore Vidal's *Myra Breckinridge* [1968], the satirical story of a man [Myron Breckinridge] who has had sexual reassignment surgery. In keeping with the novel's sustained black humour, Frank, the inveterate sign-reader, remains blind to some of the more obvious clues relevant to his true 'condition.') Banks renders his national allegory agenda especially clear when Frank offers up the following self-description:

> Often I've thought of myself as a state; a country or, at the very least, a city. It used to seem to me that the different ways I felt some-times about ideas, courses of action and so on were like the differing political moods that countries go through. (62)

Frank's unofficial existence as a 'boy' without a birth certificate (13–14) nicely parallels the state of Scotland that lacks nationhood status. Further to this, Frank's reiterated description of himself as a self-aware, guilty and fragmented individual comprised of a dark side that is 'racist' (63), 'sick' (78) and 'destructive' (80), is fittingly reflective of the eighteenth-century, post-Union stereotype of Scotland as a schizophrenic nation-state. Identity-wise, Scotland was regarded as torn between Scottish and British identity, and between the barbarian, past-obsessed Highlands and what Victor Sage nicely describes as 'rationalist, progressive, Euro-Edinburgh' (21). Frank, the isolationist and outcast, leans more toward the stereotype of the Highlander who is generally regarded as naturally superstitious, warlike,[19] 'idle, thievish, ... and separatist'.[20] Further to this, Frank's frequent engagements with the factory, his obsessive war games and his growing independence – a source of tremendous con-cern to his control-obsessed father whom Frank increasingly regards as idiotic and embarrassing – are especially indicative of his national iden-tity. In his intricately designed Wasp Factory where wasps 'select' their own particular style of gruesome death, Frank emulates his experiment-ing father. There, he essentially assumes the role of a god presiding over what Sage calls his 'little world of death and retribution' (25). In its role of predicting the future, the Factory provides yet another testament to his superstitious nature. This 'beautiful and deadly and perfect' site (118) also artistically incorporates mementoes of Frank's crimes and history (122), thus serving as both a superb Gothic sign of *memento mori* and a rich, multifaceted and even paradoxical symbol that taps a vein deep in the Scottish psyche. It yokes together at least three distinct concepts: the idea of (factory) labour, Scotland's primary role within the British Union since its establishment; Calvinism, a superstitious religious philosophy that underscores the idea of choosing one's own fate; and revenge on the 'wasps' (white Anglo-Saxon Protestants) whose patriarchal and militaristic worldview, as I will explain momentarily, is seen to have infected Scotland.

The *coup de grâce* in Banks's brilliantly conceived and executed national allegory is that Frank suffers, like Scotland in the 1980s,[21] from a deep lack of self-knowledge and self-respect. Frank's role as a typical Gothic hero-villain is nowhere in doubt: he is an obsessive and self-absorbed individual guilty of grievous crimes against his dysfunctional family in the form of three carefully planned and executed murders, one a fratricide (138). In what amounts to a wonderful twist of narrative irony, however, Frank is exposed as a secret-keeper from whom the novel's most significant secret – one involving 'his' secret identity – is kept. Frank is 'not a full man', as he describes himself (109), due to the fact, as this Female Gothic narrative reveals, that he is a woman. His deep lack of self-knowledge is compounded by an intense self-hatred. The logic runs as follows: Frank hates women (43); Frank is a woman; therefore, Frank is guilty of intense self-loathing.

Read in the light of its role as a work of national allegory, *The Wasp Factory* presents a psychological portrait that is more than a little Freudian and far from flattering, of a patriarchally obsessed Scotland. Frank's exclusion 'from society's mainland' (183) and his grotesque manipulation by a father who subjected him to a bizarre gender experiment (174) results in a warped Oedipal relationship. Indeed, the novel's prominent and sustained sheep and dog imagery essentially positions Scots in the role of mindless sheep ever subject to the bullying power of British bulldogs like the one belonging to Frank's father (Old Saul) that purportedly castrated Frank. According to Frances's retrospective lay evaluation of 'his' behaviour, his primary response to his unmanning and what she characterises as 'his' 'penis envy' was to kill as a mode of outmanning others (183). Frank simultaneously repressed his 'maternal' side, which resulted in his lack of a balanced personality and transformation into an aggressive, militaristic machine. His hippie father, ironically, produced a warmonger. Banks has explained in various interviews that *The Wasp Factory* is an attack on the British male military establishment.[22] Since the Act of Union, and particularly since the defeat of the Jacobites in the eighteenth century, an emasculated Scotland has willingly served a major role within that establishment. Banks suggests that a monstrous Scotland has been the result. In a typical Gothic boundary-blurring move, however, Banks issues the further suggestion that Frank's worldview is not limited to himself or his island. As Frank's ironic discussion with his only friend Jamie makes clear, politicians and 'leaders of countries or religions or armies' (112) constitute the world's maddest people. These leaders will ultimately come out on top, thus confirming the 'survival of the nastiest' people (112). It is Frank, ironically, who expands on this theory and articulates Banks's broader critique:

> If we're really so bad and so thick that we'd actually use all those wonderful H-bombs and Neutron bombs on each other, then maybe it's just as well we do wipe ourselves out before we can get into space and start doing horrible things to other races. (113)

In his construction of the bomb-wielding Frank, Banks creates a microcosm of said politicians and their jingoistic nations. This monstrous individual is but a mirror for a larger, global problem.

As a meditation on monstrosity that draws upon *Frankenstein*, *The Wasp Factory* indicts Frank's father as the progenitor of Frank's monstrosity. Although, as McVeigh argues, 'both Frank and his father are grotesque, lonely people whose lives are steered by a single "truth" which has become obsession ... [and] Frank is also a physical grotesque: a male castrated when he was three-years-old' (3), his father is the monster-maker. The primary sin of this father is best encapsulated in Frank's distorted and simplistic gender philosophy, which proclaims that 'Both sexes can do one thing specially well: women can give birth and men can kill' (118). Ironically, the experiment conducted on Frances fails to confirm such essentialist notions of gender: Frances becomes Frank only as a result of *both* socialisation and biochemical manipulation. Banks's clever subversion of Frank's rudimentary, black-and-white gender philosophy and his positioning of monstrosity in relation to gender, radically undermine the Aristotelian conception of femaleness as an aberration from the male 'norm'. Scottish female monsters may seem innumerable in Frank's world, as they are in Robert Wringhim's, but they are nowhere to be found in Banks's. Frank's 'death' – the traditional outcome for the Gothic hero-villain – and the concomitant 'birth' of Frances, combined with Frances's revelation at the novel's end regarding Frank's motivations, speak volumes about the nature, location and sustenance of monstrosity. Frances's ultimate and ironic recognition of her position within a 'greater machine' where her path – like the wasps in the factory – is part chosen and part determined (184), is damningly, soberingly realistic yet nonetheless re-empowering. Although she possesses a greater sense of the multifarious influences at work in the individual's life, her newfound self-knowledge constitutes the foundation for a possible, new, non-destructive beginning.

Poor Things: Allegorising Acts of Union

In at least two major ways, Alasdair Gray's *Poor Things* (1992) piggy-backs on Banks's *The Wasp Factory*: this Female Gothic work draws on the Frankenstein monster motif and thinks back through the Scottish Gothic tradition in crafting its critique of Thatcherite Britain and offering up an incisive meditation on a cross-section of pressing socio-political issues in the late twentieth century. In this typically postmodern novel where the boundary between fiction and history is consciously and frequently obscured,[23] Gray chooses to look back a century in order to render a contemporary commentary, a narrative strategy that is, appropriately, typical of the Victorian novel. *Poor Things* not only qualifies as a work of 'sham-Gothic,' as at least one reader has labelled it;[24] it may also be categorised as sham-Victorian. In the novel's tongue-in-cheek blurb prepared for the 'high-class hardcover edition', which was omitted from the American version, Gray provides an important clue regarding the agenda informing this key narrative decision. It reads, 'Since 1979 the British government has worked to restore Britain to its Victorian state, so Alasdair Gray has at last shrugged off his postmodernist label and written an up-to-date nineteenth-century novel.' In its preoccupation with such traditional Victorian concerns as Darwinism, Home Rule, poverty and socialism, as Marie Odile Pittin has noted,[25] Gray suggests that Britain has experienced a damaging socio-political regression. Read in this light, this novel's '*strange* resurrection of dead bits and pieces of Victorian literature' as Johanna Tiitinen has described it,[26] does not seem so strange. Indeed, as the combined insights of two of Gray's fake reviews maintain, *Poor Things* is 'a blackly humorous fiction' that reveals a whole society (xi). Although Gray intimates that little progress has been made in Britain over the course of a century on various issues, this explicit work of feminist Female Gothic reserves its foremost indictment for the Woman Question. It exposes the oppression and objectification of women as monsters within patriarchy, from 'the scullery maid ... [to] the master's daughter' as its protagonist, Bella, lays out the parameters (263), particularly by way of the pathologisation of their bodies by the scientific and medical establishments.

Drawing on Johanna Tiitinen's insights, *Poor Things* may be described both structurally and thematically as a fiction of resurrection. It is packaged, in traditionally Gothic fashion, as a found, 'resurrected' manuscript and is comprised of two contending, disparate narratives, one written by a husband, Archibald McCandless, and the other – a letter dated 1914 after McCandless's death in 1909 – by his wife, Bella/Victoria, after reading her husband's version of her life story. Although McCandless's narrative is intended as a testament to his love for his wife, she is grievously offended by it, calling it an 'infernal parody' (273) penned by an 'idle, dreamy fantastical [man]' (252).[27] Victoria's reaction is far from unfounded: McCandless's narrative is a Gothic, wildly implausible tale that conceives of her – in her capacity as 'Bella' – as the product of a 'skilfully manipulated resurrection' (27) conducted by Godwin Bysshe Baxter, an experimental doctor and Bella's father/wannabe husband named, in part, after Mary Shelley's visionary father, William Godwin, and her husband Percy Bysshe Shelley. If McCandless is to be believed, this female suicide was fished out of the Clyde River in Glasgow and her body revived after her brain was replaced by that of her dead foetus. Victoria is, understandably, grossly insulted by this suggestion; however, a more apt emblem of the 'monstrous' ideal of Victorian womanhood – the infantilised woman – would be impossible to conceive as would a more fitting symbolic synthesis of the mother–daughter duo of Mary Shelley and Mary Wollstonecraft (the latter denounced by Horace Walpole as a monstrous 'hyena in petticoats'), who seem jointly to comprise Bella's character portrait.[28]

Ironically, the narrative recounted by Victoria, the ostensible erotomaniac yet self-described 'practical, busy-in-the-world mother' (252), is much more rational, scientific and matter-of-fact than her husband's. As such, the traditional Gothic tug-of-war between a supernatural and a rational worldview is played out between their widely divergent accounts. Style aside, both in combination underscore the question of accurately recounting personal and national history. According to Victoria, McCandless's narrative is a patchwork of morbid Victorian fantasies (272). Among other works, it consciously draws on Hogg's *The Private Memoirs and Confessions of a Justified Sinner* (272), which problematises the question of truthful, reliable narration, and is not unlike its principal parent-text, *Frankenstein*, which employs multiple narrators with widely differing worldviews and motives in a text comprised of Chinese-box style narratives.

Gray's indebtedness to *Frankenstein* has been readily and repeatedly acknowledged in the critical literature. According to Pittin, the use of *Frankenstein* as a source text in *Poor Things* is 'glaringly apparent' although not 'without a fair amount of distortion and indecisiveness' (212). While she identifies the tangential and obvious equation between Godwin and Victor Frankenstein (212),[29] Pittin problematically concludes that the beautiful Bella is 'strikingly unlike Frankenstein's creature' (212), thus overlooking Gray's principal agenda of laying bare the cultural construction of woman as monstrous. By way of a huge dollop of parody in McCandless's narrative, initiated by Bella's Bride-of-Frankenstein-style introduction to him (29), Gray exposes the mechanics and dangers of discursive monstrosity. Bella's husband is revealed to be as instrumental to the process of female monster-making as Godwin with his innovative experiments and unconventional ideas. Archie and several other men with whom she comes into contact expend a great deal of energy trying to classify Bella, the general consensus being that she is a transgressive, monstrous woman. In opposition to Godwin's and McCandless's *construction* of a female monster in the latter's narrative, Gray undertakes her postmodern *deconstruction*, which involves exposing the culturally contingent and constructed nature of 'womanhood' and the sometimes brutal methods used to police women's adherence to this ideal.[30] Gray's deconstruction is symbolically reflected in the novel's numerous etchings of female body parts by one William Strang (a.k.a. Alasdair Gray).

Gray's self-reflexive deconstruction extends the purview of the traditional Female Gothic novel from consideration of women's vexed experiences of love and romance and the constraining roles advocated for women within the institutions of marriage and motherhood, to the limiting and imprisoning discursive aspects related to the ideology of femininity. With its account of Bella's first husband, General Blessington, and his mistreatment, neglect and brief incarceration of her in a coal-cellar (227), alongside his intention of unlawfully incarcerating her long-term in an asylum (230), Gray also blends a traditional Female Gothic narrative into a more modern variant. Stripped to its essence, McCandless's account functions as a fantastic and symbolic allegory regarding the construction of women as monsters within patriarchy. It is to highlight this position that Bella is presented as a female blank slate, a history-less monster made rather than born. Within such a scenario, Bella is revealed, ironically and tellingly, to be a monster whether she refuses or embraces the socially acceptable role of object of desire. Under the tutelage of the monstrously unattractive, masculine–feminine Godwin who is as much monster as monster-maker, Bella eschews such a role in favour of that of a liberated, intelligent woman and sexually desiring subject. In the former capacity, Godwin ensures a revolution by granting her freedom of thought: while in McCandless's narrative, Bella ends up becoming a doctor who promotes female suffrage and pens Fabian pamphlets, in her own version of events, she becomes a doctor engaged with the International Socialists. Godwin would applaud this outcome given his scathing condemnation early in the novel of an essentially monstrous Britain as a heartless plutocracy where money talks, industry rules, and people – generally of the working classes – are left to die (24). Ironically, by Victorian standards, 'Doctor' Bella/Victoria is regarded as a fully fledged monster who brazenly transgresses the established boundaries of male professionalism. By way of Bella's medical role, Gray gestures towards a substantially altered future when female authority will be recognised and celebrated, and women will assume control over their own bodies.

In her latter capacity as a sexually desiring subject who had 'never been taught to feel her body is disgusting or to dread what she desires' (69), Bella becomes subject to severe social stigma. This unconventional, anachronistic woman who does not recognise class differences (80), shamelessly enjoys sex, and rejects marriage – Duncan Wedderburn claims he has never met a 'man-loving middle-class woman in her twenties who did NOT want marriage, especially to the man she eloped with' (81) – follows what is, effectively, a traditionally male trajectory. She undertakes a Grand Tour of the continent where she comes into contact with a variety of 'gentlemen' who expose her to various popular but problematic contemporary socio-political ideas. Over the course of these encounters, Bella is demonised as a 'gorgeous monster' (91), a supernatural freak of nature, a sleepless, sexual vampire (86) who ends up literally exhibited at the Salpêtrière by the renowned French neurologist Jean-Martin Charcot to illustrate the dangers of erotomania (179). (Her claim in her own narrative of experiencing an unrequited love for Godwin would have been considered, according to Victorian mores, equally monstrous and scandalous.) Bella's categorisation as a monster also occurs in relation to the crack that circles her skull, which is notably interpreted as 'the female equivalent of the mark of Cain, branding its owner as a lemur, vampire, succubus and thing unclean' (89). Although according to Victoria's epistolary account, this horrifying scar was the result of paternal abuse (256), her objectified body is, significantly, a text she cannot read (254), a loaded situation given women's objectification within patriarchy. The idea that women's bodies are texts that only men can interpret is especially brought home by the fact that Bella's lover Duncan Wedderburn can read her hymenless, caesarean-inscribed body while she cannot (107). Ironically, Bella's painstakingly lengthy, socially acceptable transformation from the daughter of a Manchester foundry foreman into a lady well groomed for the 'marriage market' (215), as directed and paid for by Blessington, shares important resonances with Godwin's infantilising, monster-making process. After seven years in a Swiss convent, Victoria emerges, in the General's estimation, with 'the soul of an innocent child within the form of a Circassian houri – irresistible' (215).[31]

Despite their crucial divergences in style and several key plot elements, both McCandless's and Victoria's narratives, albeit in various manners, follow the direction of Shelley's *Frankenstein* in considering both the complex and fluid monster/monster-maker dialectic and the often selfish, dangerous motives underpinning scientific ventures. Both foreground the monstrously destructive nature of British patriarchy on women's lives, an ideology fundamental to British imperialism and similarly grounded, it is intimated, in hierarchy and classification. Bella is introduced to the tenets of imperialism during the course of her Tour by Dr Hooker who expounds his theory on Anglo-Saxon superiority (139–41) and Mr Astley who justifies British warfare as a type of civilising mission (141). The latter's claim that Britons possess the world's biggest (read *advanced*) brains and function as adults in comparison with infantilised colonials (139), lends support to the novel's suggestion that imperialism begins at home among Britain's 'poor things' – women and the working classes – who are taught, Godwin laments, to be tools (263). Wedderburn's role as a self-identified monster (79) who sexually mistreated countless working-class women serves as a perfect example of such imperial behaviour, as does the impregnation of a kitchen-maid by General Blessington, 'the nation's darling... [and] example to British youth' (211).

Much like Banks in *The Wasp Factory* yet to a less successful degree, Gray grafts a national allegory onto his Female Gothic fiction. While it is most graphically in evidence in Strang's etching of Bella in the role as 'Bella Caledonia' (45), it is tangentially developed in Bella's *Bildungsroman*-style narrative that involves her maturity from a sexually promiscuous woman engaging in 'Acts of Union'/'weddings' with Wedderburn (83) to her more intellectual engagement with Scottish nationalism and socialism. The amnesiac Bella's reminder of her first legal 'Act of Union'[32] with General Blessington, an arch-imperialist who was involved in every major Victorian military event (for example, the Crimean War and the Indian Mutiny), is part and parcel of her Female Gothic development towards self-awareness. It also signifies, allegorically, Scotland's imperialist history. Bella's act of confronting and disarming the General (236–8) signals Gray's hope that an amnesiac Scotland will seriously re-examine its history, confront and, ultimately, reject its imperial role in order to embrace the newfound nationalist, class-aware ideas of such thinkers as John Maclean and Hugh MacDiarmid.[33] In this way, Bella/Scotland strikes out towards independence and learns the quintessential Gothic lesson that only by confronting the ghosts of one's past is progress possible. It is Godwin himself, rather notably, who brings this lesson home in his own personal life. His courageous reconsideration of why he chose to surgically reconstruct and 'resurrect' Bella instead of resuscitating her dead baby serves as a prototypical Gothic sins of the fathers' moment that looks back to Victor Frankenstein's warring motives for fabricating his creature.[34] In a novel that reveals the often fluid boundary between monster and monster-maker, Godwin confesses to his own sexual urges and flawed human nature. He states, regretfully, that 'Our vast new scientific skills are first used by the damnably greedy selfish impatient parts of our nature and nation' (68). In what amounts to a postmodernist Gothic cautionary tale for the 1990s, Gray issues a dire warning to a Scotland on the cusp of devolution[35] – namely, that no person or nation possesses a monopoly on, or immunity from, monstrosity.

As for female 'monstrosity', *The Wasp Factory* and *Poor Things* are strikingly contemporary Female Gothic narratives that expose a peculiar form of 'feminine carceral', one in which women are made to experience their own bodies as prisons. While traditional Female Gothic novels generally take up the issue of imprisoning female roles as inherited from the mother, contemporary Female Gothic works wrestle with patriarchy's insistence on imprisoning women in their maternal bodies.[36] To opt for the female self-awareness that both novels promote, and thus espouse the role of the intellectual woman is, effectively, to embrace monstrosity. 'A thinking woman sleeps with monsters,' as this essay's epigraph from Adrienne Rich so astutely makes clear. Within the damning confines of patriarchy, a thinking woman has no other choice, nor does a woman like Bella/Victoria who celebrates her own body and exults in the role of sexually desiring subject. *The Wasp Factory* and *Poor Things*, however, expose and explode such confining modes of thought as being themselves monstrous. As pseudo-anthropological assessments, each indicts patriarchy as a form of cultural pathology wherein, as Michelle Massé has argued, 'normal' feminine development amounts to 'a form of culturally induced trauma'.[37] Frances's 'castration complex' brings this idea especially to the fore. In keeping with Hogg's *Private Memoirs and Confessions*, one of their principal literary models, both novels illustrate how such a cultural pathology requires the demonisation of an Other in order to maintain it. Women are shown to be doubly demonised – for their difference and their necessity – a situation rendered even more nefarious when national identity is figured into the equation and they also fall into the category of different-yet-necessary Scots.

Notes

1. Adrienne Rich, from *Snapshots of a Daughter-In-Law* (New York: Norton, 1963).
2. Mary Shelley, *Frankenstein; Or, The Modern Prometheus* (Oxford: Oxford UP [1818], 1993), 125–7. All subsequent references are to this edition and are given in the text.
3. On the very rich and fascinating subjects of Scotland's romanticisation and Scotland and Romanticism, see Andrew Hook, ed., 'Scotland and Romanticism: The International Scene.' *The History of Scottish Literature. Vol. 2. 1660–1880*, (Aberdeen: Aberdeen UP, 1987), 307–22; Peter Womack, *Improvement and Romance: Constructing the Myth of the Highlands* (London: Macmillan, 1989); and Leith Davis, Ian Duncan and Janet Sorenson, eds, *Scotland and the Borders of Romanticism* (Cambridge: Cambridge UP, 2004).
4. John Knox, *The First Blast of the Trumpet Against the Monstrous Regiment of Women* (New York: Da Capo [1558], 1972). All subsequent references are to this edition and are given in the text.
5. While the Witchcraft Act dates from 1563, the most intense period of witch-hunting in Scotland took place a century later between 1658 and 1662. (P. G. Maxwell-Stuart, *An Abundance of Witches: The Great Scottish Witch-Hunt* (Stroud, Gloucestershire: Tempus, 2005).)
6. Francis Lathom, *The Romance of the Hebrides; or, Wonders Never Cease!*, 3 vols (London: Minerva Press, 1809). All subsequent references are to this edition and are given in the text.
7. Catherine Smith, *The Caledonian Bandit; or, The Heir of Duncaethal. A Romance of the Thirteenth Century*, 2 vols (London: Minerva Press, 1811). All subsequent references are to this edition and are given in the text.
8. Cristie March, 'Bella and the Beast (and a Few Dragons, Too): Alasdair Gray and the Social Resistance of the Grotesque', *Critique* 43 (2002), 323–46, 328.
9. Cairns Craig, *Out of History: Narrative Paradigms in Scottish and English Culture* (Edinburgh: Polygon, 1996), 46.
10. Iain Banks, *The Wasp Factory* (London: Abacus, 1984). Alasdair Gray, *Poor Things* (San Diego, New York, and London: Harcourt Brace and Company, 1992). All subsequent references are to these editions and are given in the text.
11. Victor Sage, 'The Politics of Petrifaction: Culture, Religion, History in the Fiction of Iain Banks and John Banville' in *Modern Gothic: A Reader*, eds Victor Sage and Allan Lloyd Smith (Manchester and New York: Manchester UP, 1996), 20–37, 24. All subsequent references are to this edition and are given in the text.
12. In regard to the use of castles in his fiction and Frank's relationship to them in *The Wasp Factory*, Iain Banks has stated in an interview, 'any time a castle appears in any book, certainly in mine, in a way it stands for the

individual... Frank is almost literally cut off – literally insular in his perceptions' (Michael Cobley, 'An Interview with Iain Banks', *Science Fiction Eye* 6 [1990], 24–32, 26).

13. Andrew M. Butler, 'Strange Case of Mr. Banks: Doubles and *The Wasp Factory*', *Foundation* 76 (Summer, 1999), 17–26.

14. See Kev P. McVeigh's very cogent article on the probable non-existence of Eric: 'The Weaponry of Deceit: Speculations on Reality in *The Wasp Factory*', *Vector* 191 (1997), 3–4. By way of some very persuasive textual evidence, McVeigh theorises that Eric is 'a product of the joint imaginations of Frank and his father Angus' (3), that there is no other corroboration of Eric's existence in the text, and that Eric serves as the scapegoat who helps justify Frank's homicidal actions and onto whom Frank projects his rage and horror over his life experiences. In McVeigh's assessment, Eric represents 'Frank's demon, the artificial masculinity he has had forced upon him and which he himself has forced' (4) that is laid to rest at novel's end after Frances discovers the truth about her gender history. In terms of my argument, this 'demon' that goads Frank into aggressive action serves as a modern parallel of Hogg's Gil-Martin. This Other/Brother is a truly uncanny figure onto whom Robert Wringhim projects a repressed aspect of himself. Eric serves in a similar capacity. When he returns to the island at novel's end, Frank describes him as follows: 'His face was bearded, dirty, like an animal mask. It was the boy, the man I had known, and it was another person entirely' (176). In this instance, Eric serves as a quintessentially uncanny foreign-yet-familiar figure, a projection of Frank's own divided self.

15. Berthold Schoene-Harwood, 'Dams Burst: Devolving Gender in Iain Banks's *The Wasp Factory*', *Ariel* 30 (1999), 131–48, 134.

16. Banks publishes his fiction under the name Iain Banks and his science fiction under the name Iain M. Banks. See Butler, 'Strange Case of Mr. Banks', 18.

17. James Hogg, *The Private Memoirs and Confessions of a Justified Sinner* (Oxford: Oxford UP [1824], 1991). All subsequent references are to this edition and are given in the text.

18. This is an especially fitting mirroring as Frank also does not exist – legally.

19. Hook, 308.

20. Womack, 22.

21. This novel is very specifically set in 1981 in Thatcherite Britain. Born in 1964 (121), Frank is nearly 17 (13) when he recounts his story and Britain, notably, is on the cusp of war with Argentina in the Falkland Islands.

22. McVeigh, 3.

23. Linda Hutcheon, *A Poetics of Postmodernism: History, Theory, Fiction* (New York and London: Routledge, 1988), 113.

24. Archibald McCandless's wife, Bella, characterises it as such in her letter of response (275).

25. Marie Odile Pittin, 'Alasdair Gray: A Strategy of Ambiguity', *Studies in Scottish Fiction: 1945 to the Present*, ed. Susanne Hagemann (Frankfurt: Lang, 1994), 199–215, 209. All subsequent references are to this edition and are given in the text.

26. Johanna Tiitinen, 'Alasdair Gray's *Poor Things* and the Resurrection of Frankenstein's Monster', *Proceedings from the 7th Nordic Conference on English*

Studies, eds Sanna-Kaisa Tanskanen and Brita Wàrvik (Turku, Finland: University of Turku, 1999), 315–26, 316, emphasis added. All subsequent references are to this edition and are given in the text.

27. In this novel comprised of bits and pieces of Mary Shelley's life and works, it would seem that Gray has William Godwin's *Memoirs* of Wollstonecraft in mind in this instance. While written as a tribute to his dead wife, Godwin's *Memoirs* so bluntly discussed such things as Wollstonecraft's titillating love life and various suicide attempts that they served, for most readers, to destroy her already damaged reputation. (William Godwin, *Memoirs of Mary Wollstonecraft* (New York: Haskell House, 1969).

28. With regard to Bella's likeness to Wollstonecraft, Pittin notes, 'Victoria commits suicide by leaping from a bridge, and her brand of feminism recalls that of Wollstonecraft, as does her rhetoric in the last part of the book which could have been copied straight from the *Vindication of the Rights of Women*' (213).

29. Godwin also partakes of other aspects of characters in the Scottish Gothic literary tradition. In his act of going in and out of his house by way of the servants' entrance, for example, he is much like Stevenson's Dr Jekyll (26) (Robert Louis Stevenson, *The Strange Case of Dr Jekyll and Mr Hyde* (Oxford: Oxford UP [1886], 1987)).

30. The key method featured in the novel is clitoridectomy (218). Bella is threatened with this procedure as a 'remedy' for her so-called 'erotomania'.

31. Wedderburn's early assessement of Bella echoes Blessington's as he calls her 'a Houri, a Mahomet's paradise' (82).

32. Intriguingly, various literary works set in Scotland, such as Sir Walter Scott's *Waverley; Or, 'Tis Sixty Years Since* (1814, ed. Andrew Hook. Harmondsworth: Penguin, 1985) and Susan Ferrier's *Marriage* (1818, New York: Penguin, 1986), employ the concept of marriage as an 'act of union' in order to comment on the political Act of Union of 1707.

33. John Maclean was a left-wing Scottish politician, nationalist and pacifist. Hugh MacDiarmid was the pseudonym of Christopher Murray Grieve, a leading modernist writer involved in the early twentieth-century Scottish Renaissance, who was a committed nationalist and communist.

34. In keeping with his confusion and ambivalence throughout Shelley's novel, Victor Frankenstein identifies at least two oppositional reasons motivating the creation of his 'monster'. While the first seems philanthropic – Victor wishes to 'banish disease from the human frame, and render man invulnerable to any but a violent death' (23) – the second is selfish. Victor anticipates the day when '[a] new species would bless me as its creator and source; many happy and excellent natures would owe their being to me. No father could claim the gratitude of his child so completely as I should deserve theirs' (36).

35. As the publication of his concise political statement, *Why Scots Should Rule Scotland* (Edinburgh: Canongate, 1992) illustrates, this issue was at the forefront of Gray's mind in 1992, the year he also published *Poor Things*.

36. Claire Kahane, 'Gothic Mirrors and Feminine Identity', *Centennial Review* 24 (1980), 43–64, 59.

37. Michelle Massé, *In the Name of Love: Women, Masochism, and the Gothic* (Ithaca, NY and London: Cornell UP, 1992), 7.

Index